Gaming and the Arts of Storytelling

Gaming and the Arts of Storytelling

Special Issue Editor

Darshana Jayemanne

MDPI • Basel • Beijing • Wuhan • Barcelona • Belgrade

MDPI

Special Issue Editor
Darshana Jayemanne
Abertay University
UK

Editorial Office
MDPI
St. Alban-Anlage 66
4052 Basel, Switzerland

This is a reprint of articles from the Special Issue published online in the open access journal *Arts* (ISSN 2076-0752) in 2018 (available at: https://www.mdpi.com/journal/arts/special_issues/gaming_and_storytelling)

For citation purposes, cite each article independently as indicated on the article page online and as indicated below:

LastName, A.A.; LastName, B.B.; LastName, C.C. Article Title. *Journal Name* **Year**, *Article Number*, Page Range.

ISBN 978-3-03921-231-6 (Pbk)
ISBN 978-3-03921-232-3 (PDF)

Cover image courtesy of pixabay.com.

Contents

About the Special Issue Editor

Darshana Jayemanne is Lecturer in Art, Media and Computer Games at Abertay University and the author of "Performativity in Art, Literature and Videogames" (Palgrave MacMillan 2017). This book's title names many of his main research interests, and develops a media studies approach to performance in digital space and time. He is Co-Investigator on the AHRC-funded "Reality Remix" project. His work has appeared in *Games and Culture, The Journal of Broadcasting and Electronic Media, Fibreculture Journal*, and *Westminster Papers in Communication and Culture*.

Preface to "Gaming and the Arts of Storytelling"

The title of this collection makes use of some ambiguous terms: 'gaming' rather than 'videogames'; the plural 'arts' rather than the singular 'art'. Similarly, the concept of 'storytelling' has an ambiguous relation to the term 'narrative', which is far more commonly deployed in scholarly discussions of games. These ambiguities were designed to encourage interdisciplinary approaches which may be orthogonal to—while mindful of—the existing discourses. The issue's contributors have responded to this broad remit. Both the original symposium held at Abertay University in May 2018 and this Special Issue include work from scholars in computer science, film studies, comics studies, cultural studies, and game studies. The idea of 'storytelling' places emphasis on the process and performance and, in their artful weaving together of domains, the articles comprising this Special Issue represent important responses to far-reaching transformations in contemporary storytelling practices.

Darshana Jayemanne
Special Issue Editor

Editorial

"Gaming and the Arts of Storytelling" Introduction

Darshana Jayemanne

Division of Games and Arts, School of Design and Informatics, Abertay University, Dundee DD1 1HG, UK;
d.jayemanne@abertay.ac.uk

Received: 27 November 2018; Accepted: 30 November 2018; Published: 4 December 2018

The title of this Special Issue of *Arts* makes use of some ambiguous terms: 'gaming' rather than 'videogames'; the plural 'arts' rather than the singular 'art'. Similarly, the concept of 'storytelling' has an ambiguous relation to the term 'narrative' which is far more commonly deployed in scholarly discussions of games. These ambiguities were designed to encourage interdisciplinary approaches which may be orthogonal to—while mindful of—the existing discourses. The issue's contributors have responded to this broad remit. Both the original symposium held at Abertay University in May 2018 and this Special Issue includes work from scholars in computer science, film studies, comics studies, cultural studies and game studies. The idea of 'storytelling' places emphasis on the process and performance, and, in their artful weaving together of domains, the articles comprising this Special Issue represent important responses to far-reaching transformations in contemporary storytelling practices.

In the opening piece, Goetz (2018) utilises the analogy of 'trellis and vine' in order to conceptualise the relationship between fictionality and game rules within a single framework that is oriented towards videogames' medium-specificity. Engaging with psychological research alongside the theory of play, Goetz's trellis and vine analogy conceptualises rule-bound and make-believe play as 'bipolar and synergistic'. This yields four schemes in which trellis and vine may be related, each of which captures a particular set of play situations.

Keogh and Jayemanne (2018) explore the remediation of the *Alien* films in videogames through a central question: what does it mean to look at the alien? Reading critical responses to both the film and videogame appearances, Keogh and Jayemanne note that the alien has completely inverted its affective and storytelling functions: what once repulsed the audience's gaze comes to focus the gun-player hybrid look of the first-person shooter. These dynamics are further traced to the more recent *Alien: Isolation*, where, through what the game's A.I. designer terms 'psychopathic serendipity', players are subject to the look of the alien being. The alien look emerges from these readings as an acute locus in which to trace storytelling transformations across eras and media forms, serving as the basis for a critique of 'ego-centric design' in digital games.

Summerley (2018) invokes John Carmack's dismissive equation of the value of stories in pornography and videogames, and proceeds to pursue the question in earnest. Reviewing some key academic discussions of musicals and pornography, Summerley explores how storytelling relates to the formal aspects of videogames. Considered formally, videogames, musicals and pornography alike often involve the punctuation of fictionality with other material—gameplay, musical numbers and explicit scenes respectively. Dyer's categories of integrated, separated and dissolved forms of the musical and Williams' application of the same to pornography are extended as a framework for videogame storytelling.

Pittner and Donald (2018) also pose the question of remediation with a focus on the influence of Conrad's *Heart of Darkness* across games, film and comics. This complex draws together questions of adaptation and historical fact, where themes developed by Conrad after a visit to the Belgian Congo disseminate through media forms, time periods and storytelling functions. In *Far Cry 2* and *Spec Ops: The Line*, difficulty and frustration become game design methods through which videogames have taken up the storytelling dynamics and techniques which Conrad pursued in literary fiction.

Mawhorter et al. (2018) bring the concept of 'choice poetics' to bear on the question of videogame storytelling. Developed as support for a system for algorithmically generating interactive narrative choices, the adaptation of this vocabulary for critical appraisal of such choices represents a fruitful crossing between disciplines. Choice poetics consists of four steps: goal analysis, likelihood analysis, prospective analysis and retrospective analysis. Having described the method, the authors turn to two case studies taken from *Undertale* and *Papers, Please*. Each case represents a return by players to a decision framework which, through repetition, is formally similar but nevertheless poetically distinct. Mawhorter et al. demonstrate the utility of choice poetics through using the four steps to rigorously characterise how difference and repetition work in these choices.

Novitz (2018) explores the resonances, often noted by critics, between the videogame *Deadly Premonition* and the television show *Twin Peaks*. Both texts generate uncanny imagery and affect through storytelling techniques that invoke and subvert genre conventions, invoking tropes and states such as possession, twinned or mirrored characters, potentially animate objects and mystery narratives. *Deadly Premonition* expands the uncanny emphasis on the player–avatar relationship common to survival horror into many aspects of its design. Reading in this way allows Novitz to investigate gameplay itself as a storytelling strategy.

Koenitz (2018) provides a focused analysis of early influential research on the ontology of interactive narrative, identifying what he terms a 'foundational canon'. Many of these texts rely on different definitions of narrative, each of which necessarily influences its discussion of narrative in interactive texts. Rather than proposing another definition, Koenitz conducts a mapping of this foundational work, placing key texts on two axes: media specificity and user agency. The resulting framework and discussion are valuable both for specialists looking to take stock of the infrastructure of contemporary debates on interactive narrative, and those newer to the field who are interested in orienting their ideas in relation to existing positions.

Discussions of 'immersion' are very common in relation to videogames, but Kocurek's (2018) discussion of the topic begins from a distinctive intellectual touchstone: Walter Benjamin's essay "The Storyteller". While contemporary action games pursue immersion through overstimulating players' sensory and cognitive capabilities, for Benjamin storytelling immerses us in the communication of experience and 'counsel'. Kocurek locates this form of storytelling in the rise of contemporary independent games, such as *Depression Quest* and *I Get This Call Every Day* which can be situated not only within videogame canons, but also in 'the broader cultural web of storytelling'.

Finally, Backe (2018) explores Machine Games' *Wolfenstein II: The New Colossus* through Bakhtin's notions of the carnivalesque and grotesque along with Haraway's cyborg. The game recapitulates the anti-fascist aesthetics of preceding *Wolfenstein* games, but in shifting its setting to an alternate reality mid-century United States, intensifies the politics of resistance with intersectional dynamics including themes of race, ability and gender. For Backe, the game's carnivalesque aesthetics and scenes are storytelling techniques that allow it to explore the subversive potentials of the cyborg that are inherent in, but disavowed by, gaming's technological assemblages.

Conflicts of Interest: The author declares no conflict of interest.

References

Goetz, Christopher. 2018. Trellis and Vine: Weaving Function and Fiction in Videogame Play. *Arts* 7: 41. [CrossRef]

Keogh, Brendan, and Darshana Jayemanne. 2018. "Game Over, Man. Game Over": Looking at the Alien in Film and Videogames. *Arts* 7: 43. [CrossRef]

Summerley, Rory K. 2018. Approaches to Game Fiction Derived from Musicals and Pornography. *Arts* 7: 44. [CrossRef]

Pittner, Fruzsina, and Iain Donald. 2018. Gaming the Heart of Darkness. *Arts* 7: 46. [CrossRef]

Mawhorter, Peter, Carmen Zegura, Alex Gray, Arnav Jhala, Michael Mateas, and Noah Wardrip-Fruin. 2018. Choice Poetics by Example. *Arts* 7: 47. [CrossRef]

Novitz, Julian. 2018. Expansion, Excess and the Uncanny: Deadly Premonition and Twin Peaks. *Arts* 7: 49. [CrossRef]

Koenitz, Hartmut. 2018. What Game Narrative Are We Talking About? An Ontological Mapping of the Foundational Canon of Interactive Narrative Forms. *Arts* 7: 51. [CrossRef]

Kocurek, Carly A. 2018. Walter Benjamin on the Video Screen: Storytelling and Game Narratives. *Arts* 7: 69. [CrossRef]

Backe, Hans-Joachim. 2018. A Redneck Head on a Nazi Body. Subversive Ludo-Narrative Strategies in Wolfenstein II: The New Colossus. *Arts* 7: 76. [CrossRef]

arts

MDPI

Article

What Game Narrative Are We Talking About? An Ontological Mapping of the Foundational Canon of Interactive Narrative Forms

Hartmut Koenitz

Professorship Interactive Narrative Design, HKU University of the Arts Utrecht, Nieuwekade 1,
3511 RV Utrecht, The Netherlands; Hartmut.koenitz@hku.nl

Received: 6 July 2018; Accepted: 14 September 2018; Published: 20 September 2018

Abstract: There have been misunderstandings regarding "narrative" in relation to games, in part due to the lack of a shared understanding of "narrative" and related terms. Instead, many contrasting perspectives exist, and this state of affairs is an impediment for current and future research. To address this challenge, this article moves beyond contrasting definitions, and based on a meta-analysis of foundational publications in game studies and related fields, introduces a two-dimensional mapping along the dimensions of media specificity and user agency. Media specificity describes to what extent medium affects narrative, and user agency concerns how much impact a user has on a narrative. This mapping is a way to visualize different ontological positions on "narrative" in the context of game narrative and other interactive narrative forms. This instrument can represent diverse positions simultaneously, and enables comparison between different perspectives, based on their distance from each other and alignment with the axes. A number of insights from the mapping are discussed that demonstrate the potential for this process as a basis for an improved discourse on the topic.

Keywords: game narrative; interactive digital narrative; mapping; ludology; narratology; ludonarrative; shared vocabulary

---

1. Introduction

A foundational issue with respect to the relationship between games and narrative is the lack of a shared understanding of "narrative", as well as related terms like "story", "storytelling", or "fiction". Indeed, Jesper Juul in *Half Real* assesses the term "narrative" as "practically meaningless":

> [...] the term narrative has such a wide range of contradictory meanings and associations for different people and in different theories that it is practically meaningless unless specified in great detail. (Juul 2005)

Juul proceeds to analyze several definitions from outside game studies to support his assessment. However, so far, little attention has been paid to the differences in the understanding between different researchers and practitioners within the space of game studies, game design, and related fields broadly concerned with the theory and design of interactive digital narratives (IDN) (e.g., artificial intelligence (AI) for interactive narrative, interactive documentaries, narrative-focused installation pieces, etc.).

In this paper, I will introduce a mapping of different positions in order to acknowledge and visualize these differences, with the aim of improving the academic and professional discourse around games and narrative. The mapping is based on a meta-analysis of the ontological status of the word field surrounding "narrative" in a range of academic publications concerned with video games and other interactive narrative forms during its foundational period (1997–2006).

2. The Story So Far

A first analysis of "narrative" in a range of academic publications concerned with video games during the last two decades uncovers a variety of different meanings. These include "narrative" as a human expression extended by encounters with the interactive digital medium (Murray 1997), as the result of the engagement with a cybertextual machine (Aarseth 1997), as a means to provide context (Juul 2005), as an experiential quality during the experience of work (Pearce 2004; Salen and Zimmerman 2004; Calleja 2009; Calleja 2013), as an analytical framework to understand artefacts (Montfort 2005; Fernández-Vara 2014; Ensslin 2014), or as an analytical entity challenged by the interactive aspect of video games (Ryan 2006).

So far, I have strategically chosen to omit papers from the main phase of the narratology versus ludology debate (1999–2004), in order to show that the ontological problem this paper is concerned with is not restricted to the adversarial positions in the debate, but existed before and since.

Unfortunately, these examples represent some of the most accessible cases—publications in which the authors take great care to explicitly define their usage of the term. Implicit definitions of "narrative" and related terms are widespread in academic and professional discourse, as I have argued previously (Koenitz 2016; Koenitz 2018), and thus often neither the particular meaning of the term nor its categorical status are readily accessible. In other words, one scholar's "experience dimension" might be another scholar's "narrative", and one developer's "level design" might be an audience member's "narrative". In that sense, both exist and are interrelated—different definitions and implicit definitions. The latter requires an additional analytical effort to identify the specific definition used. The focus of this article is to address the former.

The realization that the ontological status of vocabulary has not been at the center of attention is surprising, especially if we consider the relative novelty of these areas of study, as well as their interdisciplinary nature. If—for the sake of this argument—we take Murray's *Hamlet on the Holodeck* from 1997 as a pioneering effort in the academic investigation of interactive narrative (while acknowledging earlier efforts[1]), and the first issue of the *Game Studies* journal with Aarseth's (Aarseth 2001), Juul's (Juul 2001), and Eskelinen's articles (Eskelinen 2001) as "year one" (Aarseth 2001) of modern game studies (again, while being mindful of earlier work, e.g., Huizinga 1938; Caillois 1961), then it follows that none of these scholars themselves have been originally trained in the novel fields of interactive narrative or video games. Indeed, Murray's Ph.D. is in English Literature, Aarseth's is in Comparative Literature; only Juul's is in Video Game Theory (although completed in 2003, two years after the inaugural issue of *Game Studies*). Yet, when scholars originate in different traditions, there is a danger of misunderstanding, as the respective terms and underlying categorical concepts are not automatically understood. This is especially problematic when, at first glance, the vocabulary appears to be identical, yet no attempt was made to establish a shared understanding of the word field around narrative. During the so-called "narratology versus ludology" debate, the seemingly obvious question—"what do you mean by narrative (and related terms)?" was hardly asked. Instead, the protagonists treat terms in the word field around "narrative" as transparent, then at best, they provide a definition to support their respective understanding and engage in a discourse, with the aim to prove their opponent wrong. This strategy is a scholarly dead end, and so far has not led to a satisfying conclusion to the debate. While the "hot" phase of this (in)famous debate might seem to have ended around 2005, infrequent contributions kept it alive (Calleja 2009; Ryan 2006; Simons 2007; Calleja 2013; Calleja 2015), while more recently an edited collection (Kapell 2015) discussed the topic, and Bogost's 2017 article "Video Games Are Better Without Stories" (Bogost 2017) re-iterated the original rejection of narrative in games. While it might be productive to engage with the original

---

[1] e.g., Laurel's (Laurel 1986) and Buckles' Ph.D. theses (Buckles 1985), Laurel's 1991 book (Laurel 1991) and the work by the hypertext fiction community, e.g., (Bolter and Joyce 1987; Bolter 1991; Bernstein et al. 1992; Landow 1992; Joyce 1995).

arguments once more, from the distance of nearly two decades, the purpose of this paper is instead to propose a change of perspective.

2.1. A Change of Perspective

I would like to consider the possibility that both sides might present valid arguments on the backdrop of their respective disciplinary tradition. An actual debate never took place (cf. Gonzala Frasca's contemporary insight (Frasca 2003)), as this would have meant first investigating the ontological status of terminology—for example, of Murray's "story" (e.g., in (Murray 2004)) in comparison to Aarseth's use (e.g., in (Aarseth 2004)) of the same word. This aspect has certainly not garnered the necessary attention during the debate (or since). Therefore, I would like to suggest that at least some aspects of the debate can be traced back to differences in the respective ontological understanding, as both specific meaning and categorization differ between scholars.

2.2. Examples of Ontological Differences

Markku Eskelinen criticizes Janet Murray' interpretation of *Tetris* (AcademySoft 1984) as a narrative, when Murray characterizes it as a "[…] perfect enactment of the over tasked lives of Americans in the 1990s—of the constant bombardment of tasks that demand our attention and that we must somehow fit into our overcrowded schedules and clear off our desks in order to make room for the next onslaught" (Murray 1998). In Eskelinen's view, Murray's interpretation is inappropriate because it wrongly categorizes a game as something it is not. However, Murray's reading of *Tetris* as an allegory for the continuous onslaught of daily tasks in late-20th-century capitalism is not surprising for a literary scholar, and is certainly not "wrong" in an absolute sense. Conversely, this does not mean that Eskelinen's analysis of *Tetris* as a game with specific mechanics is "wrong" either. The difference between these two analyses are rather the different levels of abstraction on which they operate. Eskelinen's concern is with the concrete material of *Tetris*, and is thus less abstract, while Murray addresses the more abstract question of the game's meaning as cultural expression. It might be helpful to consider the difference as akin to signifier and signified—two different and equally valid perspectives on the same artefact. From this perspective, Murray's 2004 declaration that "all games are narratives" is also not "narrativism"—a colonial approach that misconstrues interactive experiences as narratives—as Espen Aarseth alleges, but rather an abstract allegorical understanding of games as hero stories.

Therefore, while it might be a convenient theoretical shortcut to simply reject differing scholarly perspectives originating in other disciplines, this is actually where the work should begin rather than end. This is the purpose of a meta-study, to investigate the ontological status, respective framework, and definition. What do Murray, Eskelinen, and other scholars want to address? What is their understanding of narrative? Where does it come from? How do their concepts compare to other authors? What can we learn from the comparison?

Once we start with this perspective, Eskelinen's attempt at a clear distinction between games and narratives, which is "If I throw a ball at you I don't expect you to drop it and wait until it starts telling stories" (Eskelinen 2001), reveals itself to be less clear-cut on several levels. First, there is no generally accepted definition of what "telling stories" actually entails. While it might indeed be difficult to identify a "teller" in Eskelinen's hypothetical example, some papers (e.g., (Stern 2008; Koenitz 2016)) have argued against the categorization of game narrative as "telling". To stay with this image—the ball might not tell a story, but could still convey a narrative in a specific context. This is especially true if we consider narrative forms that operate without words. Second, there is also the possibility of imagining a game in which the ball drop is a trigger for the players to start telling stories. Lastly, Eskelinen's example itself can be construed as a micro-narrative, and in this sense, the ball game has actually created a story, the one Eskelinen tells us. Every single one of these analyses represents a different lens on the same fact, which reframes Eskelinen's foregrounding of one that excludes narrative as just that, a specific preference that should be clearly marked as such.

3. Mappings

For the time being, a generally accepted definition of "narrative" (and related terms like "story" and "storytelling") seems elusive, and thus any hope of a simple solution on that end might be naive. At the same time, this does not mean that there is no chance for a comprehensive understanding. The key here is to move beyond the binary property of definitions (what is/is not a narrative) towards a relational approach: how can we describe the relationship between different definitions? On which dimensions do they differ? For this purpose, spatial mappings are promising. Provided that the respective dimensions of such a mapping are carefully chosen, they can offer novel insights into the relationship between different positions.

N. Katherine Hayles' call for a "media-specific analysis" of digital forms of narration (Hayles 2002), provides a first dimension for this process. While she made her argument originally to point out the neglect of the aspect of mediated representation in the humanities, this question also has a more universal application that fits the present topic. I call this dimension "media specificity". It investigates the relationship to materiality—is narrative seen as media agnostic, and not affected by digital procedural media, or is it understood as considerably affected, which would mean that Interactive narrative has specific qualities, and is effectively a separate entity.

The impact of the player/interactor on the experience and their agency with regards to narrative is another important and frequently discussed aspect (e.g., (Wardrip-Fruin et al. 2009; Harrell and Zhu 2009; Knoller 2010; Mason 2013). I will use the term "player agency" for this dimension. Here, perspectives range from "not different to that of a novel" (player equals reader/viewer) to "significant change" (player has agency over the course of experience).

Thus, media specificity and user agency are represented in the two axis of the mapping. Both of these dimensions will be scored on a scale from 0 (no impact) to 6 (considerable impact) in the mapping. Individual positions on the scales on both dimensions are represented in more detail in the following tables (Tables 1 and 2).

Table 1. Scale for media specificity.

Score	0	1	2	3	4	5	6
Desc.	Narrative is not affected by the digital medium, it is the same entity as a book or film	There is some influence of the digital medium, yet narrative is properly manifested in non-digital forms	Some genres of digital narrative exist; however, these are digital versions of analog manifestations	Some aspects are specific to the digital medium, but not enough to consider them different entities	There are specific digital narrative genres, yet these are enabled by non-digital forms	There is a clear influence of the digital medium on narrative, yet some form of media agnosticism is still maintained	Narrative is considerably affected by the digital medium; it is a different entity, in contrast to a book or film

Table 2. Scale for user agency.

Score	0	1	2	3	4	5	6
Desc.	User has no impact; user equals reader/viewer	Very limited impact on frame narratives/contextual narratives	User as visitor, only indirect impact on their own experience	There is a mix—some impact exists, but core elements are understood as fixed	User makes choices within a pre-determined structure	User has considerable impact, yet only on a narrative that exists in relation to non-digital forms	User has considerable impact (decision making, sequencing, selection, co-creation)

Locating Positions

Using these scales, in the following section I briefly analyze a foundational canon of 11 publications (Murray 1997; Aarseth 1997; Juul 1998; Juul 2001; Juul 2005; Eskelinen 2001; Aarseth 2001; Jenkins 2004; Pearce 2004; Salen and Zimmerman 2004; Ryan 2006) on the topic of interactive and video game narrative, and score them on media specificity and user agency (Table 3). These scores were then used to create a two-dimensional mapping (Figure 1) which is discussed in Section 4. The selection criteria for the canon were high-impact (a google scholar citation count of at least 200 citations[2]) and from the formation years (1997–2006) of video game studies and related areas concerned with interactive forms of narration. More recent publications on the topic (e.g., (Eskelinen 2012; Ensslin 2014; Mukherjee 2015)) have not yet reached this level of impact.[3] In addition, the concentration on earlier publications is purposeful, in order to address the issue at its origin.

Table 3. Positions in the analyzed publications.

Author	Publication	Year	Media Specificity		Player Agency
Murray, Janet	*Hamlet on the Holodeck*	1997	6		6
Aarseth, Espen	*Cybertext*	1997	2		6
Juul, Jesper	*A Clash Between Game and Narrative*	1999	0		6
Juul, Jesper	*Games telling Stories?*	2001	1		6
Aarseth, Espen	*Game Studies, Year One*	2001	1		6
Juul, Jesper	*Half Real*	2005	1		6
Eskelinen, Markku	*The Gaming Situation*	2001	0		6
Pearce, Celia	*A Game Theory of Games*	2004	Experiential	6	6
			Performative	3	0
			Augmentary	3	1
			Descriptive	n/a (see text)	
			Metastory	3	1
			Story System	6	6
Jenkins, Henry	*Game Design as Narrative Architecture*	2004	Evocative	4	3
			Enacted	4	5
			Embedded	6	2
			Emergent	6	6
Salen & Zimmerman	*Rules of Play*	2004	Embedded	6	5
			Emergent	6	6
Marie-Laure Ryan	*Avatars of Story*	2006	external—exploratory	3	4
			internal–exploratory	3	2
			external–ontological	3	6
			internal–ontological	3	6

[2] Citation count on scholar.google.com, September 2018: (Murray 1997) > 5000; (Aarseth 1997) > 4000; (Juul 1998) > 300; (Juul 2001) > 600; (Aarseth 2001) > 700; (Eskelinen 2001) > 600; (Pearce 2004) > 200; (Jenkins 2004) > 1400; (Salen and Zimmerman 2004) > 6000; (Juul 2005) > 2000; (Ryan 2006) > 600.
[3] Citation count on scholar.google.com, September 2018: (Eskelinen 2012) < 100; (Ensslin 2014) < 70; (Mukherjee 2015) < 30.

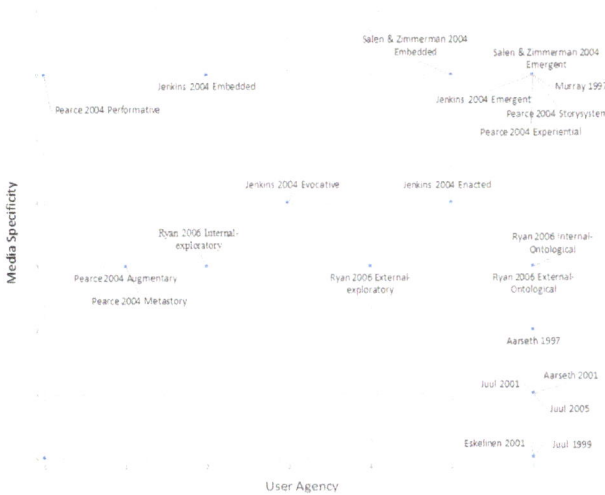

Figure 1. Spatial mapping of different ontological positions on interactive digital narrative.

Janet Murray's position in *Hamlet on the Holodeck* (Murray 1997) can be categorized as foregrounding the impact of the affordances of the digital medium (her categories of procedural, participatory, spatial, and encyclopedic) on narrative, as well as on the player's agency, which for her represents a fundamental aesthetic quality. Murray also associates an additional aspect of player agency with transformation, which is the dual quality of affecting change in the narrative, as well as being affected by the experience. This position will be ranked as high (6) on both dimensions.

Espen Aarseth in *Cybertext* (Aarseth 1997) introduced the notion of the "ergodic"—the non-trivial effort required by the audience to traverse an interactive narrative. In the present context, this translates to a high ranking on the user agency dimension (6). In respect to media specificity, Aarseth indeed champions novel narrative forms in mostly digital manifestations, for example adventure games. Yet, his insistence on a transmedial perspective on narrative (according to him, textual representations on paper can also qualify as cybertextual machines) results in a lower score on this dimension (2).

Similarly, Jesper Juul's initial rejection of narrative in games, when he says "the computer game is simply not a narrative medium" (Juul 1998), is in line with traditional perspectives in the humanities with regards to media specificity (narrative is not affected by the digital medium), as Juul understands narrative as immutable while emphasizing the difference to player agency in games. This perspective will be ranked low (0) on the media specificity dimension and high on player agency (6). Juul's later position from 2001 onward (Juul 2001) moves the position on the dimension of media specificity to 1, in line with Aarseth's later position (Aarseth 2001), while Eskelinen's pronouncement (Eskelinen 2001) of the incompatibility of narrative with games ranks lower (0). Juul's 2005 book *Half-Real* (Juul 2005) sees a role for narrative (in the guise of "fiction") in games, and thus might initially appear to open up towards a more media-specific understanding of narrative. However, Juul still preserves a dichotomic perspective, in which games represent an open structure and narrative a fixed, closed one. For him, the role of narrative in games is mostly ornamental to provide context, and thus is increasingly superfluous the more the player progresses. From the perspective of media specificity, the mapping of this positions thus remains at 1, and player agency at 6.

In 2004, Henry Jenkins published his essay "Game Design as Narrative Architecture" (Jenkins 2004), in which he argues for a media-specific perspective. He describes four specific modes for interactive digital narrative: "evocative", "enacted", "embedded", and "emergent". The evocative mode refers to narratives that reference prior stories in other media, e.g., a Harry Potter game. Enacted narratives allow the user to act out specific roles within an existing narrative universe, for example that of a Hobbit from Tolkien's *Lord of the Rings*. Embedded narratives convey information by means of spatially distributed narrative-infused encounters, as exemplified in the adventure game *Myst* (Cyan 1993). Finally, emergent narratives appear in rule-based game worlds that provide players with the tools to construct stories of their own (e.g., *The Sims* (Wright 2000)). With respect to media specificity and player agency, the different modes require individual assessment—the evocative and enacted modes cannot be ranked as fully media-specific, since Jenkins describes them as dependent on more traditional print literary or cinematic narratives. Consequently, they are ranked at 4 on this dimension. Player agency is medium (3) in the evocative mode, as it is restricted to the "satellite narratives" that cannot affect the main traditional narrative core, and higher in the enacted mode, but does not reach full agency for its dependence on the main narrative (5). For embedded narrative, media specificity ranks higher (6), yet user agency is limited to movement (2). Finally, emergent narrative ranks highly on both dimensions, as a media-specific form with extensive user agency (6/6).

Celia Pearce, in her paper "A Game Theory of Game" (Pearce 2004), foregrounds a media specific perspective and argues for a different understanding of narrative—no longer as "storytelling", but in a "play-centric context". Pearce rejects literary and film theory and proposes a path towards a specific theory of games and narrative within games that casts narrative as a mostly experiential quality. Narrative games are successful, Pearce tells us, if they apply what is engaging and interesting about narrative and "use it to enhance the play experience". On this foundation, Pearce identifies six different modes of narrative in games. The first, "experiential", is the emergent narrative that stems from the conflict of the games as experienced by the player. According to Pearce, this mode exists in every game; it is media-specific (6), and the user has agency (6). The second mode, "performative", describes the same emergent narrative, but from the spectator position. This mode still ranks high on media specificity (6), but the spectator has no agency on their own (0). "Augmentary" is Pearce's term for supplemental "layers of information, interpretation, backstory, and contextual frameworks" that enhance the experience. This mode can include media-specific elements, but could also use traditional fixed-linear narrative modes, and is thus scored at the midpoint (3) for media specificity, while user agency is low (1). "Descriptive" denotes the retelling of game experiences to third parties, either in person or through platforms such as Twitch. This narrative mode will not be represented in the mapping, as it constitutes a "second order narrative" that happens outside of the direct relationship between player/interactor and the work. "Metastory" is similar to "augmentary", and is ranked in the same way (3/1), but instead describes a fully developed narrative framework. Finally, a "story system" allows the player to build her own narrative content from generic parts. This mode is similar to Jenkins' understanding of emergent narrative (6/6).

Similar to Pearce, Salen and Zimmerman in *Rules of Play* (Salen and Zimmerman 2004) see narrative mostly as an experiential quality, but focus on the designer's task in creating said experience. They describe two possible narratives modes: embedded and emergent. Their understanding of emergent narrative aligns with both Jenkins' and Pearce', and thus is ranked the same (6/6), yet their concept of embedded is broader than Jenkins'. For Salen and Zimmerman, an embedded narrative can be experienced through all kinds of interactions (not just spatial as with Jenkin's), therefore user agency is ranked high (5); however, this narrative mode misses the highest mark for the lack of control over the global narrative. Media specificity is high in this case too (6).

Marie-Laure Ryan, in her 2006 book *Avatars of Story* (Ryan 2006), approaches the question of interactive digital narrative from a narratological perspective. While she clearly acknowledges some of the changes brought about by the digital medium, and identifies some resulting opportunities and particular structures, she ultimately considers interactivity to be in conflict with narrative: "[. . .] interactivity is not a feature that facilitates the construction of narrative meaning". Therefore, on the media specificity dimension, her position is ranked at the midpoint (3). When it comes to player agency, Ryan's position requires a closer examination, as she offers a categorization of different types of interactivity along two different trajectories, internal–external and exploratory–ontological, which result in four different modes:

1. External–exploratory: the interactor makes choices in a game of discovery; e.g., text-based hypertext fiction,
2. Internal–exploratory: the interactor as a visitor with no ability to change; e.g., 360 video,
3. External–ontological: the interactor is a god; e.g., *The Sims*,
4. Internal–ontological: Interactor is a character in the virtual world, determining the fate of the avatar and the virtual world; e.g., *Façade* (Mateas and Stern 2005).

For the mapping, these modes equate to different levels of player agency. External-exploratory is at 4 because the interactor has control over choices, internal-exploratory is at 2 with limited agency (only in movement), and finally external-ontological and internal-ontological are at 6, as the interactor has considerable impact on the narrative in both modes.

4. Discussion

Narrative under interactive conditions in the digital medium is a phenomenon that is not going to go away, instead, it will proliferate in different forms, from video games and interactive documentaries to installation pieces, not to mention journalistic interactives and AR/VR/MR (augmented reality/virtual reality/mixed reality) works. Interactive digital narrative thus represents a rich field for artistic experiments, journalistic information transfer, education, and entertainment, as well as related research. Yet so far, vague vocabulary with multiple contradictory meanings has existed, acting an impediment for both practice and research. The mapping presented in this paper addresses that challenge by identifying and positioning different perspectives on narrative. The result is an argumentative space that allows for productive critical comparisons of different positions. As a first effort of this kind, some of the values assigned might be subject to later revision. The mapping moves beyond binary perspectives and thus enables a novel perspective on the narratology versus ludology debate, no longer as a battle over the "correct" perspective, but as an encounter of different definitions of narrative within the same space.

Specifically, the mapping provides a number of insights. Two clusters exist around the maximum value of both dimensions (6 and 6), as well as around a point that is low on media specificity and high on user agency (0 and 6, respectively). These two clusters represent the opposing positions in the narratology versus ludology debate. What we can learn from identifying these clusters is that the actual disagreement in the debate is about media specificity, not on user agency, since the majority of positions are closely aligned when it comes to the dimension of player agency. The takeaway here is that the debate should properly be regarded as being concerned with the aspect of media specificity of interactive narrative. This also means that "narratology versus ludology" description is a mislabeling. Consequently, future work can now concentrate on investigating these positions towards media specificity, in order to move the discussion forward.

Another aspect worth pointing out is that Aarseth's position from 2001 onward allows for less media specificity than his earlier perspective in *Cybertext*, which means his position has moved further away from the media-specific cluster around Murray's position, while Juul's trajectory is in the opposite direction. For future work, it would be interesting to investigate if (a) these movements continue and (b) how they are motivated by the two scholars.

We can also see that Jenkins' perspective encapsulates several different positions, making him less clearly placed amongst the proponents of specific interactive digital narrative forms clustered around Murray's position. Jenkins is thus not as good a representative of that position as Aarseth especially has portrayed him (e.g., in (Aarseth 2012)). Furthermore, engaging Jenkins' perspective properly would mean engaging either all or a specific one of these positions. The same insight holds true for Pearce' several positions, as well as Ryan's analytical framework along the dimensions of internal/external and exploratory/ontological. What these three scholars describe is not a single position, but rather a space within the mapping.

A further takeaway from the mapping is that the discrepancy in the ontological status of vocabulary pertains even to qualifications like "embedded narrative". This is clearly visible in the differing positions of Jenkins' use of the term to describe "environmental storytelling", in contrast to Salen and Zimmerman's meaning of "any kind of predetermined narrative structure".

5. Conclusions

The mapping introduced in this article is an instrument for visualizing the ontological differences between different scholars' perspectives on "narrative", as expressed in the foundational canon of publications on interactive forms of narrative. The resulting space is testimony to the diversity of opinions in this matter. More importantly, this representation provides a means to compare different positions by proximity and distance, as well as alignment versus the two dimensions. In this way, the representation provides a basis for an improved discourse on interactive forms of narration, overcoming simplistic binary oppositions used earlier, e.g., in the so-called "narratology versus ludology" debate. The insights presented in the discussion section show the potential of this approach.

In future work, the instrument could be extended in various ways—for instance, with additional authors' positions, a further dimension to create a three-dimensional mapping, or through comparisons with mappings featuring different dimensions. In addition, it would be interesting to map artifacts in this way, assessing where particular works could be located in this space.

Funding: This research received no external funding.

Conflicts of Interest: The author declares no conflict of interest.

References

Aarseth, Espen J. 1997. *Cybertext*. Baltimore: JHU Press.

Aarseth, Espen J. 2001. Computer Game Studies, Year One. *Game Studies* 1: 1–15.

Aarseth, Espen J. 2004. Genre Trouble. In *First Person: New Media as Story, Performance, and Game*. Edited by Noah Wardrip-Fruin and Pat Harrigan. Cambridge: MIT Press, Available online: www.electronicbookreview.com/thread/firstperson/vigilant (accessed on 6 July 2018).

Aarseth, Espen J. 2012. A Narrative Theory of Games. In Paper presented at FDG'12 Proceedings of the International Conference on the Foundations of Digital Games, Raleigh, NC, USA, May 29–June 1; pp. 1–5, ISBN 978-1-4503-1333-9.

AcademySoft. 1984. *Tetris*. Lyon: Infogrames Entertainment.

Bernstein, Mark, Michael Joyce, and David Levine. 1992. Contours of Constructive Hypertexts. In Paper presented at ECHT'92 Proceedings of the ACM Conference on Hypertext, Milan, Italy, November 30–December 4; New York: ACM, pp. 161–70. [CrossRef]

Bogost, Ian. 2017. Video Games Are Better without Stories. *Theatlantic.com*. April 24. Available online: https://www.theatlantic.com/technology/archive/2017/04/video-games-stories/524148/?utm_source=atlfb (accessed on 6 July 2018).

Bolter, Jay David. 1991. *Writing Space*. Mahwah: Lawrence Erlbaum.

Bolter, Jay David, and Michael Joyce. 1987. Hypertext and Creative Writing. In Paper presented at HYPERTEXT'87 Proceedings of the ACM Conference on Hypertext, Chapel Hill, NC, USA, November 13–15; New York: ACM, pp. 41–50. [CrossRef]

Buckles, Mary Ann. 1985. Interactive Fiction: The Computer Storygame 'Adventure'. Ph.D. thesis, University of California, San Diego, CA, USA.

Caillois, Roger. 1961. *Man, Play, and Games*. New York: Free Press of Glencoe.

Calleja, Gordon. 2009. Experiential Narrative in Game Environments. Paper presented at Digra 2015 Conference, Beijing, China, July 11–12; Available online: http://www.digra.org/wp-content/uploads/digital-library/09287.07241.pdf (accessed on 6 July 2018).

Calleja, Gordon. 2013. Narrative Involvement in Digital Games. Paper presented at Foundations of Digital Games 2013, Crete, Greece, May 14–17.

Calleja, Gordon. 2015. Game Narrative: An Alternate Genealogy. In *Digital Interfaces in Situation of Mobility*. New York: Springer Press.

Cyan. 1993. *Myst*. Eugene: Broderbund.

Ensslin, Astrid. 2014. *Literary Gaming*. Cambridge: MIT Press, pp. 1–217.

Eskelinen, Markku. 2001. The Gaming Situation. *Game Studies 1*. Available online: http://www.gamestudies.org/0101/eskelinen/ (accessed on 6 July 2018).

Eskelinen, Markku. 2012. *Cybertext Poetics*. New York: Bloomsbury Publishing USA.

Fernández-Vara, Clara. 2014. *Introduction to Game Analysis*. Abingdon: Routledge.

Frasca, Gonzalo. 2003. Ludologists Love Stories, Too: Notes from a Debate That Never Took Place. Paper presented at Digital Games Research Conference 2003, Utrecht, The Netherlands, November 4–6.

Harrell, D. Fox, and Jichen Zhu. 2009. Agency Play: Dimensions of Agency for Interactive Narrative Design. Paper presented at 2nd AAAI Spring Symposium on Intelligent Narrative Technologies, Stanford, CA, USA, March 23–25.

Hayles, N. Katherine. 2002. *Writing Machines*. Cambridge: MIT Press.

Huizinga, Johan. 1938. *Homo Ludens: A Study of the Play Element in Culture*. Boston: The Bacon Press.

Jenkins, Henry. 2004. Game Design as Narrative Architecture. In *First Person: New Media as Story, Performance, and Game*. Edited by Noah Wardrip-Fruin and Pat Harrigan. Cambridge: MIT Press, Available online: http://www.electronicbookreview.com/thread/firstperson/lazzi-fair (accessed on 6 July 2018).

Joyce, Michael. 1995. *Of Two Minds*. Ann Arbor: University of Michigan Press, Available online: http://press.umich.edu/script/press/10599 (accessed on 6 July 2018).

Juul, Jesper. 1998. A Clash between Game and Narrative. Paper presented at the Digital Arts and Culture Conference, Bergen, Norway, November 26–28.

Juul, Jesper. 2001. Games Telling Stories. *Game Studies* 1: 45.

Juul, Jesper. 2005. *Half-Real*. Cambridge: MIT Press.

Kapell, Matthew Wilhelm. 2015. *The Play versus Story Divide in Game Studies*. McFarland: Jefferson.

Knoller, Noam. 2010. *Agency and the Art of Interactive Digital Storytelling*. Berlin/Heidelberg: Springer, pp. 1–4.

Koenitz, Hartmut. 2016. Interactive Storytelling Paradigms and Representations: A Humanities-Based Perspective. In *Handbook of Digital Games and Entertainment Technologies*. Singapore: Springer, pp. 1–15.

Koenitz, Hartmut. 2018. Narrative in Video Games. In *Encyclopedia of Computer Graphics and Games*. Cham: Springer, vol. 1, pp. 1–9. [CrossRef]

Landow, George P. 1992. *Hypertext*. Baltimore: Johns Hopkins University Press.

Laurel, Brenda. 1986. Toward the Design of a Computer-Based Interactive Fantasy System. Ph.D. thesis, Ohio State University, Columbus, OH, USA.

Laurel, Brenda. 1991. *Computers as Theatre*. Boston: Addison-Wesley.

Mason, Stacey. 2013. On Games and Links: Extending the Vocabulary of Agency and Immersion in Interactive Narratives. In *Interactive Storytelling, Proceedings 6th International Conference, ICIDS 2013, Istanbul, Turkey, 6–9 November 2013*. Edited by Hartmut Koenitz, Gabriele Ferri, Mads Haar, Digdem Sezen, Tonguc Ibrahim Sezen and Güven Catak. Lecture Notes in Computer Science. Cham: Springer, vol. 8230, pp. 25–34. [CrossRef]

Mateas, Michael, and Andrew Stern. 2005. Structuring Content in the Façade Interactive Drama Architecture. In Paper presented at AIIDE'05 Proceedings of the First AAAI Conference on Artificial Intelligence and Interactive Digital Entertainment, Marina del Rey, CA, USA, June 1–3.

Montfort, Nick. 2005. *Twisty Little Passages*. Cambridge: MIT Press.

Mukherjee, Souvik. 2015. *Video Games and Storytelling*. Berlin/Heidelberg: Springer. [CrossRef]

Murray, Janet Horowitz. 1997. *Hamlet on the Holodeck: The Future of Narrative in Cyberspace*. New York: Free Press.

Murray, Janet. 1998. *Hamlet on the Holodeck: The Future of Narrative in Cyberspace*. Cambridge: MIT Press.

Murray, Janet H. 2004. From Game-Story to Cyberdrama. *Electronicbookreview.com*. January 5. Available online: http://electronicbookreview.com/thread/firstperson/autodramatic (accessed on 6 July 2018).

Pearce, Celia. 2004. Towards a Game Theory of Game. In *First Person: New Media as Story, Performance, and Game*. Edited by Noah Wardrip-Fruin and Pat Harrigan. Cambridge: MIT Press, Available online: http://www.electronicbookreview.com/thread/firstperson/tamagotchi (accessed on 6 July 2018).

Ryan, Marie-Laure. 2006. *Avatars of Story*. Minneapolis: University of Minnesota Press.

Salen, Katie, and Eric Zimmerman. 2004. *Rules of Play*. Cambridge: MIT Press.

Simons, Jan. 2007. Narrative, Games, and Theory. *Games Studies 7*. Available online: http://gamestudies.org/0701/articles/simons (accessed on 6 July 2018).

Stern, Andrew. 2008. Embracing the Combinatorial Explosion: A Brief Prescription for Interactive Story R&D. In *Interactive Storytelling, Proceedings First Joint International Conference on Interactive Digital Storytelling, ICIDS 2008 Erfurt, Germany, 26–29 November 2008*. Lecture Notes in Computer Science. Berlin/Heidelberg: Springer, vol. 5334, pp. 1–5. [CrossRef]

Wardrip-Fruin, Noah, Michael Mateas, Steven Dow, and Serdar Sali. 2009. Agency Reconsidered. Paper presented at DiGRA Conference 2009, London, UK, August 30–September 4.

Wright, Will. 2000. *The Sims [Video Game]*. Redwood City: Electronic Arts.

arts

MDPI

Article

Approaches to Game Fiction Derived from Musicals and Pornography

Rory K. Summerley

Games Academy, Falmouth University, Penryn Campus, TR10 9FE Penryn, UK; rory.keir@gmail.com

Received: 26 June 2018; Accepted: 17 August 2018; Published: 27 August 2018

Abstract: This paper discusses the construction of consistent fictions in games using relevant theory drawn from discussions of musicals and pornography in opposition to media that are traditionally associated with fiction and used to discuss games (film, theatre, literature etc.). Game developer John Carmack's famous quip that stories in games are like stories in pornography—optional—is the impetus for a discussion of the role and function of fiction in games. This paper aims to kick-start an informed approach to constructing and understanding consistent fictions in games. Case studies from games, musicals, and pornography are cross-examined to identify what is common to each practice with regards to their fictions (or lack thereof) and how they might inform the analysis of games going forward. To this end the terms 'integrated', 'separated', and 'dissolved' are borrowed from Dyer's work on musicals, which was later employed by Linda Williams to discusses pornographic fictions. A framework is laid out by which games (and other media) can be understood as a mix of different types of information and how the arrangement of this information in a given work might classify it under Dyer's terms and help us understand the ways in which a game fiction is considered consistent or not.

Keywords: games; video games; game fiction; game narrative; game storytelling; pornography; musicals; ludonarrative dissonance

---

1. Introduction

This paper sets out to establish the common links between humanities theories applied to musicals, pornography, and games and to identify the ways in which game fictions can be understood to be constructed around the formal aspects of games. This research is particularly concerned with cases where fictional consistency might be more reliably achieved in a game. This research was undertaken using a humanities approach because understanding fiction in musicals and pornography in relation to the structure of games and the experience of fiction by players is not an empirical problem with a quantifiable answer. Many have identified gaps between the fictions and rules-oriented qualities of games (Polansky 2015; Tocci 2008; Juul 2005; Hocking 2007; Murray 1997) and the understanding of these gaps is a prime concern here. Often neglected are those media which, I will argue, have structural similarities to games and thus could reveal much about how they operate alongside fiction. Since games are examined here as a vector for fiction (consistent or otherwise) it may be worth looking at how fiction does not comfortably gel with formal processes in other media. Fictional inconsistencies are not unique to games and other media also feature different types of information that may not always mesh. In the course of this research many cases were examined where fiction is broken or played with by its author: breaking the fourth wall; metafictional stories; and cases where fictional plausibility is stretched to the breaking point. While games are often compared to film, theatre and literature in order to understand them as media for storytelling I believe it may be more fruitful to take a more general approach and look at games as media for relating fictional information. Two practices, musicals and pornography, stand out alongside games where fiction is often challenged by the formal affordances of their media. Like games, these practices are not primarily associated with telling stories and even challenge traditional notions of fictional representation.

2. Musicals and Pornography

Linda Williams once observed that 'it is commonplace for critic and viewers to ridicule narrative genres that seem to be only flimsy excuses for something else—in particular, musicals and pornography are often singled out as being really about song and dance or sex.' (Williams 1999, p. 126). In a similar way, game fictions can often be interpreted as just an excuse—they exist for the game's own sake. Pornography, musicals and games are all forms that can be enjoyed apart from a fictional context and it is surprising that they are not compared more often given their remarkable structural similarities. For pornography, games and musicals an explicit narrative is arguably optional and their formal structure means that they often come across tensions when trying to convey fictional information. Fiction in pornography is fraught with difficulty when reading it mostly due to the nature of pornography and its audience. Like games, there are those who would question whether there is even any need for any kind of fiction, narrative or story in pornography. Game developer John Carmack made the infamous analogy that, 'Story in a game is like a story in a porn movie. It's expected to be there, but it's not that important' (Kushner 2003, p. 120). However, this does not detract from the fact that there are audiences that engage with stories in both games and pornography. It merely highlights an interesting commonality that I argue is one of many. The formal core of each is related to the sensory pleasures of sound, sexual arousal, and victory rather than storytelling.[1]

To make sure there is no confusion at this stage, I define music as organized sound chosen for performance (prerecorded or otherwise) and musical theatre and film (hereafter referred to as musicals) as productions that use music as a foundation for exploring a narrative or theme. My definition of musicals does not presently include opera, as Taylor (2012) notes the two are very distinct forms and so the theoretical discussions of musicals presented here are not necessarily applicable to opera. I define pornography as any material made in any medium for the primary purpose of instilling or aiding sexual desire and/or arousal in its audience. Notice that these definitions neither include nor exclude the possibility of fictional information in music or pornography (yet in practice they very often exclude it). I realize these definitions are quite broad and I will discuss many cases that function in different ways. A pornographic pin-up functions differently to a pornographic film or erotic literature but all examples will come under my definition of pornography. My discussion of musicals is similarly broad as I will primarily be discussing examples from musical theatre but also of classical compositions and popular musical genres. These extra examples, even though they are music, do not strictly fall in the same realm as musicals. However, this diverse range of case studies still provide useful comparisons to the ways fiction functions in games. Games, musicals and pornography are all practices that are not tied to a particular medium and so caution is raised here not to confuse my discussion in this section as making definitive claims about any of the media these practices use. They are only discussed to

---

[1]   The thing that caused me to see a link between these very different practices was the revelation of the inseparable role repetition plays in games. Repetition is also a hallmark of musicals and of pornography. Oliver Sacks, in his study of the cognition of music, emphasiszs the importance of repetition in music:

> There are, of course, inherent tendencies to repetition in music itself. Our poetry, our ballads, our songs are full of repetition. Every piece of classical music has its repeat marks or variations on a theme, and our greatest composers are masters of repetition; nursery rhymes and the little chants and songs we use to teach young children have choruses and refrains. We are attracted to repetition even as adults; we want the stimulus and the reward again and again, and in music we get it.
> (Sacks 2007, p. 47)

Similarly, when discussing video games in relation to other media, Dovey & Kennedy observe ' . . . no other kind of cultural consumption requires this kind of repetition. Instead we find it in cultural activities where musicians or sports players are called upon time and again to repeat actions in order to achieve a preferred performance or a kind of virtuosity' (Dovey and Kennedy 2006, p. 100).

help understand how fictions function in cases similar to games (where fiction is not strictly necessary or of primary focus).

Take the concept of a pin-up for example. In a pin-up illustration or photograph, a model is displayed in either an abstract or fictional setting. In the case of a pin-up that describes a limited fictional world, the significance of the fiction is a curiosity. The mere appearance of erotic stimuli (typically the nude or partially clothed human body in an erotically charged scenario) is enough for pornography to fulfill its function. Either the fiction enhances the pornographic function (as in the case of a particular role-playing or uniform fetish) or it serves as 'window dressing', a non vital bonus that gives the pin-up a degree of distinctiveness from other pin-ups. Likewise, it could be said of a game that as long as the design of a game is functionally adequate and ludically compelling then the fictional world of the game is also 'window dressing'. In both cases, the fictional aspect may not be as separate as we imagine.

Pornographic films of the latter half of the 20th century, as documented by Linda Williams (1999), would more commonly feature narratives specifically structured around erotic subject matter. In the film *Insatiable* (Stu 1980) the plot centers on a wealthy and powerful woman's quest to have satisfying sex. In this instance, a fiction gives explanation for the formal pornographic elements (i.e., the revelation of sexual stimuli to the audience). While these more fictionally explicit films do exist, the majority of pornography rarely features a narrative. The subgenre of porn parodies (Simon 2003) and the hardcore feature films that Williams (1999) examines are seen as exceptions to the norm when compared to more 'gonzo' films or nonfictional sex scenes. Modern games have also had a similar trajectory regarding narrative where a heavy focus on story is marketed as a unique selling point as in games such as *Heavy Rain* (Quantic Dream 2010) or *Gone Home* (Fullbright 2013).

Williams (1999) notes that in pornography a formal structure, similar to that found in musical theatre, is at play. Drawing from '*The Film Maker's Guide to Pornography*' (Ziplow 1977), Williams shows how 'numbers' and narrative work in parallel in pornographic films. These numbers are not unlike the formal musical numbers that exist in musicals (duet, solo etc.). Distinct from narrative, numbers merely describe a formal template on which narrative may or may not be transcribed. In pornography, according to Ziplow, the numbers are:

1. Masturbation
2. Straight sex
3. Lesbianism
4. Oral sex
5. Ménage à trois
6. Orgies
7. Anal sex
8. S&M (Sadism and Masochism)

While this is not a comprehensive list of numbers, it is clear that these numbers do not prescribe many specifics about fiction. Likewise, in musical numbers such as a solo, duet, or ensemble number, fiction is not yet established, only the formal musical structure is described. We can see similarities in games where a boss fight, hub-world, or puzzle can be thought of as numbers which do not prescribe any specific fictional information but might serve as the foundation for it later.

In music, and more prominently in musicals, fiction is communicated alongside formal musical information. Typically, a distinction can be made between music and lyrics, and in the case of musicals this extends to stagecraft, dance choreography, libretto, acting, and costumes. The question is, where is fiction communicated in music? Lyrics can be read as making fictional statements that are merely set to music but in some cases can be abstract as in doo-wop, wordless choir, or scat singing. Can music itself make fictional statements? Ludwig van Beethoven's sixth symphony—*Pastoral Symphony*—(Beethoven 1951) is often cited as an example of music that features no lyrics yet represents a fictional setting. This is known as 'program music', which is thought of as having 'content', as opposed to 'absolute music' which is purely abstract, nonrepresentational and textless (Dahlhaus 1989). Beethoven's *Pastoral Symphony* features titles for each movement which describe different aspects of an idyllic countryside and the music itself features identifiable sounds such as the imitation of bird-calls and the sounds of thunder by musical instruments (as can be seen in bar 130 of *VI Symphonie F Major "Pastorale" Op.68.* by Beethoven (1951)). While some instrumental music integrates these aspects of fictional representation, a large proportion of music features very little explicit fictional information partially because it does not need to in order to function as music in much the same way as pornography or games do not need fiction to function. An example of a musical without a fiction would be the abstract segment of Fantasia (Joe and Huemer 1940) depicting Bach's *Toccata and Fugue in D Minor*.

Richard Dyer (1992) suggested the formal nonrepresentational parts of music are in contradiction with representational signs in musicals, making them a contradictory medium. 'What film musicals do, he proposes, is to manage these contradictions so that superficially they seem to disappear.' (Taylor 2012, p. 10). Music theorist Millie Taylor suggested that the discontinuity of musical theatre is where the pleasure they offer may be derived. Musicals take on an unrealistic, almost escapist sense about them due to how the formal aspects rule over the narrative. Taylor describes how romantic couples in musicals can be identified by the fact that they have a similar vocal range that compliments one another (Taylor 2012, p. 27). Other character archetypes are often signified by their musical performance showing a unique connection between formal music and fictional information. Taylor's analysis of *The Rocky Horror Picture Show* (Sharman 1975) shows how musical styles inform us about characters.[2] This connection may make it easier for audiences to intuitively understand the fiction of a musical without having to feel that the fiction is an excuse for the music to happen, as is often the case in pornography.

Richard Dyer developed a theory about how different musicals work and categorized them into three broad types: integrated, separated and dissolved (Dyer 1992, p. 28; Williams 1999). These terms were applied to pornography by Linda Williams (1999, p. 160) and perhaps the concepts they discuss can also be applied to game fiction given their marked similarities. According to Dyer, integrated musicals are musicals where the songs are directly woven into the narrative. This is usually done by naturally setting up a fictional explanation that cues a song (as opposed to spontaneously bursting into song in any given context) or by making the songs part of the diegesis. In other words, characters are given reasons for why they might be singing, as in *Chicago* (Fred and Kander 1975). Separated musicals are ones where narrative and number have no relation and characters frequently express their thoughts and feelings through song but for no apparent reason as in *Grease* (Jim et al. 1971) or *West Side Story* (Leonard and Sondheim 1957). Dissolved musicals are musicals where the fictional world is fantastical to a point of being utopian. The nature of dissolved musical fiction is such that singing is a means of dealing with the fictional world and metaphorically represents a character's existence in relation to the narrative via music (an example could arguably be *The Wizard of Oz* (Fleming 1939) as seen through the lens of a childish protagonist's imagination). In dissolved musicals the world is so pleasurable that it seems to call forth music but not 'for no reason'. It is just how things operate in that utopian fictional universe (Dyer 1992, p. 30).

Linda Williams took these three categories of musical and noted similarities to the way that narrative and number are connected in pornographic films. Integrated pornography gives fictional explanations for why characters have sex. Separated pornography does not bother with fictional explanations for sex or often any kind of fiction at all. Lastly, dissolved pornography features characters in a fictional world where sexual congress and promiscuity are commonplace.[3] It would be simple to

---

[2]   Pop is virginal and conventional, and so Brad and Janet sing in this style. This contrasts with Dr. Frankenfurter's sexually
       deviant and flamboyant glam rock style or Eddie's rugged and manly rock and roll vocals and so on.
[3]   Williams highlighted that the connection between musicals and pornography demonstrated the similarities between how
       the human body is configured in both practices. However, I would like to emphasize that they are closely related structurally.

transpose the categories of integrated, separated and dissolved narratives to games and the analogies are clear. However, the concern of this research does not stop at the identification of texts that feature gaps. Within pornography and music, techniques have been developed to adjust to the quirks of their own forms that attempt to sew together fictional information and the unique formalities of their respective medium.

In the case of music, mickey-mousing and sound painting are two that are used to signify something halfway between musical and fictional information (Taylor 2012; Whalen 2004). Mickey-mousing refers to the synchronized mimicry of a character's actions by the non-diegetic musical score. It is so-called after the musical scores of early Disney cartoons which helped signify scenes such as a character angrily walking away by a thumping rhythm that crashes over the background score. Sound-painting is a similar technique whereby the score is used to create rudimentary sound effects with musical instruments. The music in this case is used as a mimicry for a genuine sound such as birdsong or a punch. Foley recordings could be used in these cases but these sounds when played musically add to the musicality of the fictional universe and join what is seen and heard in a novel way.

In pornography, fetishes are often a way into fiction. Costume role-play can naturally lead to many different narratives, such as the fictional perversion of a nun used as a pretext to the religiously charged breaking of taboo. There are many common narratives found in pornography organized around different fantasies and fetishes. The accidental discovery of someone in a vulnerable or sexually compromising situation; the arrival of a workman to fix someone's pipes; or the seduction of a young person by an experienced one. These are all fictions that are not required for pornography to function yet they attempt to meld fiction with that function in order to enhance that function. These melding attempts are not always successful but it points to one thing being clear. There are multiple parts of these media, of which fiction is one part, where stable fictional consistency is achieved by making sure nonfictional parts do not conflict, but actively combine with fictional ones as well.

3. Defining Information in Games

Let us suppose that in pornography and musicals there is information that can be termed fictional information. Obviously (and especially in the case of music) it is possible to have abstract pieces that either forego fiction (such as 'absolute music' as categorized by Dahlhaus (1989)) or are representative as a matter of document (as in 'gonzo' pornography or commonly amateur pornography). These cases are not being ignored, but for now let us focus on the fictional information as it exists in certain cases. This fictional information may be consistent or inconsistent but it is there. The question turns to what other information is communicated if it is not fictional? In games, this information is commonly associated with rules and rules are often established as a separate or opposite category to fiction by game scholars (Juul 2005; Salen and Zimmerman 2003), but having examined other media more closely it is perhaps more proper to say that it is a type of information common to all forms of media. The rules of a game are certainly a part of this other type of information (as they can't really be said to be describing fictional events directly) but the sense is that it doesn't stop there. In music this other information could be said to be the 'formal conventions' of music: time signatures, tempo, harmony and other concepts (primarily from western music theory). Yet I would suggest that it is not just the abstract information that describes a medium but rather the medium itself that communicates this other type of information. It just so happens that most media can also communicate fictional information alongside their native and inherent character (which may be why the discussion has centered on a dualistic interpretation of how games function—rules versus fiction). For lack of a better

---

'This extended analogy to the musical has allowed us to assess qualities of body performance that, although inherent to hard core, are often overlooked because sex, in contrast to song and dance, appears so natural and unperformed. I have therefore emphasized the reverse of the truism that dance in the musical is really about sex by suggesting the ways in which sexual numbers are like dance; in showing how sexual performances are choreographed, placed in a scene, and deployed within a narrative context, I have tried to get beyond the 'fact' of sex to its rhetorical function in texts.' (Williams 1999, p. 270).

word, I suggest that the information unique to a medium might be termed 'significant' as a means of differentiating it from fictional. While fiction can certainly be thought of as significant (in the colloquial sense) to a novel or film, there also exist films and books that contain no fiction but still represent things with information unique to that medium (i.e., the information is organized on pages or rolls of film stock). Etymologically, one can take a derived meaning of 'significant' from its Latin roots: *signum*, meaning 'distinguishing feature' (Jones 2016, p. 182) and *fico*, 'I make' (Jones 2016, p. 39). *Signa* + *ficant* thus means 'a quality that makes distinct'. Without this information there is no medium, thus it is significant to that medium. The notes of Beethoven's 6th Symphony are presenting us with significant information which helps to represent, but is not actually, the fictional information of the work. The erotic stimuli of the human body and its display in pornography could be considered the significant information that may lead us to imagine a fiction surrounding various sexual acts. So it is with all fictional works. However, when there is a gap between significant and fictional information (at least in the cognition of the audience), fictional inconsistencies may be experienced.

This analogy could be applied to the concepts of separated, integrated and dissolved fictions in musicals. Separated fictions often feature apparent fictional inconsistencies as the significant form of the musical has little to no conceptual or contextual connection to its fictional content (although this is not to say they are qualitatively better or worse than other fictions—a fiction can be inconsistent or good, consistent and bad simultaneously). A solution here is to just take separated musicals at face value and ignore the potential disruptions or inconsistencies or embrace separation as an aesthetic decision (e.g., parody, metafiction, satire etc.). Integrated musicals feature a conceptual and contextual union between the two and dissolved musicals operate in a fictional world in which the significant aspect is a natural part (e.g., it is expected in the world of the musical for one to burst into song). The goal for fictional consistency in games, it seems, would be to focus on how to integrate and dissolve fictional and significant information together rather than leave them separated.

In summary, significant information is so called not because it is more important than fictional information but because it holds significant meaning to the medium it is communicated by, which cannot be classed as explicitly fictional. For games, significant information refers to information that describes the operation of a game, how it is played and what is ludically possible and/or legal. It can be thought of as the rules of a game however this is not the only thing it covers. While the rules certainly do constitute significant information there are cases where significant information is not explicit and can even be hidden from players. Significant information is information that relates only medium-specific meaning not otherwise fictional. In a game, it consists of the rules, goals, situations and materials for the playing of a game. Thus we have a name for the component that is commonly referred to as 'game' or 'rules' within the model. As a bonus, this also lets the model be freed from just discussing games.

To give a practical example of significant information: before beginning a game of Monopoly, players might discuss which version of Monopoly they will play with (digital or analog?), whether they are playing the game with a time limit, whether trading should be allowed, how best to determine who goes first or what the rules for rolling doubles or getting out of jail should be. All of these discussions revolve around significant information. In a video game some significant information is usually hidden from the player due to the fact that they are partially automated. Explicit information about hitboxes, frame data, statistical information, and other (partially) hidden information is significant but is usually approximated, guessed at or not considered by a (human) player during play. What is certain is that without significant information there is no game.

Fictional information is a little easier to define. It is information that pertains *only* to the fictional world of a work (in short, its fiction). Generally speaking, the fictional setting, fictional events, characters, flavor text/dialogue, art assets, or character names can all be considered fictional information. A practical example of fictional information would be the fact that the character Mario (in *Super Mario 64* (Nintendo EAD 1996)) has an Italian accent and wears overalls. There is no practically ludic purpose for why this should be but it does give the character some recognizable traits and provides information about the world of the various games in which Mario stars. To simplify further, one can think of significant and fictional information influencing the statements we make about games. For instance, 'I lost the game' would be a significant statement. 'Stanley died' would be a fictional statement. Fictional information does not often depend on qualities specific to a medium and so, in this way, it is not significant. As with significant information, we can now rename fiction as specifically 'fictional information' within our model.

Fiction (as distinct from fictional information) is a little harder to define. There is an agreed understanding of what it means in most cases but for the sake of this discussion it should probably be pinned down before misunderstandings accumulate. Walton (1990), Ryan (2001, 2007) and others (Castañeda 1979; Kit 1982; Howell 1979; Woods 2009) have encountered similar ambiguities in their examinations of definitions that oppose fiction to reality, nonfiction or truth. Walton uses it quite broadly and interchangeably with the term 'representation' and links it closely to imagination. It is not restricted to literary fictions and includes all forms of depiction. Ultimately, Walton does not settle on a definition as the very word is so ambiguous that it would be difficult, if not impossible, to come to an agreeable definition that is not incredibly vague or restrictively narrow. One thing Walton does focus on is the idea of fiction as possessing the function of 'serving as a prop in games of make-believe' (Walton 1990, p. 91). This is to say that fiction is simply an anchorage point from which the audience's imagination may develop a 'game of make-believe' which, in practice, can be as simple as viewing a painting and imagining that its depictive content exists in a fictional world.

Marie-Laure Ryan (2001, p. 109) assesses Walton's theory of representation as a game of make-believe stating: 'The assimilation of representation to fiction and the definition of the latter as a prop in a game of make-believe make the embarrassing prediction that texts designed to elicit belief, rather than make-believe, are not representations'. If belief (versus make-believe) is a condition on which we judge the fictionality of a text, as Walton (1990) suggests, then we must scrutinize whether something is understood to be fiction because we make-believe that it is so, or assess it as something other than fiction because we are led to genuinely believe it. Ryan writes that 'make-believe ... often confuses, two distinct phenomena: (1) regarding texts that describe obviously made-up situations as report of true facts ('willingly suspending disbelief'); and (2) engaging in an act of imagination ... ' (Ryan 2001, p. 110) the latter of which does not necessarily involve fiction. Ryan suggests that the concept of mental simulation is helpful in analyzing what make-believe might be understood to be. Imagination as an act of simulation is situated as both similar and different to fiction because of the intended usage and the quality of what is imagined. In Ryan (2007) discussion of a definition of narrative, she suggests that the status of fiction is partially a question of authorial intent.

> If ... we are presented with unknown texts and asked: "is this fiction or nonfiction," our answers will be right or wrong, because they will not be an assessment of what the text is all about, but a guess of the author's intent. Fictionality is indeed a type of game that authors invite readers to play with texts: a game variously described as make-believe, suspended disbelief, or immersion in an imaginary world. The same text could, at least in principle, be presented as a creation of the imagination or as a truthful account of facts, and we must be guided by extra-textual signs, such as generic labels ('novel', 'short story') to assess its fictional status. Because judgments of fictionality affect what the reader will or will not believe, they are much more important than judgments of narrativity. (Ryan 2007, p. 32)

Fictional information comprises all of the information in a game that is exclusively fiction (as opposed to significant information). What determines its status is somewhat dependent on reading the creator's intent and is partially informed by intersubjective convention such as Ryan's example of 'generic labels'. Fiction's function, as Ryan and Walton note, can differ greatly depending on the context it is presented in and for what purpose its audience seeks it out.

> What counts as fiction will depend on how its maker intended or expected it to be used; or on how, typically or traditionally, it actually is used; or on what uses people regard as

proper or appropriate (whether or not they do so use it); or on how, according to principles, it is in fact to be used (whether or not people realize this); or on one or another combination of these. (Walton 1990, p. 91)

As is clear from Walton and Ryan's work, fiction covers many things and defining it becomes a muddy task. I understand it to be identified in much the same way Walton's representations are defined: as a prop in a game of make-believe. To put it succinctly (but by no means conclusively) fiction is information constructed by an author for the sake of imagination (and not necessarily belief) by an audience. The audience (in the case of musical, pornographic or game fictions) can arguably ignore the fiction of those works in preference of the significant information each of these provides. In the case of games this can take the form of subversive or purely instrumental play (such as speed-running) but ignoring fiction is not unique to games. Ignoring the significant information in any of these cases is arguably impossible given that it is to do with the very medium these practices are communicated through. One could arguably play on a lower difficulty or skip sections of gameplay but these decisions are not always made in preference of fictional information and still require some interaction with a system that is rooted in significant information. Likewise, it would be unusual if not impossible for the audiences of pornography and musicals to ignore the significant information unique to each in favor of their fictional information.

In order that our observations about the structure of fictions in musicals and pornography might be of use to games it is worth discussing some case studies that might come under my appropriation of Dyer's terminology. What is the structure of an integrated or dissolved game?

4. Case Studies—Integrated and Dissolved Games

Jesper Juul correctly identifies level design as an aspect of games that has potential for fictional consonance: 'The level design of a game world can present a fictional world *and* determine what players can and cannot do at the same time. In this way, space can work as a combination of rules and fiction' [Juul's emphasis] (Juul 2005, p. 163). Further to this he states: 'Level design, space and the shape of game objects refer simultaneously to rules and fiction. This is a case in which rules and fiction *do* overlap' [Juul's emphasis] (Juul 2005, pp. 188–89). As an example, if there is a fence that physically blocks the player in the world then ludically the fence prescribes a rule that the player cannot walk through the fence. The fence is also fictionally a fence and its depiction prompts the player to imagine that a fence exists in this fictional world and all that that implies. This dual nature of level design is usually unremarkable as the connection between significant and fictional information is made automatically and effortlessly. The physical layout of a game level naturally makes fictional statements.

I would like to take this principle of level design a step further and consider how Dyer's terminology reflects the structure of games. The three types of musicals (as recounted by Taylor 2012) presented a useful way of thinking about how fiction relates to musicals. The terms 'separated', 'integrated' and 'dissolved' refer to the different ways in which significant information may connect to a fictional world in a given work. To clarify, separated games are those where the fictional information and significant information are divorced from one another. Integrated games and dissolved games are those where the fictional and significant information are joined to create a mostly consistent imaginable world. 'Dissolved' describes integration that is so all-encompassing that even seemingly abstract game mechanics are simply another part of a stylized fictional world. For the purposes of elaborating on world-building in games, I will apply these terms to several case studies. I propose *Dark Souls* (From Software 2011) as an example of an integrated game and *Beat the Beat: Rhythm Paradise* (Nintendo SPD and TNX Music Recordings 2011) as an example of a dissolved game. Specific case studies of separated games are not explored in this paper, but it is suggested that, currently, the majority of games constitute separated fictions in which the fictional and significant information have little to no overlap. A more in-depth study of separated games (specifically those that reflexively engage with fictional inconsistency) alongside other separated fictions is needed to determine the full use of Dyer's terminology for games and whether separation constitutes a problem for games or if it is simply a different aesthetic consideration.

Dark Souls is set in a dark fantasy world which tasks the player with exploring a dangerous and dying world that exists in the aftermath of various conflicts between dragons, gods and humans. A key plot device in the game is the existence of a curse of the undead. This curse spreads much like a disease and the player begins the game locked in an asylum to which the cursed are sent. The curse's main symptom is that the cursed person cannot perish upon death. Instead they resurrect near bonfires, doomed to undeath. This process of continually dying takes its toll on various characters in the world, often resulting in them losing their sanity. If a cursed one completely loses their sanity then they become 'hollow', a hostile, undead shell of a person.

This curse makes for an intriguing plot device in *Dark Souls* but it also has significant, mechanical implications[4]. Since the player character is cursed they cannot die in the permanent sense and will always return to a bonfire (functionally the checkpoints of the game) upon 'death'—fire being implied to be the magical source of all life. This shows a remarkably rare case of player character death and apparent resurrection being given a fictional explanation. This is not to say that every game system must be explicitly tied to a fictional explanation, only that the player is directed towards a potential explanation rather than their imagination be left frustrated by a lack of information.[5] Cursed ones are also branded with a Darksign by which they are recognized. This darksign, a symbol featured in the *Dark Souls* logo, is also a usable item within the player's inventory. Upon 'using' it, players will die losing all their accumulated souls and humanity (two forms of currency in *Dark Souls*) and resurrect at a bonfire. Interestingly, using it is almost never advantageous, it is almost always preferable to die in the conventional way.

In *Dark Souls*, death features prominently as a theme and as a ludic event. To strengthen this connection the conceit of the curse of the undead resolves tensions relating to the apparent resurrection of the player-character upon death. Juul (2005) recalls an example of such a tension in the explanation players give for Mario's ability to apparently resurrect through the use of extra lives in *Donkey Kong* (Nintendo Research and Development 1 1981). He argues that, while the fictional world of *Donkey Kong* is fairly simple to imagine (a gorilla has kidnapped Mario's love interest):

> It is harder to understand why Mario has three lives: Being hit by a barrel, by a fireball or by an anvil should reasonably be fatal. Furthermore, the player is rewarded with an extra Mario at 10,000 points. This is not a question of *Donkey Kong* being incomplete, but a question of the fictional world being incoherent or unimaginable. While, technically, any world can be imagined, and we could explain Mario's reappearance by appealing to magic or reincarnation, the point here is that nothing in *Donkey Kong* suggests a world where people magically come back to life after dying. [Juul's emphasis] (Juul 2005, pp. 123–30)

Death (and the implicit structural repetition that follows) is rarely factored into the fictional world in a game. If anything, it is the most common disruption of a player's experience of fiction (Tocci 2008).

---

[4] A similar conceit where repeated death is fictionally integrated can be found in the role-playing game *Planescape Torment* (Black Isle Studios 1999).

[5] Other notable explanations are given to account for game systems that normally go unexplained. At one point the player's character meets Solaire of Astora a knight who introduces the summoning mechanic whereby players can summon, or be summoned by, other players with a 'soapstone' to help one another. To explain this Solaire states that

> The flow of time itself is convoluted; with heroes centuries old phasing in and out. The very fabric wavers, and relations shift and obscure There's no telling how long your world and mine will remain in contact. But, use this [white soapstone], to summon one another as spirits, cross the gaps between the worlds, and engage in jolly co-operation!

(From Software 2011)

This accounts for how enemies reappear upon sitting at a bonfire, how players are able to join the worlds of other players and also speaks, fictionally, to the disturbed situation of the world.

One of the earliest examples of a designer acknowledging this effect death has on games can be found in the *Zak McKracken and the Alien Mind-benders* (Lucasfilm Games 1988) manual where the Lucasfilm game design philosophy reads:

> We believe you buy games to be entertained, not to be whacked over the head every time you make a mistake. So we don't bring the game to a screeching halt when you poke your nose into a place you haven't visited before. In fact, we make it downright difficult to get a character "killed". We think you'd prefer to solve a game's mysteries by exploring and discovering. Not by dying a thousand deaths. (Moriarty 2015)

Brian Moriarty (2015) points out that Lucasfilm did this to best competition at the time and as an act of good will towards players who were often given intentionally frustrating puzzles to pad the play time of relatively expensive graphic adventure games. However, the relevant point is clear that death can be distracting. Failure necessarily commands the attention of the player and so can take attention away from the fictional world. Game designer David Cage notes how he finds 'game over' screens distracting when considering the narrative and offered another approach to reconciling failure with fiction (Academy of Interactive Arts & Sciences 2017). In David Cage's game *Heavy Rain* (Quantic Dream 2010), players control four characters involved in a murder mystery. The player's choices and skill determine the outcomes of the narrative and if a playable character dies, the narrative continues another character's story without them. There is not just one path to incorporating the structural quirks of games into their fictional worlds but player failure is tricky to account for. The graveyards and resurrection mechanics in *World of Warcraft* are highlighted by Klastrup (2008) as another example of death being aesthetically incorporated into the fictional world.

Dark Souls would seem to provide an explanation for what is left as incoherent in *Donkey Kong* and the games that Lucasfilm derides. Juul notes player's responses to the *Donkey Kong* case: 'In an informal survey of Donkey Kong players, all players explained the three lives by appealing *to the rules of the game*: With only one life, the game would be too hard' [Juul's emphasis] (Juul 2005, p. 130). Juul follows this train of logic to suggest that as long as we focus on the rules, the game is not incoherent, we merely shift the discussion to rules. In practice, the seemingly inconsistent interruption of death in the course of gameplay is something that regular players of games can be said to be literate in. It is not such a jarring inconsistency that we classify these 'incoherent' games as aesthetically deficient because we are used to 'reading' death as a normal process of ludic failure. However, *Dark Souls* shows that it is possible to marry constant death with a consistent fiction and so we might ask what is stopping any game from achieving this rare feat? What is the structural meaning of death within games given death's dual purpose as fail state and dramatically-charged fictional occurrence? How different information in games overlaps (or doesn't) is what needs to be understood. In any case it is clear that *Dark Souls* is achieving integration through its explanations for how death operates in its world. We could say that *Dark Souls'* fictional and significant information are integrated in much the same way Williams (1999) states 'narrative' and 'number' can be in pornography or as Dyer (1992) does in musicals.

Beat the Beat: Rhythm Paradise (hereafter referred to as *Rhythm Paradise*), on the other hand, features a universe that is dissolved. The game's fiction revolves almost entirely around the mechanics and goals of the game. In *Rhythm Paradise*, the player plays through various rhythm-based minigames that require them to tap out a beat or repeat a call-and-response rhythm. These minigames usually feature a framing device that gives context for the action they must perform. The subsequent fictions that result from these framing devices are usually absurd or comical but still help the player intuitively understand the game. One infamous example is set during an interview with a professional wrestler. 'Ringside' has the player control a wrestler's responses during a post-match interview. They have three responses that are all rhythmically signaled by a fictional occurrence. If the interviewer asks a question (via a pseudo-nonsense rhythmic refrain: 'wubba-dubba-dub, is that true?') to which the player must nod to, on the beat, by pressing a single button. If the interviewer expresses enthusiasm for the wrestler (indicated by her statement 'Woah, you go, big guy!') the player must tap the button twice in quick rhythmic succession to raise the wrestler's arm and perform a bicep flex. Lastly if the crowd of journalists yells 'pose for the fans!?' the player must press two buttons simultaneously to pose for a picture, again on the beat of the accompanying musical track.

Another example from *Rhythm Paradise*, 'Double Date' involves a couple of high-school students on a date near a sports field. For whatever reason, the female student is fascinated by a couple of weasels in the ground nearby. As the couple sits on the bench various types of ball bounce from the sports field and threaten to startle the weasels, which in turn upsets the girl potentially ruining the date. The player plays as the male student and is required to kick the balls away so as not to disturb the date. Each ball's bounce denotes a particular rhythm which the player must 'kick' the last beat.

Rhythm Paradise's fictional set-ups are very simple but allow for an entertaining frame in which to understand the purely formal rhythmic challenge of the game. While it could be argued that the fiction doesn't make sense (the Ringside reporter's comments are gibberish) one has to look at the context in which the fiction takes place. *Rhythm Paradise* (to the extent that it presents a continual fictional universe) concerns a fiction which surrounds rhythm in a highly unrealistic manner. However, realism is not the same as consistency (although they are related in some cases). One clue to this is how the beginning of the Ringside game shows an establishing shot of the stadium where the interview takes place. As the music starts up the entire stadium literally pulsates to the rhythm of the beat. This is not realistic but it shows how the significant information of the game naturally flows alongside its fiction. Indeed, they are dissolved. Not only does the fiction and significant information inform each other (as is the case in *Dark Souls*), they are related so much that the fiction is essentially overtaken by significant information, giving it an abstracted and quasi-fictional status. It is simply a natural part of this world for rhythmic movements and situations to unfold in everyday events. *Rhythm Paradise* does not seem realistic or sensible when assessed alongside our reality but it is certainly internally consistent when observed in its dissolved context.

A similar observation is made by Melanie Fritsch (2014) in her discussion of gameworlds that specifically frame themselves around music and thus construct a 'fantasy diegetic environment' that is consistent but not realistic or even necessarily narrativized. This is the case with Fritsch's analysis (Fritsch 2014, pp. 170–71) of *Vib-Ribbon* (NanaOn-Sha 1999) which, like *Rhythm Paradise's* world, does not offer explicit narratives so much as it uses music as a framework for an unrealistic but dissolved fictional world. Fritsch argues that games like this are constructed from a 'music-based gameplay gestalt' and that: 'It is music with all its features and contexts that blurs the borders of fantasy and reality by being the "real thing" within these gameworlds' (Fritsch 2014, p. 175). In this way a synaesthetic gestalt blends the abstract concerns of significant information in games and music with fictional information put forth by the representation of the game's world.

Rhythm, as we know, incorporates repetition, one of the hurdles to clear to achieve fictional consistency in a game. Repetition has been acknowledged as a structural certainty and potential problem in various areas of game design (Kirkpatrick 2011, pp. 186–87; Grodal 2003; Andersen 2016; Quinn 2015). Grodal in particular stresses the repetitious experience of a video game as similar to the same repetitive requirements of musical appreciation:

> ... this aesthetics of repetition is based on the sequence: first unfamiliarity and challenge, then mastery, and finally automation. The experience is thus in some respects similar to the way in which we enjoy music—musical appreciation is also strongly based on repeating the listening process until it has reached a stage of automation. (Grodal 2003, p. 148)

Rhythm Paradise taps into repetition in a natural way. *Rhythm Paradise's* minigames all account for the need, fictionally, for there to be a depiction of the repetition the player mechanically engages in—in this case it is the rhythm of the game's music. Ringside uses the frame of an interview, an event likely to have its own structural repetitions (e.g., question, response, question, response, photo opportunity etc.). *Double Date* (while it makes little sense in a comparable real-world scenario) is set up so that a repetitive series is plausible and will require an equally repetitive series of actions (being set near a sports field, balls are likely to interrupt the date and since balls are most quickly removed by kicking them, the player and character are called upon to kick them away). *Rhythm Paradise* features a world that is completely about rhythm, and thus repetition. Each character is wholly involved in some musical or rhythmic activity regardless of an explicitly musical context. Even nature itself is shown to be rhythmically motivated (in minigames such as *Micro-Row* where bacterium pulsate to the beat). The fictional and significant information here are totally aligned and thus we can say that *Rhythm Paradise* is a dissolved game.

5. Conclusions

Musicals and pornography have provided a novel means of analyzing game fictions and developing some medium-agnostic terminology (fictional and significant information) for discussing fictional structure in games (and potentially other media). Williams' work on pornography shows that there is a solid theoretical precedent for importing Dyer's terminology to describe another medium and the games examined here indicate there is a good fit for the same terms within game studies.

Dark Souls and *Rhythm Paradise* form internally consistent fictions because they frame their fictional information and significant information in a congruent way. Repetition, for instance, does not prescribe worlds just like that of *Rhythm Paradise* where every fictional depiction is slavishly in service of repetitive rhythms. Rather, a game should have plausible reasons why the same enemies, actions and objectives keep occurring, and these reasons should factor into the world-building itself. Repetition is not appropriate to fictionalize in *every* case. Plausible circumstances in a game should cue imagination to interpret repetition as natural. The 'numbers' of repetitive dialogue, animations, level design, and many other aspects of games all risk incurring disruptive experience of the fiction, as they do in musicals or pornography. Death and repetition are two frequently encountered states within games due to their structural make-up and integration or dissolution of these states with the fiction of a game is difficult to navigate. This is not to say that every fictional world in a game should focus on death or repetition, but should be able to offer plausibly imaginable reasons for at least some of the structural features of games.

Funding: This research received no external funding.

Acknowledgments: Thanks are due for the support of Tanya Krzywinska, Douglas Brown, and Rob Gallagher in reading and assessing this research.

Conflicts of Interest: The author declares no conflict of interest.

References

Academy of Interactive Arts & Sciences. 2017. The Game Makers: Inside Story—E05 on Structure. Available online: https://www.youtube.com/watch?v=w0yJ_nVtBFM (accessed on 26 February 2017).

Andersen, Martin. 2016. A Game that Listens—The Audio of INSIDE. *GDCvault*. Available online: http://www.gdcvault.com/play/1023731/A-Game-That-Listens-The (accessed on 13 February 2017).

Beethoven, Ludwig. 1951. *VI Symphonie F Major "Pastorale" Op.68*. Paris: Imp. Rolland/Heugel et Cie.

Black Isle Studios. 1999. *Planescape Torment*. Microsoft Windows. Los Angeles: Interplay Entertainment.

Castañeda, Hector-Neri. 1979. Fiction and reality: Their fundamental connections: An essay on the ontology of total experience. *Poetics* 8: 31–62. [CrossRef]

Dahlhaus, Carl. 1989. *The Idea of Absolute Music*. Translated by Roger Lustig from German to English. London: University of Chicago Press.

Dovey, Jon, and Helen W. Kennedy. 2006. *Game Cultures: Computer Games as New Media*. New York: Open University Press.

Dyer, Richard. 1992. *Only Entertainment*. London: Routledge.

Fleming, Victor. 1939. *The Wizard of Oz*. Los Angeles: Metro-Goldwyn-Mayer.

Fred, Ebb, and John Kander. 1975. *Chicago*. New York: Broadway.

Fritsch, Melanie. 2014. Worlds of Music: Strategies for Creating Music-based Experiences in Videogames. In *The Oxford Handbook of Interactive Audio*. Edited by Karen Collins, Bill Kapralos and Holly Tessler. New York: Oxford University Press.

From Software. 2011. *Dark Souls*. Playstation 3, Xbox 360 and Microsoft Windows. Tokyo: Bandai Namco Entertainment.

Fullbright. 2013. *Gone Home*. Microsoft Windows, OS X and Linux. Portland: Fullbright.

Grodal, Iorbeh. 2003. Stories for Eye, Ear and Muscles—Video Games Media and Embodied Experiences. In *The Video Game Theory Reader*. Edited by Wolf Mark J. P. and Bernard Perron. New York: Routledge.

Hocking, Clint. 2007. Ludonarrative Dissonance in Bioshock: The Problem of What This Game Is about. *Click Nothing*. Available online: http://clicknothing.typepad.com/click_nothing/2007/10/ludonarrative-d.html (accessed on 14 April 2016).

Howell, Robert. 1979. Fictional Objects: How they are and how they aren't. *Poetics* 8: 129–77. [CrossRef]

Jim, Jacobs, Warren Casey, and John Farrar. 1971. *Grease*. Chicago.

Joe, Grant, and Dick Huemer. 1940. *Fantasia*. Burbank: Walt Disney Productions.

Jones, Peter. 2016. *Quid Pro Quo. What The Romans Really Gave The English Language*. London: Atlantic Books Ltd.

Juul, Jesper. 2005. *Half-Real: Video Games between Real Rules and Fictional Worlds*. Cambridge: The MIT Press.

Kirkpatrick, Graeme. 2011. *Aesthetic Theory and the Video Game*. Manchester: Manchester University Press.

Kit, Fine. 1982. The Problem of Non-Existents. I. Internalism. *Topoi* 1: 97–140.

Klastrup, L. 2008. What makes World of Warcraft a World? A Note on Death and Dying. In *Digital Culture, Play, and Identity: A World of Warcraft Reader*. Edited by H. Corneliussen and J. Walker. Cambridge: The MIT Press.

Kushner, David. 2003. *Masters of Doom: How Two Guys Created an Empire and Transformed Pop Culture*. New York: Random House.

Leonard, Bernstein, and Stephen Sondheim. 1957. *West Side Story*. New York: Broadway.

Lucasfilm Games. 1988. *Zak McKracken and the Alien Mind-benders*. Amiga, Commodore 64 and MS-DOS. San Francisco: Lucasfilm Games.

Moriarty, Brian. 2015. Classic Game Postmortem: Loom. *GDCvault*. Available online: http://www.gdcvault.com/play/1021862/Classic-Game-Postmortem (accessed on 26 February 2017).

Murray, Janet. 1997. *Hamlet on the Holodeck*. Cambridge: The MIT Press.

NanaOn-Sha. 1999. *Vib-Ribbon*. Playstation. Tokyo: Sony Interactive Entertainment.

Nintendo EAD. 1996. *Super Mario 64 [Video Game]*. Nintendo 64. Kyoto: Nintendo.

Nintendo Research and Development 1. 1981. *Donkey Kong*. Arcade. Kyoto: Nintendo.

Nintendo SPD and TNX Music Recordings. 2011. *Beat the Beat: Rhythm Paradise*. (A.K.A. *Rhythm Heaven Fever*). Nintendo Wii. Kyoto: Nintendo.

Polansky, Lana. 2015. Coherence and Dissonance. Available online: http://sufficientlyhuman.com/archives/1006 (accessed on 30 June 2017).

Quantic Dream. 2010. *Heavy Rain*. Playstation 3. Tokyo: Sony Interactive Entertainment.

Quinn, Zoe. 2015. Comedy Games an Underexplored Genre. *GDCvault*. Available online: http://www.gdcvault.com/play/1021867/Comedy-Games-An-Underexplored (accessed on 14 April 2016).

Ryan, Marie-Laure. 2001. *Narrative as Virtual Reality: Immersion and Interactivity in Literature and Electronic Media*. Baltimore: The John Hopkins University Press.

Ryan, Marie-Laure. 2007. Toward a Definition of Narrative. In *The Cambridge Companion to Narrative*. Edited by Herman David. Cambridge: Cambridge University Press, pp. 22–36.

Sacks, Oliver. 2007. *Musicophilia: Tales of Music and the Brain*. New York: Random House Inc.

Salen, Katie, and Eric Zimmerman. 2003. *Rules of Play: Game Design Fundamentals*. Cambridge: The MIT Press.

Sharman, Jim. 1975. *The Rocky Horror Picture Show*. Los Angeles: 20th Century Fox.

Simon, George. 2003. *Shaving Ryan's Privates*. London: Channel 5 Broadcast Ltd.

Stu, Segall. 1980. *Insatiable*. Canoga Park: Caballero Home Video.

Taylor, Millie. 2012. *Musical Theatre: Realism and Entertainment*. Farnham: Ashgate Publishing Ltd.

Tocci, Jason. 2008. "You Are Dead. Continue?": Conflicts and Complements in Game Rules and Fiction. *Eludamos. Journal for Computer Game Culture* 2: 187–201.

Walton, Kendall. 1990. *Mimesis as Make-Believe: On the Foundations of the Representational Arts*. Cambridge: Harvard University Press.

Whalen, Zach. 2004. Play along—An Approach to Videogame Music. *Game Studies—The International Journal of Computer Game Research* 4: 214.

Williams, Linda. 1999. *Hard Core: Power, Pleasure and the "Frenzy of the Visible"*. Berkeley: University of California Press.

Woods, John. 2009. *The Logic of Fiction*, 2nd ed. London: College Publications.

Ziplow, S. 1977. *The Film-Maker's Guide to Pornography*. Drake Publishers.

arts

MDPI

Article

Trellis and Vine: Weaving Function and Fiction in Videogame Play

Christopher Goetz

Department of Cinematic Arts and the Public Humanities in a Digital World Cluster, University of Iowa, Iowa City, IA 52242, USA; christopher-goetz@uiowa.edu

Received: 1 July 2018; Accepted: 10 August 2018; Published: 17 August 2018

Abstract: This paper reviews and synthesizes ideas in the philosophy of play and relevant psychology research in order to address videogame medium specificity, with particular focus on the notion of videogame play as simultaneously "rule-bound" and "make-believe." It offers the sustained analogy of "trellis and vine" for provisionally sorting through the tangle (the "mess" or "assemblage") of function and fiction in games.

Keywords: gaming; videogames; play; fantasy; psychology

1. Introduction

> There was a time when, though my path was rough,
> This joy within me dallied with distress,
> And all misfortunes were but as the stuff
> Whence Fancy made me dreams of happiness:
> For hope grew round me, like the twining vine,
> And fruits, and foliage, not my own, seemed mine.

Samuel Taylor Coleridge (1996)
"Dejection: An Ode"

One day in the late 1990s, during a moment of quiet reverie, Shigeru Miyamoto noticed a line of ants carrying leaves past his patio seat. Watching the workers disappear under tall blades of grass spurred his imagination: *what if the ants were people?* The story of how *Pikmin* (2001) was born in a garden is well known (e.g., Whitehead 2013; Collin 2014; LeJacq 2014). It was not the first instance in Nintendo lore of Miyamoto attributing inspiration to unusual sources, such as daydreaming in his bathtub or recollecting the bamboo forests and caves from his childhood in rural Sonobe, Japan. In his story on *Pikmin's* genesis, *Kotaku's* Yannick LeJacq observes that Miyamoto is an oddity since it is rare for most game designers to even talk about inspiration for a game: " ... there's a reason the developers at Sledgehammer don't reflect during interviews about sitting in their gardens and suddenly realizing that this was the way they wanted to have players shoot at bad guys." (LeJacq 2014). As a developer of the *Call of Duty* series (2011–present), Sledgehammer knows well that "[s]hooting at bad guys isn't a new or groundbreaking concept in video games anymore" (LeJacq 2014). Of course, the flipside of Miyamoto's flash-of-genius approach to mapping new game-design terrain is a cool disinterest in the creative endeavors of industry peers: it is avowedly not by refining existing game designs that Miyamoto plots new directions for his creative work. This is just one way, the *Kotaku* story suggests, that Miyamoto (with Nintendo) is unabashedly out of sync with a risk-averse industry prone to focus-group testing, incremental change, and the careful emulation of past successes.

The question of what inspires a videogame is a big one, whether its answer relies on authorial intent, evokes the relation of one game to another, or raises consideration of how games both influence and are influenced by other media, intellectual or artistic pursuits, or even banal, everyday life in the home; unavoidably, the answer also opens onto the even wider concern of how one defines videogames in the first place.[1] That is, what happens within any game influences how we think of the space between games: what inspires games, how they change over time, and what influences or is influenced by them.

This paper is intended as a way to think about the space between games. However, for that reason, it is also about how one moment of play is bridged with the next and, like Miyamoto, this paper is inspired by the garden. Its extended analogy for thinking about videogame play draws on the relation between a *trellis* (a carefully patterned structure intended to facilitate the growth of climbing plants) and a *vine*, which becomes imbricated with such structures in its pursuit of sunlight. Trellis is to game as vine is to play: the trellis is artificial, rigid, inert, mechanically repetitive in structure, and incomplete on its own (deliberately gap-filled); the vine is organic, dynamic, unpredictable, goal-driven, and can be taken to new heights by the support the trellis offers. The vine may, of course, ignore the trellis altogether and shoot its coiled tendrils in any direction—over time, the lianas woven across various structures may grow and thicken, reinforcing the very objects they had once relied on for support. The analogy is useful for speaking to the relation between play inflected with the structure of rules, and play that abandons rules and stretches out with no more "support" than its own free-form creative energy.

In this regard, there are four key permutations of *trellis and vine*: vines growing without trellis support; empty patches of trellis (where no vine grows); areas where trellis and vine are tightly intertwined and inseparable without the violence of cutting (analysis); and areas where a vine that has already climbed across the full length of the latticework then overshoots the structure in a new direction (having been first carried to places it might not have otherwise reached). Tending to these trellis/vine permutations is perhaps overkill for simply thinking through broad categories like "game" and "play." However, each arrangement is helpful for conceptualizing the relation between rule-bound and make-believe play—or, by extension, for thinking about the relation between a game's structured repetitions (its rules, systems, algorithms, mechanics, and "loops") and its story elements (fictions, themes, settings, characters, and plot events).

The trellis/vine framework serves as a rejoinder to the central argument of *Half-Real: Video Games Between Real Rules and Fictional Worlds* (2005), namely Jesper Juul's claim that " … a video game is a set of rules as well as a fictional world" (Juul 2005, p. 1). Why devote an entire book to advancing such a seemingly non-controversial claim? The full answer requires contextualizing Juul's writing within contemporaneous conversations about videogame medium specificity, which was a heated topic early in game studies.[2] For introducing the trellis/vine framework, it suffices to focus on how

---

[1] While definitions of games occur throughout this essay, engaging in a sustained manner with the wider question of how the videogame has been historically defined as a medium would exceed the paper's intended scope. I recommend consulting excellent primers for such a review, such as Salen and Zimmerman (2004) foundational book (especially Chapter 7, "Defining Games"), or Stenros' more recent article, "The Game Definition Game" (Stenros 2016).

The range of literature implicated in the question of what inspires a game is also quite vast. Some approaches inherently value some combination of market forces and the authorial intent of a game's developers, such as most journalistic or chronicle-style histories of the medium, as in Kent (2001), Altice (2015). Critical perspectives such as Bogost (2007) also rely on notions of authorial intent, and could be contrasted with approaches that privilege meanings made by players, such as with Galloway (2006) notion of "countergaming" or Henry Jenkins' argument before the United States Congress about the importance of fan communities (Jenkins 1999). Genre analysis often thinks about games relationally (defining and tracking common terms as they recur and change over time). See Clark et al. (2015) and Faisal and Peltoniemi (2015) for two recent and innovative approaches to defining and classifying videogame genres. For examples of work exploring how games both influence and are influenced by other media, see Jenkins (2006) and Murphy (2011). See Parker (2013) for a helpful primer on games influenced by installation art practices, and Apperley (2010) for a helpful introduction to gaming's relation to everyday life.

[2] Juul's book represents a meticulous effort at tracking and organizing different ways of conceiving of rules and fictions in videogames. It is positioned as a stopgap for the phenomenon of game scholars talking past one another (failing to agree on the meaning of basic terminology) on the topic of videogame medium specificity (aka, the narratology/ludology debate). Apperley and Jayemane (2012) describe the narratology/ludology debate as being "somewhat unsatisfying on its own terms because discussion often stalled at an inability to agree on basic premises" (Apperley and Jayemane 2012, p. 7). Juul's response to this debate is very much in keeping with a widespread tendency within recent game studies of explicitly disengaging from what has often been conceived of as a narrow terminological squabble. For instance, Janet Murray

Juul approaches the formal question of this debate (i.e., whether narrative analysis is appropriate for thinking structurally about videogames).

2. A Straw Man Tangled in the Garden of Rules and Make-Believe

In 2005, Jesper Juul reversed his position that "fiction in games is unimportant" for the study of games qua games. His reversal takes aim at Caillois (1961) oft-cited foray into play theory. Caillois first argues that "the sentiment of *as if* replaces and performs the same function as do rules" and then concludes that "games are not ruled and make-believe. Rather, they are ruled *or* make-believe" (Caillois 1961, pp. 8, 9; original emphases). Taking Caillois to mean "that rule-based games *do not* have a make-believe element," Juul contends that such a "division is . . . contradicted by most modern board games and video games. Most videogames are ruled *and* make-believe" (Juul 2005, pp. 12, 13; original emphases). This distinction may seem like a quibble. However, the stakes here are quite high when it comes to how we think of videogame medium specificity (see note 2 above). Without second-guessing Juul's progressive embrace of game fiction, I argue that this reading makes Caillois into a bit of a straw man. In effect, Juul's eagerness to acknowledge the co-presence of both rules and fictions in games flattens an important distinction in Caillois' writing—a distinction I argue is useful for thinking about the *relationship* between rules and fictions in games.

In the passage Juul cites, Caillois' main example is Chess, a game that clearly combines both rules and elements of make-believe (i.e., a Medieval theme). It is doubtful Caillois would have overlooked Chess' thematic dimension. Nor does Caillois' argument shunt off the representational qualities of Chess. Rather, Caillois works to distinguish two frames of mind or modes of engagement that, by definition, exclude ("replace and [perform] the same function" as) one another. For example, "One easily can conceive of children, in order to imitate adults, blindly manipulating real or imaginary pieces on an imaginary chessboard, and by pleasant example, playing at 'playing chess'" (Caillois 1961, p. 9). If one knew the rules, one could play chess *"for real,"* meaning that the rules of chess are not mimetic of some real-world phenomenon: the game that is created by the rules "is separated from real life where there is no activity that literally corresponds" (p. 8). Caillois' point is that our motives for following and working within rules (as in a game like Chess) are different from the motives involved with engaging in free-form, make-believe play (such as *pretending* to play Chess). Although one physical object—one board game—could clearly sustain both kinds of play, to speak of rules or make-believe is to speak of two different sorts of play, in turn: thus, his provocation that "games are ruled *or* make-believe."

If it is accepted that Caillois does not actually mean one game cannot contain both rules and elements of make-believe, then there is not much in Caillois' model that Juul's prohibits, not even the former's problematic hierarchizing of rule-based play above make-believe play.[3] For Juul, "a videogame is a set of rules as well as a fictional world," and "[t]o play a video game is therefore to interact with real rules while imagining a fictional world" (Juul 2005, p. 1). Caillois does not preclude the possibility of following the rules of chess (playing chess, in his terms, *"for real"*) while, at moments, also playing at some additional game, such as acting out or imagining the chivalry of Medieval combat. That play generally represents a special frame of mind unique from the experience of everyday life has

---

argues that "Game studies, like any organized pursuit of knowledge, is not a zero-sum contest, but a multi-dimensional, open-ended puzzle that we are all engaged in cooperatively solving" (Murray 2005, p. 2).

3   One area where I would suggest breaking with Caillois is in the subtle condescension he holds for make-believe play. Caillois' binary implicitly positions the rule-bound play of mature adults ("ludus") above the free-form improvisational play he observes in children, animals, and "primitive" peoples ("paidia"). That these two poles of play tend to fall in line with (and reinforce) the gendered and colonialist ideas strewn throughout *Man, Play and Games* is problematic, to say the least. Ian Bogost has observed that there is *still* "an ontological pecking order" (where one part of a game is "more real than another") in the "embrace of syncretism" that Juul and other ludologists have expressed in the past decade (Bogost 2009). This paper's analogy of trellis and vine is meant to maintain a meaningful distinction between rule-bounded and make-believe play without reinforcing this "pecking order." The image of a vine creeping across a trellis does create a contrast of center and periphery, but "periphery" here is less about the margins than the vanguard.

been a much-discussed topic in play theory.[4] Caillois' opposition of rule-based play to make-believe play calls for a further distinction: two separate and somewhat opposed frames of mind that can only with difficulty be said to openly operate in relation with the same element of a game during the same moment of play.

To an extent, Caillois' differentiation seems to be confirmed by literature in clinical psychology that focuses on the role of make-believe play in children's development. On one hand, make-believe and rule-bound play are treated as two distinct modes of engagement; however, on the other hand, shifts between these modes are considered both routine and difficult to track. Singer and Singer (1990) suggest that make-believe is "a commonplace of human thought," adding that "even 'games with rules,' such as the board game 'Monopoly,' often involve additional pretend elements or are the focus of private or shared fantasies well into adult life" (Singer and Singer 1990, p. 42). And Weisberg (2015) emphasizes the difficulty researchers face when attempting to disentangling the two:

> [I]t is sometimes difficult to draw sharp lines between episodes of pretend play and other types of play. Are children engaged in rough-and-tumble play just interacting physically, or are they pretending to be superheroes in a fight? Is a child who stacks blocks just manipulating these objects according to their physical properties, or is she pretending to create a fortress? Even though some kind of imaginative or nonliteral quality is necessary for an action to count as pretence, the presence of this quality is not always immediately apparent to an outside observer, as it is part of the child's internal state ... Researchers struggle with such questions of delineation whenever pretend play is studied (Weisberg 2015, p. 250).

Weisberg goes on to say that make-believe "may not occur throughout the entire episode" of play (e.g., superhero fights or block stacking)—instead, it is more likely that "the activity switches back and forth between being physical play and pretend play," even though it is difficult for outside observers to determine which is which at any moment (Weisberg 2015, p. 250).

The difficulty of "drawing sharp lines between episodes of pretend play and other types of play" during observation might seem to support prevailing attitudes in game studies towards formal analysis. This includes Juul's (2005) assumed simultaneity of rules and fictions, as well as Bogost's (2009) proclamation that "videogames are a mess" of different elements not worth making "tidy" by neatly organizing or analyzing separately, and even Taylor's (2009) suggestion that we make sense of games as "assemblages" of "actors ... , concepts, practices, and relations" that are "interwoven in complex ways at particular historical moments" and are inherently resistant to controlled experimentation or direct, ordered analysis (Taylor 2009, p. 332). It is, perhaps, wishful thinking that conversations about videogame medium specificity will cease—and every call for the topic to be "put to rest" seems, in turn, to inspire more scholars to take up the question, even if just to express a position—a position that likely resembles those mentioned in this paragraph. For the psychologists who study symbolic play in the developmental process, however, distinctions between make-believe and other kinds of play are regularly sought experimentally. Their efforts to conceptualize this distinction are helpful

---

[4] Play theory that thinks of play as a special frame of mind has been influenced largely by Bateson (1972, p. 178) psychological notion of "metacommunication" (the various ways animals and people signal "this is play," thus changing how communication within that frame is to be interpreted), as well as Goffman (1961) writings about play, which include the notion of "rules of irrelevance," echoing Caillois' and Huizinga's definition of play as a separate space where unique meanings are generated by arbitrary rules and values. That Goffman would emphasize the irrelevance of "whether checkers are played with bottle tops on a piece of squared linoleum, with gold figurines on inlaid marble, or with uniformed men standing on colored flagstones" reflects a wider contemporary philosophical interest in the unique social and psychological values games introduce (Goffman 1961, p. 19). Goffman proposed the term "transformation rules" (p. 27) to account for how aspects of the real world nevertheless enter the game in some form. The interest play theorists hold in the unique contexts games generate has been recently mistaken as an assertion that games are hermetically sealed "magic circles," unrelated to any real-world issues. For a thorough consideration of how the "magic circle" has been maligned in game studies (e.g., Consalvo 2009), see (Stenros 2014).

towards the meager end of even temporarily prolonging the need to yield to gaming's complex, unanalyzable "tangle."

If make-believe and rule-bounded play involve distinct and opposed frames of mind, then play, as an action, likely flits from one mode to the other and back again in much the same way behaviorism conceives of two behavioral systems that are incompatible with one another: via the mechanism of *inhibition*. That is to say that two distinct behavior systems can tend to come into conflict, so that though both are active, the weaker of the two is inhibited from being expressed.[5] When one such activity is fully engrossing (even flow-like), then the exclusion of other activities would become even more pronounced.[6] In short, there are behavioral phenomena that cannot be easily explained without conceiving of distinct systems operating episodically.

Are make-believe play and rule-bound play examples of this? For this question, it is helpful that there exists a subfield of psychology investigating behavior motivation called *reversal theory*, which posits that "deep human values" often "come in opposites," and that since "every value has a contradictory value," it is, therefore, "difficult for an individual or a group to pursue all values at the same time" (Apter 2017, p. 2). Reversal theory sees play as a "metarepresentational" state—akin to Bateson's concept of "metacommunication" (psychological frame)[7]—where a certain "bipolarity" is stimulating and pleasurable rather than aggravating and stressful. In this sense, reversal theory's application to play seems to suggest that where an option exists between exaggerating or else fusing two opposites, play's preference seems to lie with the former. Kerr (1991) identifies the distinction between the "real" and the "imaginary" as one such reversal pair which, in play's dramatic oscillations, becomes *"synergistic"* (i.e., distinct but mutually reinforcing) (Kerr 1991, p. 71). Apter and Kerr (1991) identify another pair as *mastery* and *sympathy*, where *mastery* is a state epitomized by "competitive sports" (akin to Caillois' agôn, which focuses on competition and rules), and *sympathy* is a state epitomized by "aesthetic experience," "exposure … to works of art," or, one could add, taking pleasure in a game's fictional and aesthetic dimension (Apter and Kerr 1991, pp. 165–66).

Though these examples are helpful for thinking about ruled and make-believe play as episodic poles, the benefit for thinking of them this way perhaps more clearly lies with the question of motivation.[8] That these two different modes of play might correspond to two distinct motivations for playing would be a valid reason for conceptually distinguishing the two. One approach might note how ruled and make-believe play seem to correspond to the different personality dimensions Lillard et al.

---

[5] As Bowlby (1982) says of behavioral systems, "Any one pattern … occurs only episodically, the reason being that the activity of one pattern is commonly incompatible with the activity of others" (Bowlby 1982, p. 85). Consider, further, how the axiom that "a rabbit cannot simultaneously graze grass and hide in a burrow," reflects the notion that different behavior systems sometimes "require different sorts of environments" (Manning and Dawkins 2012; Bowlby 1982, p. 85). If a bird on the feeder is nervous about the proximity of human voyeurs, it may become conflicted (between the need to feed and need to seek safety) and then "exhibit most of the behavior of take-off without actually doing so," a sort of compromise known as an "intention movement" (Bowlby 1982, p. 98).

[6] For instance, Csikszentmihalyi (1997) research on "flow" describes a mode of intense engagement that saturates a person's attention so fully that other demands for attention (including even basic bodily needs) tend to be suppressed. It is significant that the rubric of flow is often applied to videogames as especially engrossing activities (when optimally, both balancing and maximizing challenge and skills), as opposed to representational media, which Csikszentmihalyi has argued are less stimulating (Csikszentmihalyi 1997, pp. 31, 67).

[7] See note 4 above.

[8] This paper draws on existing scholarly work in order to map out a *conceptual space* for thinking about the dynamics of videogame play in a way that extends beyond what has currently been empirically demonstrated. It would be remiss to not mention recent empirical work on player motivation, such as papers by Kahn et al. (2015) or Ratan et al. (2015), both of which build on Yee (2007) paper, "Motivations for Play in Online Games." These studies in the uses and gratifications tradition rely on self-reported survey data, and are useful for identifying distinctly grouped motivation types. However, they are not intended as finely-ground methodologies for identifying the relationship of different frames of mind during any moment of play. In addition, they rely on the assumption that players can accurately identify motivations and reliably parse (in this case) tricky concepts like story, fantasy, conflict, character, challenge, etc. Since story is a prevalent cultural schema for making sense of the world, its use to describe motivations for playing could in effect capture (and obscure) other motivations that are more difficult to describe in words.

(2011) describe in their research on sociodramatic play and theory of mind: *dramatists* and *patterners*.[9] That distinct personality types display tendencies towards either rule-based or make-believe play hints at the presence of distinct, underlying motivations for each mode.

In fact, Caillois (1961) himself alludes to motivation throughout his book, especially in the chapter on the "The Corruption of Games," which paints the impulses underlying his taxonomy of games in an especially Freudian light. He argues that when games become corrupted (their free spirit and illusion of separateness destroyed), "the tyrannical and compelling psychological attitude that selects one kind of game to play rather than another" is all that would remain (p. 45). This is because games, he argues, "[provide] formal, ideal, limited, and escapist satisfaction" for the "powerful drives" that underlie these "distinctive attitudes" (p. 45). In corruption, each drive corresponds to "a specific perversion which results from the absence of both restraint and protection" the game provides (p. 45). Agôn's self-reliance in play breaks down to the violent assertion of the self in play's corruption ("Now competition is nothing but a law of nature") (p. 46). When mimicry (make-believe) becomes corrupted, a game of pretending to be someone else or imagining a fictional universe lapses into the dissolution of the self. Together, these drives appear to rehearse Freud's famous perversions (sadism and masochism). As is likely clear at this point, the question of player motivation, once again, does lead back to how we define games.[10] For Caillois, games are mechanisms for channeling powerful drives and different sorts of games (e.g., ruled and make-believe games) connect with different drives. Beyond this point, however, Caillois' argument remains under-developed, mostly implicit.

3. The Ball is a Mouse, the Thumb is a Breast: *"As If"* as a *Function*

Perhaps the clearest account of psychological motivation in games comes from Gombrich [1963] (1978), who posits that games become "substitutes" for players by picking a "psychological lock" and thereby enabling pleasure to "cross a boundary which is usually regarded as closed and sealed" (Gombrich [1963] 1978, p. 4). Bateman (2011), who has also written about Skinner Box reward schedules in game design, argues that Gombrich's framework is apt for thinking of how videogames effectively *hack* players by serving a substitutive function related to (or propped upon) some biological need:

> For in this sense 'substitutes' reach deep into biological functions that are common to man and animal. The cat runs after the ball as if it were a mouse. The baby sucks its thumb as if it were the breast. In a sense the ball 'represents' a mouse to the cat, the thumb a breast to the baby. But here too 'representation' does not depend on formal similarities, beyond the minimum requirements of function. The ball has nothing in common with the mouse except that it is chasable. The thumb nothing with the breast except that it is suckable. As 'substitutes' they fulfill certain demands of the organism. They are keys which happen to fit into biological locks, or counterfeit coins which make the machine work when dropped into the slot (Gombrich [1963] 1978, p. 4).

As Bateman aptly notes (and directly in relation to questions of videogame medium specificity), Gombrich's substitutes emphasize *function* over *representation*. It is extremely interesting to see "as if" (make-believe) return, but not on a representational register. Rather, through imagined psychological needs, it is the *function* of a substitute object that evokes the thing it stands for. In this sense, when

---

9   According to Lillard et al., "Dramatists frequently enacted plots involving other people, whereas patterners' play was more object-dependent and tended not to involve social or communicative exchanges" (Lillard et al. 2011, p. 301).

10 It should be noted that not all definitions of games emphasize motivation. For instance, Suits (1978) defines games as goals reached only by "inefficient means," a notion that appears, at first, to say little of motivation, or what would make one want to play one game of inefficient means over another (Suits 1978, p. 22). Galloway (2006) claim that videogames are "software systems" that share more in common with accounting programs than traditional board games is meant, provocatively, to flaunt a dismissal of motivation. However, Suits' definition may only appear to benefit from the addition of a clearer account of player motivation, or what leads one to adopt a "lusory attitude" (Suits' term for the mindset required to play a game) (Suits 1978, p. 359). This is discussed further below.

a rule-bounded game is compelling (when players feel intrinsically motivated to play), that game is no longer "for-" or "in itself," as Caillois would say. Instead, the game becomes, once again, and at all points, an "as if" for players who find pleasure centers unlocked by play that has made use of (or referred to) some privileged *thing* in the world via a logic of function (not resemblance).

Gombrich's distinction between biological substitutes (those meeting the "minimum requirements of function") and fictional representations of imagined satisfaction (e.g., a pictorial representation) seems to reflect one of Vygotsky (1967) paradoxes of play:

> . . . in play [the child] adopts the line of least resistance, i.e., he does what he feels like most because play is connected with pleasure. At the same time he follows the line of greatest resistance, for by subordinating themselves to rules children renounce what they want since subjection to rule and renunciation of spontaneous impulsive action constitute the path to maximum pleasure in play (Vygotsky 1967, pp. 13–14).

Vygotsky reasons that "to observe the rules of the play structure promises much greater pleasure from the game than the gratification of an immediate impulse" (p. 14). This idea more or less tracks Freud's (Freud [1911] 1958) distinction between the "pleasure principle" (a mode of mental functioning akin to seeking the shortest path to pleasure) and the "reality principle," which seeks a greater (and more reliable) sense of satisfaction by temporarily resisting the most direct conclusion.[11] Gombrich's "psychological lock" implies a circumstance where something real (i.e., functionally evocative and concrete) breaks into the store of pleasure that has been built up by prolonged resistance to this shortest path. Freud's two principles of mental functioning could also be thought in relation to Bernard Suits' definition of games as "inefficient means," helping explain why the shortest path to the goal is unsatisfying and, in Suits' words, rules are "inseparable from ends" (Suits 1978, p. 24).[12]

If rules help pick psychological locks (whether through delay, subordination, or their functional resemblance to something "real"), and if make-believe seems, in turn, relegated to the hallucinatory (direct) path to satisfaction that the reality principle forecloses—then what accounts for the affective power of fictional/representational elements in the player's experience of the game? Though Bateman (2011) associates rules and mechanics with Gombrich's substitute, he nevertheless maintains that fictions strongly influence the pleasure these picked locks release. In his example—*Shadow of the Colossus* (2005)—rather than conceiving of each colossus as a series of mechanical obstacles, Bateman (2011, p. 190) argues that "[e]mbodying the foe as a beast, a mighty colossus, *does* affect the emotional experience of victory against it".[13] Bateman (2011, p. 190) concludes that though it is possible to "separate out the functional and representational elements" in a game as a kind of academic exercise, "it is not so easy to distinguish between Juul's rules and his fictions—the two are intimately intertwined". The image Bateman depicts is one where fictions seem to stow away on rules or mechanics, the former amplifying the pleasures produced by engagement with the latter. This represents perhaps one small step beyond the familiar twining of the two poles of play as a "mess" or "assemblage."

Bateman has chosen a difficult, tangled-up example in *Shadow of the Colossus*, where rules and "fictions" seem impossible to separate during play. Indeed, research into the psychology of credulity (Gilbert 1991) suggests that it would be difficult to disbelieve what we see during play's tense moments, even if we wanted to. Our baseline credulity in the face of what we see or hear is amplified during

---

[11] In Freud's (Freud [1911] 1958) theory, this shortest path to pleasure is the one we imagine or hallucinate based on a memory of satisfaction from the past. Freud theorizes that our ability to sense reality around us ("reality testing") relies on this shortest path's first becoming blocked off (along with the associated stores of pleasure), leaving only the arduous, roundabout path to satisfaction, winding through reality. This condition brings us into the world.

[12] See note 10 above.

[13] Admittedly, *Shadow of the Colossus* is a fraught example for Bateman to choose, since its emblazonment in game studies academic literature over the past decade is often due precisely to its emotional complexity. For a helpful review and breakdown of the game's effect on people who think about games for a living, I recommend Cole (2015) DiGRA paper, "The Tragedy of Betrayal".

moments of stress, or "resource depletion."[14] Make-believe, as a mode, would clearly predominate if we were to imagine, in Bateman's example, what the colossus' life was like before the player showed up—what it eats, what it dreams about, or other examples of fleshing out the diegesis. We may take pleasure (or pleasurable pain) in summoning such images in accordance with the rules mediating interaction. However, clearly, such rules are subordinated here to the imaginative process. However, Bateman's example of the colossus' massive size (the difficulty of attain visual, let alone spatial control over it) and its autonomy from the player (its apparent patterns of behavior) are not simply "fictions." Rather, they help comprise the colossus as a functional 'substitute' in Gombrich's sense (i.e., one does not make-believe the size, nor the uncanny way the colossus' movements seems to resemble deeply embedded behavioral patterns we have observed in life).

The expression, "the beast is a colossus several stories tall," contains a "dual representation."[15] It is both functional and fictional at the same time. However, when thrown into the challenge of scaling and defeating the colossus, it is required to recognize a series of obstacles and spatial puzzles. And the more completely this task occupies attention (mind and body), the more a functional substitute in Gombrich's sense will dominate our engagement. However, this engagement does not fully exclude consideration of the colossus as a fictional being (for whom we are meant to feel remorse),[16] nor with considering it as an aesthetically charged, polygonal, textured, and procedurally-animated entity. During spatial negotiation, these other means of referring to the objective seem reduced to a kind of linguistic shorthand. They are momentarily in the backseat. However, it is perhaps from here that they do their best work.

4. Trellis and Vine: Four Moments

Caillois' opposition of rules to make-believe ought to be extended to videogames in the sense that "rules" (in the broadest sense here as Gombrich's "minimum requirements of function") render concrete,

---

[14] Forget Coleridge's famous adage about needing to *suspend disbelief* before narrative fiction. Research into how belief functions has found that credulity is the older and more fundamental state, and that reminding oneself of the un-reality of what one sees *requires effort*. As Gilbert (1991) both argues and carefully substantiates in a review of empirical research into inherent credulity, Spinoza was correct when he postulated "that unacceptance is a secondary psychological act in which the initial accepting that invariably accompanies comprehension is subsequently undone" (Gilbert 1991, p. 108). To understand is to believe. The negation of a proposition (disbelief) is a more complex and difficult operation than belief: it comes later in development and relies on an initial consideration (a belief) that is then negated. This more complex process is capable of being disrupted.

Empirical research shows that when the mind is overwhelmed through stress or distraction, *disbelief* is disrupted but not *belief*: "Resource depletion did not cause subjects to believe that affirmed propositions were false, but it did cause them to believe that denied propositions were true" (Gilbert 1991, p. 113). For example, when distracted or under stress, subjects told something like "President Obama was not born in Kenya" would first consider the affirmative (that he *was* born there) and then struggle and only negate that affirmative proposition with partial success. These findings have been connected with political rhetoric, propaganda, and brainwashing (torture) strategies. However, for the present discussion, one might expect a stressful or difficult videogame to also produce resource depletion.

[15] Recent research on "dual representation"—what psychologists call the capacity to see a "symbolic artifact" as "both the concrete entity itself and, at the same time, its abstract relation to its referent"—suggests that "it is generally difficult for young children to have two active representations of a single entity," and that "the concrete features of a symbolic artifact can interfere with young children's ability to notice its relation to what it stands for" (DeLauche 2011, p. 321). This research explores sign-referent relations that break down when the object-as-sign loses its intended connection to its referent because that object is "a highly salient, attractive, interesting object in and of itself," something which "invites direct physical activity" or *play* and so makes it more difficult "for young children to treat [the object] as standing for something other than itself" (p. 321).

Videogames indeed make matters messier. The question about whether a game's image is functional-mechanical (i.e., it plays a role in a wider system of rules) or else is representational-fictional (i.e., it plays a role in a wider narrative setting or scenario) attends to a perceived schism at the level of *signified* (i.e., it leaves out the question of the *material salience of the signifier itself*—the aesthetics of the pixelated image, for instance). Who can really say whether, at any precise moment in play, a player is primarily engaging with an aesthetic and material object (pixels on a screen behaving in a way that stimulates embodied play), a narrative-signified content ("this is a mushroom, like the things I ate for lunch"), or a functional element of a wider mechanical system ("this power-up gives me the ability to break bricks and sustain one unfavorable enemy collision without dying")? Research only suggests that there is some basic competition at work, and our capacity to simultaneously sustain multiple, competing meanings in one object is challenged the more highly "salient" and interesting that object becomes along one of its potential dimensions of meaning.

[16] See note 13 above.

consistent, and reliable what imagination might otherwise only conjure ephemerally. However, the above discussion demonstrates how "make-believe" is perhaps not the best term for thinking about our relation to narrative, fiction, and representation in videogames. What does the concrete and uninterrupted presence of a thing do to one's capacity to imagine it? If functional objects pick biological locks, and our baseline relation to what we encounter in the world is credulity, then make-believe proper would appear to play very little role in our engagement with videogame images we encounter during play. Nevertheless, make-believe *is* an important part of videogames with diegetic content.

In videogames, systems, rules, and mechanics enter into a kind of dialectic with fictional elements. To borrow the language of reversal theory, the two constitute a "reversal pairing." Their relationship is bipolar and synergistic. Like a vine weaving in and out of gaps in a trellis, there are moments when fleshing out the diegesis (extending its scope beyond what is functionally present) is prominent, and moments when what occupies the foreground of player activity is engaging with a rigidly-structured set of rules, mechanics, and images (whose make-believe element is temporarily subordinated to their concrete immediacy, their presence before us). That an alternation between the two poles can spur player activity (one providing foil and inspiration to the other) is supported by developmental literature on make-believe play.[17] I propose the metaphor of a trellis and vine to help to conceptually organize these dynamics into four permutations.

4.1. Vines Growing without Trellis Support

The first vine/trellis permutation—*vines growing without trellis support*—stands for autonomous make-believe play: play that has rescinded its dependence on concrete objects in the world. Of course, it is difficult to conceive of make-believe play that *draws on no medium for structural support whatsoever*. Imaginary play draws on internalized objects: memories of encounters with the material of the doll or action figure, the tone of one's voice, the body's musculature. Even closed eyelids could be said to offer darkness as a kind of support, a stage for creative demonstrations.

Strictly speaking, no videogame play could fall into this category, since the presentation of representational images, sounds and narrative spaces clearly all lend some support to the imagination's winding tendrils. Even rules themselves lend support. Thus, in this first (largely hypothetical) permutation, the image of a vine that coils against its internal structures, or some other medium, but not *the structural support—material or ruled—of a videogame*.

4.2. Empty Patches of Trellis (Where No Vine Grows)

Empty patches of trellis (where no vine grows), would correspond to rules or procedural interactions built into the videogame that aren't tightly connected to play or that deliberately flaunt their resistance to play. In a broad sense, these patches could be conceived of as a potential interaction beyond the reaches of player skill (or taste), such as secret endings, well-hidden "Easter eggs," seldom-accessed game states or, simply, unpopular games. This permutation could also refer to unused code or assets that remain in the software after release. Websites such as The Cutting Room Floor, or YouTube series such as Shesez's Boundary Break videos (2016–present), which hack games in order to reveal "developer techniques or sometimes unused content that's out of the boundaries of a videogame," could

---

17 Literature on make-believe and rule-bound play describes instances where, in each case, one form of play becomes an "out-of-frame" inspiration for the other. For instance, Singer and Singer (1990) admit that "although the wider reaches of pretending are inevitably constrained by games with rules, it is apparent that some children at least will persist in introducing additional components of imaginativeness into such games," such as with a girl who creatively links situations that emerge in the board game, *Clue*, with a television show she watched, *Murder She Wrote* (Singer and Singer 1990, p. 241). They later also identify the possibility that "a spontaneous fantasy game can be organized into a game with rules," such as an observed example of their children inventing a rule-bound game involving catching leaves as they fall from trees (p. 242). Lillard et al. (2011) identify a range of studies that discuss the "social-cognitive skills" that children build both through "in-frame pretending" and "out-of-frame negotiations," the latter of which appear in "an increasing proportion" as children mature (Lillard et al. 2011, p. 300).

demonstrate the desire to cover or extend play's activity across these unused patches of algorithmic material, and thus negate them as such (Shesez 2018). Play that actively imagines or seeks out these unused spaces (or that realizes the impulse to flesh out and visit them) likely belongs below, in the fourth trellis/vine permutation, and is itself generative of hacking techniques that essentially create a new game (i.e., a new trellis that supports this exploration beyond boundaries).

Looser or more-inclusive definitions of play (and games) will likely oppose the designation of "empty" trellis, as it smacks of the problematic *formalist* hierarchy from debates over videogame medium specificity.[18] However, scholars hoping to counter the prevalence of play in videogame analysis would likely embrace this trellis-vine pairing, which can relate to aspects of the game that exceed conventional definitions of play as well as the player's domain of experience altogether. One prominent example is what Galloway (2006) identifies as "nondiegetic machine acts" in his taxonomy of games—a taxonomy both inspired by Caillois, but also meant to eschew play theory (and decenter the human player) in favor of gaming's wider material and technological properties (thus, Galloway's preference for "operator" rather than "player"). In this sense, "empty" trellis could also correspond to the "software systems" (e.g., Quicken or Microsoft Word) that Galloway provocatively identifies as gaming's most closely related kin, where operators interact with systems, but not in a way most would characterize as play.

In fact, any computer-mediated act of designing or programming a videogame (either professionally or as a modder) would seem to exemplify *empty patches of trellis*, since this work entails using interactive software for materially productive ends. However, I think examples of mods that, *even when played*, best fit this permutation of trellis and vine are those implicated in Galloway's notion of "countergaming," (following Peter Wollen's theses on countercinema), which involves modifying games for aesthetic or political reasons. "Countergaming" generally opposes the self-contained fictional bubbles of popular entertainment (and, thus, eschews most forms of pleasure-hacking) and, instead, pursues an aesthetic of estrangement, commentary, and truth (Galloway 2006, pp. 109–10).

It must be emphasized that although the notion of "empty trellis" is introduced as an algorithmic system that lacks recognized forms of play, this "lack" is meant to be a *productive or even subversive*. In the past decade, there has been an eruption of fascinating and creative experimental games that comment upon gaming as a practice and that deliberately frustrate conventional notions of what it means to "play" a game. Prominent examples include games such as Quinn's *Depression Quest* (2013) or Rohrer's *Passage* (2007). However, there is a vital movement underway of *queer games* that explicitly oppose the naturalization of terms like "fun," which are often defined by and for a narrow demographic of white, male players.[19] Though these games are often, happily, made by diverse independent authors, Ruberg (2015) also extends this queer potential to commercial games, which are designated as "disappointing" (e.g., Atari's E.T., 1982), "annoying," (e.g., Sega's *Super Monkey Ball*, 2001–2012), "boring," (e.g., Mystique's *Custer's Revenge*, 1982), "sad," (e.g., Fullbright Company's *Gone Home*, 2013), or even intentionally hurtful, as in they "communicate negative emotions, like frustration or sadness" (e.g., Cavanagh's *Super Hexagon*, 2012) (Ruberg 2015, pp. 118–20). In each case, Ruberg embraces the *queer failure* of an algorithmic latticework that operates outside the bounds of empowering, enabling, intrinsically motivating play.

In this sense, the second moment of empty patches of the trellis takes on the coloring of a queer refusal to facilitate the weaving of normative (and normalizing) play, which, in this case, is characterized by pleasure and experiences of power.

---

[18] See notes 2 and 3 above.

[19] The metaphor of an empty trellis—a trellis that does not satisfy cultural expectations about the kinds of (mostly upward) growth it is supposed to facilitate—happily corresponds to recent work of queer theorists and queer videogame scholars who draw productively on notions of failure and stunted growth. Ruberg (2015), for example, discusses the "queer potential" of games that eschew traditional notions of fun. And Ruberg and Shaw (2017) edited volume, *Queer Game Studies*, offers a helpful introduction to queerness and videogames more generally.

4.3. A Vine Closely Woven into the Trellis

The third permutation—the condition of *a vine closely woven into the trellis*—corresponds to a mode of play tightly wound up with the terms of a game's structural support to such an extent that it presents a tangle of prolonged activity (during which it is difficult to conceptually disentangle play and game). Further, though the game's support is mechanical and procedural (images and actions that are rule-bound or "functional"), it can also be conceived of as representational, fictional, and (kin)aesthetic. That is, both ruled and make-believe play (or "mastery" and "sympathy" play) can predominate at particular moments (*inhibit* without completely banishing their counterpart). In this metaphor, the vine's twining does really rely on the game's mechanical supports, the domain of rules and systems, what Bateman calls gaming's "grip and grind" (Bateman 2011, p. 31). This is in reference to reward schedules and the process of building skills over time (in short, where the game most clearly serves as a Gombrich *substitute*, a key for a "biological lock"). Yet, when focused, prolonged play reverberates (such as the "Tetris effect"), the memory often features internalized aesthetic or representational imagery and sounds, which, in this permutation, have become inseparable from the rules governing their interaction. The pleasure "unlocked" during play has fused the circuits and bridged disparate metarepresentational polarities.

Play generated through negotiation of the videogame's rules becomes an intense nexus of player energy and attention over long periods of time.[20] As they work through a game's reliably repetitious processes, players become stitched into the game's algorithmic loops, and the game's strange rhythms become embedded as muscle memory. As new aspects of the game's system are revealed, skills and abilities expand in a rhetoric of growth and progress, which appears to speak as much to player as avatar. However, to a regular gamer, *growth* also characterizes gaming itself, which in each new game (we hope, at least) seems to push marginally outward towards new interactive terrain.

In the third permutation, the non-differentiation of this embedding into muscle memory of rules and procedures, as well as fictions and representations is reflected in simple linguistic utterances—and, to be clear, this happens in "standard" input schemas, as well as dance and exercise games. To say that *the sun is setting* in a game like *Super Mario World 2: Yoshi's Island* (1995) speaks perhaps narrowly to the game's fictional backdrop, so that contemplating this notion may pull players across the clear boundary that separates foreground and background as well as the domain of gameplay from that of the game's fictional setting. However, to say the same thing during *Minecraft* (2011) is unavoidably to encounter a more precarious *dual representation* that includes, on one hand, a fictional backdrop (i.e., there is no actual "sun" in *Minecraft*, just a fictional representation of one), as well as, on the other hand, a cluster of significant rules structuring the action of play—rules about what is visible and what is not, how and where monsters spawn, and whether players should explore or retreat. The fictional term ("sun") serves as a kind of linguistic short-hand for the full range of rules instantiating Gombrich's substitute objects. Our access to fictional shorthand likely works constantly in the background to stitch together and lend coherence to a game's virtual spaces and encounters as play winds around the trellis. While Gombrich's substitute functions, as affective intensities swell, even bizarre and

---

[20] Nicoll (2015) essay on the Neo Geo and the domestication of arcade games notes that, when games entered the home, their address to players shifted, including their relationship with *duration*:

> Rather than focusing on the blunt thrills and excessive spectacles of arcade gaming, home video games now aspired to provide long-term appeal with their engrossing stories and intellectually stimulating—but not punishing or overly challenging—gameplay. Magazine review criteria were even adjusted to factor in the longevity of a game, often quantified under a "value" or "replay-value" rubric. This also coincides with a time when games adhered less to established arcade genres and became more multifaceted and innovative in terms of their gameplay mechanics and modes of presentation. (Nicoll 2015, p. 215).

arbitrary fictional elements (sounds, gestures, appearances, actions) take on a quality of necessity and immediacy, moving from "as if" to "as is."[21]

In short, the third permutation is gaming's mainstay, both conceptually and commercially—what distinguishes videogames from other sorts of software and from other representational arts, as well as what underlies the "grip and grind" that fuels gaming as an industry. However, it is also in this third permutation that I would include most mods, hacks, speedruns, and exploit-seeking. To be precise, modifying an existing game (or building a new one out of existing code and assets), like game design more generally, is a process that stretches across multiple trellis/vine permutations. It expresses the twining of trellis and vine insofar as the creative process—the meticulous, iterative, nature of designing and programming—combines a nuanced consideration of a game's structural support with the play that defines it as support. A vine has grown in the programmer's mind, so to speak, leading to an intense focus of some sort that stitches together a pleasurable oscillation between code and its execution. This stitching action is discussed further in the final section.

Exploit-seeking could be understood as an effort to locate and activate overlooked or as-yet poorly understood aspects of the trellis and to fold them back into play (to grow a vine there too). In a related vein, speedrunning could be understood as combining the pursuit of exploits (exceptional vine grown in overlooked places) with the meticulous drawing of the trellis into the self as "structural support" (i.e., muscle memory) until the near approximation of perfection is achieved and recorded (a vine absolutely inseparable from trellis—perhaps actualized in machine-assisted speedrunning). Notably, exploit- or glitch-seeking and speedrunning both eschew gaming's representational contents and fixate to the point of a productive obsession with game rules or processes. Further, for these practices, it is unimportant whether play is sanctioned by designers, or else clearly exceeds expected boundaries for play—in both cases, the trellis itself (as it comes to be understood) serves a powerful *author function*, even as one's understanding of it grows and transforms over time.

4.4. A Vine, Having Climbed Across the Entirety of the Latticework, Overshoots the Structure in a New Direction

Finally, the fourth permutation, areas where *a vine, having climbed across the entirety of the latticework, overshoots the structure in a new direction*, corresponds with a kind of make-believe play inspired at the point rules no longer combine with (and support) play's creative action. Rules still may play a background role, since the creative energy that extends play beyond the trellis' formal "limits" is often built upon many hours of activity stabilized and held in view by that trellis. When make-believe play that has been strongly imprinted by rules stretches out autonomously in a new direction, it seems to long for new support that would *capture* and sustain its imagined actions. In other words, it seeks out something familiar in its imagining of something new. Like a vine coiling back upon itself, its growth may seem inefficient. However, unlike the hypothetical coiling tendril in the first permutation, this autonomous vine is explicitly imagined as having a particular kind of momentum—it has been drawn across the familiar paths of a videogame's structural support, and because of this it appears to call for a modification of the trellis itself.

One way to think of this fourth permutation is that make-believe play that overshoots the trellis tends to predict and precede genre development in terms of gameplay. Edge-of-trellis is a kind of ludic vanguard. How does an industry track the vine's overgrowth and respond? Whether by focus groups or sparks of genius, the "vine" is clearly also a vein (lifeblood) for industry profits. Player-made mods are hailed, perhaps, for their greater autonomy and lower overhead—in other words, for their flexible cobbling together, fixing, and rapid extension of an existing trellis infrastructure in response to momentary creative offshoots. Perhaps the boundaries of a game's algorithmic support often, in practice, take the form of a narrative fiction that launches a make-believe impulse beyond the trellis'

---

[21] See note 14 above.

frame. In short, if it cannot be directly programmed yet, then at least it can be captured in narrative; as an invisible wall, it gestures to something beyond.

A teleology emerges: decades of narrative cinema and television about daring escapes into space vessels (e.g., *Star Wars: The Empire Strikes Back*, 1980), precede punctuated moments during bookended cutscenes in popular videogames where a protagonist must return to a space ship and flee an exploding planet (e.g., *Super Metroid*, 1994), which in turn precede a new genre of games where the passage into and out of the space craft is a seamless, fluid, and regular part of play (e.g., *StarMade*, 2012; *No Man's Sky*, 2016). A narrative fiction built beyond the outer limit of a sidescroller's trellis of play (Samus' ship that waits for her at game's end) finds, in a new genre we might call *Minecraft* in space, a new trellis to support such dramas of venturing from, and returning to, the vessel's protective hull.

It should be noted that many games actively seek out this fourth permutation, the outer boundary of the trellis, but not in order to imagine its future extension. Or, put otherwise, they are deliberately sparse in their trellis. Prominent examples include industry-produced games featuring quick-time-events or build-your-own-adventure narratives. During these games' interactive cutscenes, a trellis of play has been reduced to the literal presentation of a button on the screen, and mechanics simply include pressing that button, or not pressing that button. A perhaps more significant example would be independently produced narrative games, such as those created on Twine (e.g., *Quing's Quest VII: The Death of Videogames!*, 2014). A minimalist structural support is intended, in these games, to spur make-believe play and then to get out of the way. The vine overshooting the trellis is, here, precisely the point of play during play, rather than a commercially-driven connective fiber between game iterations.

What the fourth permutation perhaps illuminates about the relationship between rules and make-believe is that rules seem to unburden imagination, to extend its reach, to offload the labor of imagining by pulling that work into the body as a whole (into the nervous system, body schema, muscle memory) by way of the body's role in testing reality, knowing its world implicitly. Though present in significant ways during play that focuses on rules (the *dual representation* of the vine wound around the trellis), make-believe is often second-fiddle, most clearly present as a valence, backdrop, or linguistic shorthand for play's action. As with a reversal pair that has neglected one of its poles, make-believe play returns with gusto at moments when the trellis falters or fails. Or, perhaps, when imagination wanders away from the game and to unexpected places.

Funding: This research received no external funding.

Conflicts of Interest: The author declares no conflict of interest.

References

Altice, Nathan. 2015. *I Am Error: The Nintendo Family Computer/Entertainment System Platform*. Cambridge: MIT Press.

Apperley, Thomas. 2010. *Gaming Rhythms: Play and Counterplay from the Situated to the Global*. Amsterdam: Institute of Network Cultures.

Apperley, Thomas, and Darshana Jayemane. 2012. Game Studies' Material Turn. *Westminster Papers in Communication and Culture* 9: 5–25. [CrossRef]

Apter, Michael. 2017. Ideology and Societal Values: A Reversal Theory Perspective. *Journal of Motivation, Emotion, and Personality* 6: 1–7.

Apter, Michael, and John Kerr. 1991. The Nature, Function and Value of Play. In *Adult Play: A Reversal Theory Approach*. Edited by John Kerr and Michael Apter. Leiden: Swets & Zeitlinger, pp. 163–76.

Bateman, Chris. 2011. *Imaginary Games*. Alresford: John Hunt Publishing.

Bateson, Gregory. 1972. *Steps to an Ecology of Mind*. New York: Ballantine Books.

Bogost, Ian. 2007. *Persuasive Games*. Cambridge: MIT Press.

Bogost, Ian. 2009. Videogames are a Mess. DiGRA Keynote. Available online: http://bogost.com/writing/videogames_are_a_mess/ (accessed on 15 May 2018).

Bowlby, John. 1982. *Attachment and Loss: Volume 1: Attachment*, 2nd ed. New York: Basic Books.

Caillois, Roger. 1961. *Man, Play, and Games*. Translated by Meyer Barash. London: University of Illinois Press.

Clark, Rachel, Jin Ha Lee, and Neils Clark. 2015. Why Video Game Genres Fail: A Classificatory Analysis. *Games and Culture* 12: 445–65. [CrossRef]

Cole, Tom. 2015. The Tragedy of Betrayal: How the design of Ico and Shadow of the Colossus elicits emotion. Paper presented at 2015 DiGRA International Conference, Lüneburg, Germany, May 14–17.

Coleridge, Samuel Taylor. 1996. Dejection: An Ode. In *English Romantic Poetry: An Anthology*, Dover Thrift ed. Edited by Stanley Appelbaum. Mineola: Dover Publications.

Collin, Robbie. 2014. Nintendo's Shigeru Miyamoto: 'What Can Games Learn from Film? Nothing. *The Telegraph*. November 10. Available online: https://www.telegraph.co.uk/culture/film/film-news/11201171/nintendo-super-mario-pikmin-tokyo-film-festival-mandarin-oriental-tokyo-sega-mario-kart-zelda-wii-oculus-rift.html (accessed on 21 May 2018).

Consalvo, Mia. 2009. There is no magic circle. *Games and Culture* 4: 408–17. [CrossRef]

Csikszentmihalyi, Mihaly. 1997. *Finding Flow: The Psychology of Engagement with Everyday Life*. New York: Basic Books.

DeLauche, Judy. 2011. Early Development of the Understanding and Use of Symbolic Artifacts. In *The Wiley-Blackwell Handbook of Childhood Cognitive Development*, 2nd ed. Edited by Usha Goswami. Hoboken: Wiley-Blackwell.

Faisal, Ali, and Mirva Peltoniemi. 2015. Establishing Video Game Genres Using Data-Driven Modeling and Product Databases. *Games and Culture* 13: 20–43. [CrossRef]

Freud, S. 1958. *Formulations on the Two Principles of Mental Functioning*, stand. ed. London: Hogarth Press, vol. 12, pp. 213–26. First published 1911.

Galloway, Alexander. 2006. *Gaming: Essays on Algorithmic Culture*. Minneapolis: University of Minnesota Press.

Gilbert, Daniel. 1991. How Mental Systems Believe. *American Psychologist* 46: 107–19. [CrossRef]

Goffman, Erving. 1961. *Encounters: Two Studies in the Sociology of Interaction*. London: Penguin University Press.

Gombrich, Ernst. 1978. *Meditations on A Hobby Horse*. London: Phaidon Press. First published 1963.

Jenkins, Henry. 1999. Congressional Testimony on Media Violence. Available online: http://web.mit.edu/m-i-t/articles/dc.html (accessed on 17 June 2018).

Jenkins, Henry. 2006. *Convergence Culture: Where Old and New Media Collide*. New York: New York University Press.

Juul, Jesper. 2005. *Half-Real: Video Games between Real Rules and Fictional Worlds*. Cambridge: MIT Press.

Kahn, Adam, Cuihua Shen, Li Lu, Rabindra Ratan, Sean Coary, Jinghui Hou, Jingbo Meng, Joseph Osborn, and Dmitri Williams. 2015. The Trojan Player Typology: A Cross-Genre, Cross-Cultural, Behaviorally Validated Scale of Video Game Play Motivations. *Computers in Human Behavior* 49: 354–61. [CrossRef]

Kent, Steven. 2001. *The Ultimate History of Video Games*. New York: Three Rivers Press.

Kerr, John. 1991. 'A Structural-Phenomenology of Play' In Context. In *Adult Play: A Reversal Theory Approach*. Edited by John Kerr and Michael Apter. Leiden: Swets & Zeitlinger, pp. 31–42.

LeJacq, Yannick. 2014. *Pikmin Has the Best Origin Story. Kotaku*. Available online: https://kotaku.com/pikmin-has-the-best-origin-story-1657571859 (accessed on 21 May 2018).

Lillard, Angeline, Ashley Pinkham, and Eric Smith. 2011. Pretend Play and Cognitive Development. In *The Wiley-Blackwell Handbook of Childhood Cognitive Development*, 2nd ed. Edited by Usha Goswami. Hoboken: Wiley-Blackwell.

Manning, Aubrey, and Marian Dawkins. 2012. *An Introduction to Animal Behavior*, 6th ed. Cambridge: Cambridge University Press.

Murphy, Sheila. 2011. *How Television Invented New Media*. New Brunswick: Rutgers University Press.

Murray, Janet. 2005. The Last Word on Ludology v. Narratology. Paper presented at DiGRA "Worlds in Play" Conference, Vancouver, BC, Canada, June 16–20.

Nicoll, Benjamin. 2015. Bridging the Gap: The Neo Geo, the Media Imaginary, and the Domestication of Arcade Games. *Games and Culture* 12: 200–21. [CrossRef]

Parker, Felan. 2013. An art world for artgames. *Loading . . .* 7: 41–60.

Ratan, Rabindra, Nicholas Taylor, Jameson Hogan, Tracy Kennedy, and Dmitri Williams. 2015. Stand by Your Man: An Examination of Gender Disparity in *League of Legends*. *Games and Culture* 10: 438–62. [CrossRef]

Ruberg, Bonnie. 2015. No Fun: The Queer Potential of Video Games that Annoy, Anger, Disappoint, Sadden, and Hurt. *QED: A Journal in GLBTQ Worldmaking* 2: 108–24. [CrossRef]

Ruberg, Bonnie, and Adrienne Shaw. 2017. *Queer Game Studies*. Edited by Bonnie Ruberg and Adrienne Shaw. Minneapolis: University of Minnesota Press.

Salen, Katie, and Eric Zimmerman. 2004. *Rules of Play: Game Design Fundamentals*. Cambridge: MIT Press.

Singer, Dorothy, and Jerome Singer. 1990. *The House of Make-Believe: Children's Play and the Developing Imagination*. Cambridge: Harvard University Press.

Stenros, Jaakko. 2014. In defense of a magic circle: The social, mental and cultural boundaries of play. *Transactions of the Digital Games Research Association*. p. 2. Available online: http://todigra.org/index.php/todigra/article/view/10/26 (accessed on 10 June 2018).

Stenros, Jaakko. 2016. The Game Definition Game: A Review. *Games and Culture* 12: 499–520. [CrossRef]

Suits, Bernard. 1978. *The Grasshopper: Games, Life and Utopia*. Peterborough: Broadview Press.

Taylor, T. L. 2009. The Assemblages of Play. *Games and Culture* 4: 331–39. [CrossRef]

Vygotsky, Lev. 1967. Play and its Role in the Mental Development of the Child. *Soviet Psychology* 5: 6–18. [CrossRef]

Weisberg, Deena Skolnick. 2015. Pretend Play. *Wiley Interdisciplinary Reviews: Cognitive Science* 6: 249–61. [CrossRef] [PubMed]

Whitehead, Thomas. 2013. Feature: A Brief History of Pikmin. *NintendoLife*. Available online: http://www.nintendolife.com/news/2013/07/feature_a_brief_history_of_pikmin (accessed on 21 May 2018).

Yee, Nick. 2007. Motivations for Play in Online Games. *CyberPsychology & Behavior* 9: 772–75.

Shesez. 2018. Boundary Break. Available online: https://www.youtube.com/playlist?list=PLYfhW_P-MkU7vBmWwwyqdIWNDzXfEZwnO (accessed on 28 June 2018).

arts

MDPI

Article

Gaming the Heart of Darkness

Fruzsina Pittner [1],* and **Iain Donald [2]**

1   School of Humanities, University of Dundee, Dundee DD1 4HN, UK
2   Division of Games and Arts, School of Design and Informatics, Abertay University, Dundee DD1 1HG, UK;
     i.donald@abertay.ac.uk
*   Correspondence: f.pittner@dundee.ac.uk

Received: 30 June 2018; Accepted: 27 August 2018; Published: 4 September 2018

Abstract: The history of Joseph Conrad's *Heart of Darkness* has been one of adaptation and change. The enduring story is based upon Conrad's experiences in the Congo in the 1890s and was published as a novella in 1902. Since then, the story has been criticised for racism by Nigerian writer Chinua Achebe and relocated to Vietnam by Francis Ford Coppola as *Apocalypse Now*, influencing computer games such as *Far Cry 2* and *Spec Ops: The Line*. In examining the adaptations of *Heart of Darkness*, we can consider how the story evolves from the passive reading of post-colonial narratives through to the active participation in morally ambiguous decisions and virtual war crimes through digital games: examining Conrad's story as it has been adapted for other mediums provides a unique lens in which to view storytelling and retelling within the context of how we interpret the world. This paper compares the source material to its adaptations, considering the blending of historical fact and original fiction, the distortion of the original story for the purpose of creating new meaning, and reflects on whether interactivity impacts upon the feeling of immersion and sense of responsibility in audiences of different narratives.

Keywords: storytelling; digital games; transmedia; literary adaptation

1. Introduction

From theatre performances of mythological themes and novels built upon arrays of folktales to the relatively modern term 'transformative works' referring to the plethora of fan-created work published online, audiences and creatives have proven the need for space to explore, complete, and re-imagine existing stories and the tropes and themes surrounding them (Coker 2017). With the emergence of new tools and technologies, the opportunities artists have to explore popular and obscure narratives and imagine them anew are ever increasing.

Stories of adventure and discovery (of faraway lands or the depths of human experience) have always had the power to induce curiosity and creativity. Sometimes regardless of their actual, often widely debated artistic value, certain narratives become powerful enough that their influence can be felt through multiple mediums over a significant period of time. What separates these works from others around their time can be attributed to multiple factors of varying significance: whims of the audience both past and present, message, controversy, academic debate, new themes and tropes and historical context (Jauss 1970). Classic and popular literature or stories spanning through multiple universes often see adaptations of varying fidelity and purpose (e.g., *The Great Gatsby*, Fitzgerald [1925] 1994, or the Marvel Cinematic Universe).

Joseph Conrad published *Heart of Darkness* as a serial in Blackwood's Magazine in 1899 after visiting Belgian King Leopold II's Congo Free State in the 1890s. Since its debut, the novella has been a topic of discussion concerning the effect of colonialism on Africa and the general public's view of the colonies and their inhabitants—arguments about Conrad's work and its place in colonial and postcolonial literature are still prevalent in academic circles. Beneath a story of adventure lies a narrative much scrutinised and discussed: while demonstrating a critical attitude towards western colonising efforts in Africa, the novella also tells a story of European values inevitably degrading in the oppressive atmosphere of the African jungle. This view—the effect of the other on widely accepted western morality—permeates not only the novella, but its subsequent adaptations from the big screen to the interactive.

Heart of Darkness has seen multiple different adaptations in a variety of mediums throughout the years since its release. From film *Apocalypse Now* (Coppola 1979) to the release of well-known and critically successful computer games *Far Cry 2* (Ubisoft Montreal 2008) and *Spec Ops: The Line* (Yager Development 2012), these vary greatly in how closely they follow the original narrative, what kind of message they attempt to convey, and how they use the different tools of each medium to achieve that goal.

The process of adaptation takes the skeleton of its original source and layers new meaning on it based on its original connotations and any new context that is applied to it throughout. Different approaches (e.g., remakes, re-imaginings, reboots) are commonly used to achieve the same purpose: to use the source material, its relevance and context as building blocks to present the story through a new lens, add relevant historical and societal commentary or call upon well-known elements of the original work to underline its message, all by using the tools of their designated medium to their advantage. As Jenkins says in his 2017 essay (Jenkins 2017) 'Adaptation, Extension, Transmedia':

> Anyone who thinks seriously about adaptation knows that each makes some unique contributions—in terms of their selection and interpretation of material and how they use the affordances of the new medium in ways unavailable to the original producer, if nothing else.

Retellings are naturally framed by the format, how the source material is considered at the time of its adaption, as well as by the new creators—the prevalent influence of the old adds to the depth of interpretation of the new, and through the process more nuanced meaning is created.

That *Heart of Darkness* has been adapted so many times and in such variety is unsurprising. The signature elements of Conrad's writing: faraway settings, dramatic conflicts between human characters and the brutal forces of nature, themes of individualism, the violent side of human nature and prejudice all make for an intriguing world to build upon. Its themes are universal enough to be relevant in the context of the Vietnam War as seen in *Apocalypse Now*, and the novella itself with its historical background and wider literary impact still influences works such as the 2010 graphic novel adaptation. These can be considered traditional adaptations in a sense that they adopt a linear story into another linear medium: film or graphic novel, the audience is presented with a static narrative that is unchanged after its release regardless of the context they transplant the source material into.

What *Far Cry 2* and *Spec Ops: The Line* provide in contrast to these other mediums is that they implement a linear story into a nonlinear medium using a genre (first-person shooter) in which the primary emphasis is not traditionally on deep storytelling. Through the games' interactive nature, the role of the audience changes from passive spectator to active participant: players have the ability to significantly shape the story through their actions.

As opposed to many other games, *Far Cry 2* and *Spec Ops: The Line* also focus on hostile game mechanics and emphasise disempowerment systems that are designed to be part of their message. The games are not only difficult to play, but systems players can generally rely upon when playing similar titles (time investment results in character progression, reliable weapon system, regenerative health, etc.) are not in place anymore, or are altered to serve a different purpose. This results in a peculiar and frustrating experience that serves to emphasise the underlying message of Conrad's original story.

Elements of adventure and other well-liked storytelling tropes present in the novella return to some degree in all four adaptations, striving to drive their messages forward while preserving select aspects of the original work forming a scale that ranges from works of faithful adaptation (*Heart of Darkness—A Graphic Novel*) to those using the novella and its cultural footprint as inspiration that informs a separate story (*Spec Ops: The Line*). These archetypes—a journey upriver as a metaphor for the journey to the depths of the human self, war, violence, the brutal forces of nature, the overarching mission, the idea of home (Europe, America) as a counterpoint to these faraway places—are all prevalent in the pieces examined. Adaptations of *Heart of Darkness*, despite the variety in their medium, execution and fidelity to the original text, have, amongst others, something very important in common: they all attempt to deliver a message that goes beyond the experience of adventure, and into questioning whether violence, exploitation and following a system that enables those is worth the cost of lives and the crisis of identity that will inevitably follow on a personal, national, or global level.

This article examines Joseph Conrad's *Heart of Darkness* and select subsequent adaptations: *Apocalypse Now* (Coppola 1979), *Heart of Darkness—A Graphic Novel* (Anyango and Mairowitz 2010) and computer games *Far Cry 2* (Ubisoft Montreal 2008) and *Spec Ops: The Line* (Yager Development 2012) in search of recurring patterns, character archetypes and messages that prevail through these various interpretations. It reflects on the effectiveness of storytelling methods different mediums use and the messages these adaptations carry in comparison to the original novella, while considering how all stories blend historical fact with the original fiction and its new intended meaning, and how these morph or distort the source material.

2. Contextual Review

2.1. Joseph Conrad: Heart of Darkness

2.1.1. Meaning and History

The Congo Free State is one of the most horrific and well-known examples of colonising efforts in Africa. Leopold II's laborious political manoeuvring resulted in a colony 76 times the size of Belgium, much of it covered by unexplored jungle and populated by indigenous tribes with varying degrees of hostility towards the newcomers on their land (Pakenham 1991). Accounts of the atrocities committed by trading companies and locals in their employ in search of first ivory and later rubber came to horrify the European population (Van Reybrouck 2010).

Conrad's journey to Africa fell around the time when the Congo's main source of wealth was still ivory and some semblance of order was still preserved, but the degradation and self-serving cruelty of the system was already beginning to very obviously show its teeth. Examples of mistreatment of the native population witnessed by the author himself are reflected in the text on multiple occasions (Hochschild [1998] 2012).

When stripped from the contextual history and response the novella received in the literary world, *Heart of Darkness* follows the recipe many other adventure stories do. It features exotic lands, violence, excitement, and the exploration of fragile human morality wrapped into the narrative of a journey both physical and metaphorical in nature: an Englishman joins a Belgian trading company in the Congo Basin where his job is to take a steam boat upriver to reach an outpost established on the edge of scarcely explored jungle.

Looking at the immediate undercurrent of meaning, however, the novella also tells of a man's first-hand experiences facing the results of European occupation in Africa and the effects of it on Europe and its agents in return. The narrator's experiences in the Congo shake him, and this starts the process of his questioning his views on the idea of colonialism and the relationship between Europeans and Africans, reflecting Conrad's state of mind after his own return from Africa.

Yet Conrad's intent in expressing the horrors he witnessed is still deeply tied to Europe's view of Africa, the colonies, their inhabitants and the difference between them and the 'civilised world'. This Eurocentric view, deliberate or not, permeates the novella and its adaptations to varying degrees in showing stories that all ask the same question in some capacity: What happens to civilised people when faced with the "dark places of the earth"? (Conrad [1899] 2017, p. 5).

2.1.2. Story and Structure

Heart of Darkness is structured as a story within a story. The narrator, Marlow, spends a night on the Thames in England in the company of several others. This scene acts as a frame for him to describe his past experiences on the Congo, much like Conrad is sharing his own story through this novella with his audience—Marlow is, in essence, a substitute for the author himself, through whom he can safely convey his message while simultaneously allowing him to distance himself from his own narrative. In this *Heart of Darkness* is really threefold. Marlow's story is nestled into his audience's view of him narrating it, witnessed both by his in-fiction companions and the readers themselves, and around it exists Conrad's own experience (Watt 1979).

Marlow's journey up the Congo River is hindered by the many hardships the landscape has to offer—both natural and led by the incompetence and lethargic attitude of the Europeans holding office on the riverbank. He learns of the mysterious Mr. Kurtz through his encounters with various characters from different steps on the hierarchy of the Company he is employed by.

By the time his reputation reaches Marlow through word of mouth, Kurtz ceases to be a mere trading-post commander, which he is by designation, and becomes somewhat of a legendary figure in the area through the power of his personality and apparent competence. He is, as described by the Company's chief accountant in the novella: "a very remarkable person" (Conrad [1899] 2017, p. 19). What this exactly means, however, Marlow must find out for himself.

The true depth of Kurtz's effect on those who have met him is uncovered piece by piece through the information Marlow slowly gathers. There are the facts of his birth, of his position, of the Company's high hopes for him. There is the often grudging but undeniable respect other officers pay him, even in his absence. There is his manifesto, his own words describing his comprehensive opinion on 'natives' that leaves Marlow unsettled and in awe at the same time. As he travels deeper and deeper into the jungle, Marlow's interest in Kurtz's larger-than-life figure slowly becomes an obsession.

The long-awaited and hard-fought final encounter, however, turns into something completely unexpected: in his long stay at the Congo, Kurtz succumbs to terminal illness in both body and mind, abandoning the morals of 'civilised society' to abuse his authority over the area's population to his own ends. The highly praised, upstanding, mysteriously grand figure of Mr. Kurtz turns into a horrific example of all that can go wrong with European ideals faced with the unforgiving, stifling and unpredictably *other* African jungle. Kurtz's widely quoted last words, "The horror! The horror!" (Conrad [1899] 2017, p. 69) underline this message with unsettling accuracy.

Despite—or perhaps because of—the controversy surrounding it, *Heart of Darkness* is still revered as one of the most significant literary works of its time, a story that stands out for its efforts in criticising western imperialism, exploitation, and the effect of those on the individual. Its weaknesses, its Eurocentric view of the world, its unwillingness to commit to the belief of equality and the other arguably questionable meanings it carries are not excusable, but are reflective of its historical context.

Regardless of its value and controversial undercurrents of meaning, however, the novella's influence is undeniable: as a commentary on colonialism, the darker side of human nature and violence as a justifiable means to an end, it has influenced academic discussion and creative work in a variety of fields for a variety of purposes ever since its release.

2.2. Linear Adaptations

2.2.1. Heart of Darkness: The Graphic Novel

The 2010 graphic novel by David Zane Mairowitz (text) and Catherine Anyango (illustration) follows the novella most faithfully out of all adaptations examined. The comic uses parts of the novella's original text, as well as excerpts from Conrad's own travel diary of his journey to the Congo for added depth to recreate the story (Faber 2010). By using Conrad's personal accounts, Mairowitz and Anyango effectively place emphasis on the relationship between the author and his narrator Marlow, while using the text to further enhance the effect of immersion within the piece (Whitlock 2007).

Visuals through the comic reflect the progressive downward spiral of Marlow's state of mind in the novella, the artwork grows grotesque and exaggerated as the story proceeds. Graphite greys and blacks, use of stark lighting, abstract shapes and close-up shots of faces magnified to the point of disturbing detail underline the atmosphere of *Heart of Darkness*, giving the original text another layer of emphasis on the unreal, the other, the nightmare-like quality of the narrative building to the end.

This adaptation adds an interesting piece of visual flavour to the connection between Marlow and Conrad: the Marlow depicted on the comic pages bears significant physical resemblance to portraits of Conrad himself. This small detail speaks volumes about the power visual representation can have in storytelling—with this decision the creators have immediately established a firm connection between the fictional figure and the author himself. With erasing the distinction between Marlow and Conrad, the comic does not allow the author to distance himself from his own narrative, making his message all the more prominent.

2.2.2. Apocalypse Now

Novel-to-film adaptations often divide opinion as to whether they honour (rather than alter or sensationalise) the original text, storyline, and characters. Adapting literature for film has been a popular tool for filmmakers since the emergence of the medium in the 20th century: taking established works of classic and popular literature seemed to be a recipe for potential success. These stories are, either directly or indirectly, already alive in the collective awareness of the audience and this pre-established sense of familiarity serves as a way for the filmmaker to build on the success of the original work and reach potential new audiences. As John Ellis in his 1982 article 'Literary Adaptation' describes:

> The adaptation trades upon the memory of the novel, a memory that can derive from actual reading, or, as is more likely with a classic of literature, a generally circulated cultural memory.

Apocalypse Now is a film originally released in 1979, directed by Francis Ford Coppola and written by himself, John Milius and Michael Herr. Coppola's film is not a direct adaptation of *Heart of Darkness*, rather it uses the skeleton of the original story and retains its basic structure to express a message much more relevant to his time. He puts the core narrative elements of the novella—a grueling journey upriver, moral deterioration, the dynamic between the narrator and Kurtz—into the setting of the Vietnam War (1955–1975).

The message he uses Conrad's framework for is not that far from the original: instead of imperialism, he uses the narrative to criticise the idea of the war. In his own words, as quoted by Kinder in her article 'The Power of Adaptation in Apocalypse Now' (Kinder 1979):

> The most important thing I wanted to do in the making of *Apocalypse Now* was to create a film experience that would give its audience a sense of the horror, the madness, the sensuousness, and the moral dilemma of the Vietnam war ... I tried to illustrate as many of its different facets as possible. And yet I wanted it to go further, to the moral issues that are behind all wars.

Parallels between *Apocalypse Now* and *Heart of Darkness* are unquestionable. The film's narrator, U.S. Army Captain Willard, is tasked to find and assassinate an errant army officer, Col. Kurtz. Marlow's Kurtz and Willard's Col. Kurtz also carry much the same message: a man of impeccable moral standing gone astray in the face of the horrors of African and Asian jungles in turn. His image looms over both narrators as they journey through a landscape of madness and violence made especially explicit and gruesome in the context of the Vietnam War. The viewer witnesses this slow collapse of integrity and sanity foreshadowed all the way from the film's introductory scenes and Willard's commentary underlined by haunting imagery of military violence to him committing war crimes in the name of the mission that is growing larger and larger within his own imagination.

The film characterizes Willard's mission as the epitome of hypocrisy—in the midst of senseless killings, the U.S. military is wasting energy and lives on killing one of its highest-ranking military officials. In that *Apocalypse Now* strives to spotlight the ironies that accompany the Vietnam War and western imperialism at large.

The film uses some of the same narrative devices the novella does: the image of a journey upriver, the hostile environment, the questionable actions of American officers holding positions along the coast, the discovery of self and how in the face of violence it can darken beyond recognition. The way Col. Kurtz is introduced makes use of the ambiguity of second-hand information (word of mouth, a military file, photographs, voice recordings) very much like *Heart of Darkness*. Through its imagery, the film conveys a very similar atmosphere to that of the novella: an overwhelming sense of decay, uncertainty, and paranoia in the face of the unknown.

It is interesting to note not only the parallels observed between the stories' plot, atmosphere, and the characters they feature, but a parallel in the underlying meaning of the film's message (Harrison 2012). Much like Conrad setting Africa as a counterpoint to European morals, *Apocalypse Now* primarily focuses on the war's effect on American ideals and identity and the effect of violence on the American consciousness, and much less so on Vietnam and its population itself. It uses the display of war crimes as a device to underline the characters' descent into moral and psychological decay. In that *Apocalypse Now* is not necessarily a story about the horrors of the Vietnam War—it is a story about how the war affects American soldiers who fight it in an environment so disquietingly unfamiliar with no real code of conduct to measure themselves and each other against.

2.3. Interactive Adaptations

Adaptation of linear narratives into interactive computer games pose some unique challenges. Games by their nature require a different kind of mindset for engagement; their audiences have different expectations towards the kind of experience they are to be presented with than those of film or other non-interactive mediums.

Games use player interaction as their primary tool to push a narrative forward. Hunicke et al. (2004) define the three major components a game can be built and interpreted by as Mechanics, Dynamics, and Aesthetics. These describe, in essence, the cornerstones of game design and refer to a game's components as follows:

- the interactions a player has to perform while playing;
- the effects of those interactions on the game itself;
- the desired emotional response the player is to experience while engaging with the piece.

Based on this framework, the challenge of adapting a literary piece to this medium is clear to see. Developers must translate a story designed to be told in a pre-established order into game mechanics; either through a series of interactions the player can perform, or events within the game world that affect the gameplay itself; while preserving the message of the original narrative and making sure players hit key points through their progress to understand the story as a whole.

In the case of narratives that can be easily broken down into quest-like elements (e.g., heavily action-based stories or adventure stories), this is a relatively straightforward task. Where the narrative's focus is less on adventure and action and more on abstract concepts where there is no hero figure or easily exploitable string of plot points to be identified within the story, breaking it down into a series of interactions proves to be much less clear-cut (Cutting 2011).

Despite the hardships of taking linear narratives and translating them into a medium where a significant part of effective storytelling depends on the way individual players interact with the platform, computer games have a unique power to retell stories within a completely new context. Through giving up a measure of control to the audience, the meaning and message of these stories earn nuance with the actions players themselves take by taking charge of the narrative and through it experience a sense of shared responsibility (Kwastek 2013).

2.3.1. Far Cry 2

Far Cry 2 is an open-world first-person shooter computer game, part of the *Far Cry* franchise published by Ubisoft. This game is the second in a series of five main games and several spinoffs, developed by Ubisoft Montreal and published in 2008.

After the largely technical focus of the first game in the series (Crytek 2004), *Far Cry 2*, while still putting a heavy emphasis on pushing the capabilities of the technology available at the time with a dynamic weather system, semi-open world and realistic physics, presents a great example of interactive storytelling in which elements of the gameplay and game world work together to create a sense of immersion into an overarching cohesive narrative. These technological advancements contribute significantly to the success of creating a game environment suitable for the story to be told.

Far Cry 2 is not a faithful remake of *Heart of Darkness*. The novella serves more as inspiration, a story framework that is analysed and elements of it integrated into the game, using some of the same narrative tropes and devices: the message, the environment, the overarching mission, the moral ambiguity of its villains. These elements are observed, then altered to be effectively transplanted into the expected format of a computer game.

The story is set in a modern African country affected by a serious military-political conflict. The player is tossed between two warring factions—the United Front for Liberation and Labour (UFLL) and the Alliance for Popular Resistance (APR)—with an initial contract to assassinate a local weapons dealer called the Jackal. After a short, armed skirmish, the player will end up running errands for one faction or the other, gaining reputation and currency in the area with the final goal of reaching the Jackal acting as the overarching driving mission.

Through diverse quests—both those that advance the plot and repeating errands aimed for collecting arms and currency in exchange for malaria medication—the player is forced to adopt increasingly violent behaviour as the story progresses. These missions are designed to be morally ambiguous and follow the idea of moral deterioration heavily present in all of Conrad's adaptations.

The game's main theme—violence—is the gameplay's driving force. Within the context of a first-person military shooter, which is by and large designed around the concept of war and combat, at first glance this is not an unusual mechanic. But the role of violence in *Far Cry 2* is different in that the narrative makes the player aware of it, its effect on the player character, his environment, his in-game companions and the progressively destabilising political situation that unfolds as the story moves ahead. In the end, it is the game's proposed main antagonist who calls out violence to be what it is: a disease, a plague that infests people and causes immense destruction both within the person and in their environment. This manifests quite literally with the player character's illness and the carnage the player causes throughout the game.

Gameplay mechanics emphasise this continuous destructive spiral: weapons degrade and jam over time, enemies respawn on the road and in camps the player has previously cleared out and weather conditions force the player to change tactics in similar situations. All this is underlined by the player character's malaria—dizzy spells affect him at random intervals (often midcombat) and the game forces the player to run special errands in order to top up his medication and survive. These mechanics are designed to work against the player and create a highly stressful environment, reminiscent of the atmosphere permeated by frustration, incompetence, and helplessness Marlow faces in the Congo jungle, successfully integrated into the flow and set mechanics system of a modern first-person shooter (Jeffries 2009).

Instead of nominating one Kurtz-like figure as antagonist, developers chose a more ambiguous approach in creating a character who embodies the disintegration of morality in all of *Heart of Darkness'* adaptations. At first glance, the Kurtz of *Far Cry 2* is the Jackal—a weapons dealer the player is tasked to assassinate as his first and most important overarching mission. The ambiguity of second-hand information plays an important role in this interpretation of the narrative as well: through running errands for the journalist Reuben Oluwagembi who is writing an account of the armed conflict in the area, the player collects cassette tapes through which the Jackal shares what is essentially *Far*

Cry 2's equivalent of Kurtz's manifesto in *Heart of Darkness*. The character archetype of a journalist documenting the deeds of the 'Kurtzes' appears in the novella and in *Apocalypse Now*.

As opposed to meeting him at the end of the story in the shape of a final shakedown mission, however, the player encounters the Jackal multiple times during the game—he is, in fact, one of the first characters the player talks to when he first arrives in the area. The Jackal appears at key turning points of the plot, going as far as taking care of the player in his illness and offering him valuable advice. This is where the clear identity of *Far Cry 2*'s Kurtz becomes questionable.

The Jackal is introduced to the player gradually, each encounter revealing more of his personality, views, and goals. Much like Kurtz in the novella, the player is never quite sure where the Jackal's character lies. With this, *Far Cry 2* introduces its final boss only to throw him in the player's path over and over again, slowly revealing his views to be aligned with the player character's goals after all. At the third in-person meeting, the Jackal wakes the player up with the words: "Wake up. I used to be you." This neatly underlines the shift of the Kurtz-identity from the Jackal to the player: through his increasingly effective violent behaviour, morally questionable decisions and the influence he cultivates in the war-torn country, the game's deliberately hostile design puts the player through the same experience as Kurtz, causing their integrity and identity to shift and deteriorate.

In this it is easy to see *Far Cry 2*'s Kurtz as both the Jackal and the player himself—by leading the player to be the narrator and the villain at the same time, the game effectively highlights its message in the consequences of violence and war through the player's actions themselves, placing the responsibility for those consequences on the player's own shoulders.

2.3.2. Spec Ops: The Line

Spec Ops: The Line is a third-person military cover-based shooter designed around the idea of violence, war and their effects on those who fight it similarly to *Far Cry 2*. The game was developed by Yager Development and published by 2K Games in 2012.

While *Far Cry 2* was praised at the time of its release as an impressive technological feat, the gameplay of *Spec Ops: The Line* is in line with a regular third-person shooter of its time, with all the successful and less successful combat and exploration mechanics included. What sets this game apart is its story: Yager Development had free reign in designing the game's narrative, as long as they kept the game's genre and mechanics in line with the rest of the series released between 1998 and 2012. The narrative the game lets the player explore is a surprising critique of war and entertainment that idolises war, laden with subtle symbolism and irony (Raycevick 2017).

Similarly to *Far Cry 2*, *Spec Ops: The Line* takes inspiration from both Conrad's *Heart of Darkness* and Coppola's *Apocalypse Now* in its distinctly American military setting and themes of war. This time the story takes place in a speculative Middle East where the city of Dubai is hit by natural disaster and is buried under a wall of sand. The area still populated by civilians and affected by heavy wind, sandstorms, riots, and limited resources is controlled by a deserted U.S. army battalion under martial law, led by PTSD (Post-Traumatic Stress Disorder) troubled Colonel John Konrad.

The player enters the scene as the captain of a special forces unit sent to this no-man's land with the mission to find out what exactly happened to the planned evacuation attempt and to figure out the meaning of Col. Konrad's cryptic last radio broadcast:

> This is Colonel John Konrad, United States Army. Attempted evacuation of Dubai ended in complete failure. Death toll . . . too many.

As Captain Martin Walker and his team fight their way deeper and deeper into the city, hindered by enemies and hostile environmental conditions, the true depth of the horrifying events and the acts the deserted 33rd Battalion committed against the civilian population slowly come to light. The game's story then shifts from that of a straightforward shooter to a narrative that takes the player down the path of destruction: the player must fight the protagonists' own people-turned-antagonists by this disaster-hit city, operating under constant threat from the environment, committing war crimes and still being unable to protect civilians and those from his own squad. The game's aesthetic reflects this downwards spiral well: scenes become progressively darker in colour and lighting, and the player character Martin Walker's appearance gradually changes to reflect the rough conditions that affect him both physically and mentally.

The mechanics that make this environment a hostile and stressful territory to explore further enhance this feeling of disempowerment. Where most games set the player up for forward momentum, gaining skills and becoming more powerful with experience, *Spec Ops: The Line* does the opposite. The traditional video game hero (the strong, masculine figure of a soldier) is declining into a tragically flawed and mentally unstable person. The sandstorm that buried Dubai serves as a chaotic force of transformation, turning the player's expectations for the narrative, the mechanics, the experience of a game to its reverse: a personal journey into madness with the game's mechanics ready to complement it.

Spec Ops: The Line, rather than taking direct plot points from either *Heart of Darkness* or *Apocalypse Now*, uses references and subtle visual and textual symbolism to replicate and push further the environment set as an example by Conrad. The game's Kurtz-figure is Col. Konrad, whose name is a direct reference to that of the novella's author. His intent to help, turned and twisted in the face of disastrous conditions, is very much in line with the novella, the film, and their treatment of Kurtz. As the player explores the game world, he is continuously harassed and taunted on broadcast by a character titled the Radioman who serves as the game's chronicler archetype familiar from *Heart of Darkness*, *Apocalypse Now* and *Far Cry 2*.

These concrete allusions to the original story and its subsequent adaptations are underlined with subtle visual and textual cues indicating distress and the deterioration of the situation: the game's main menu displays the American flag upside-down as a sign of distress, and in the loading screens—where other games would generally display tips and useful information for the player to see—*Spec Ops: The Line* taunts the player with lines recounting the crimes they commit in-game. With this the responsibility of the player themselves for the consequences of Walker's actions becomes clear to see.

As with *Far Cry 2*, *Spec Ops: The Line* is not a faithful game adaptation of *Heart of Darkness*. It takes the novella's initial meaning that is further explored by Coppola in *Apocalypse Now* and using the tools and narrative elements of the previous adaptations effectively tells its own story of madness and psychological decay. The game and *Apocalypse Now* both allude to a narrative of American military identity crisis—their protagonists' (eventual) mission is to fight their own side with no reliable chain of command to control the situation—placing the story in a setting relevant to both their audiences at the time.

On the surface, *Spec Ops: The Line* caters to a specific audience (players of military shooter games) and, with its seemingly patriotic themes, so does *Apocalypse Now*. Yet using the medium of film and game respectively, they both make clever commentary on war and violence against the backdrop of the Vietnam War and a fictional Middle-Eastern military conflict. This disintegration of identity can also be observed when reading *Heart of Darkness*. Marlow, although not exempt from the prejudices of his time, starts questioning the legitimacy of the colonisation of Africa, and in consequence what he believes to be the true European ideals of morality.

By fulfilling players' preconceptions about military shooter games and turning them into a plot device that further drives the point home, *Spec Ops: The Line* takes full advantage of the medium—starting from the main menu through loading screens to the actual gameplay itself, every element works together to make this game a unique and fascinating example of effective video game storytelling.

3. Discussion

Paul B. Armstrong, editor of the Fifth Norton Critical Edition of *Heart of Darkness* (Armstrong 2017) says in his introduction:

One of the peculiarities of great literary works is that they have a life that goes beyond what their authors originally intended.

The message *Heart of Darkness* carries is something literary historians, critics, and novelists have debated, analysed, and re-interpreted over and over since its publication. For where it sits within history, both in literature and in the movements of the economic and political powers of the world, it stands out as a piece that criticises the system ultimately leading to its birth. Yet a very important point to consider when reading *Heart of Darkness* is that Conrad—voluntarily or involuntarily—still falls into setting Africa as a counterpoint to Europe, its jungles and local population capable of eroding the moral standards it stands for (Said 1993). He sets the two continents in opposition: one of history and civilisation, another one of an impenetrable wilderness and a sense of oppressive separation (Achebe 1977).

In a sense, Conrad's criticism of imperial efforts is blind to many of the injustices it carries. Chinua Achebe, Nigerian novelist in his article 'An Image of Africa: Racism' in Conrad's "Heart of Darkness" (1977) says:

> Conrad saw and condemned the evil of imperial exploitation but was strangely unaware of the racism on which it sharpened its iron tooth.

Part of the reason for Conrad's prejudices lies within the context of his time, his view of Africa and its inhabitants is by no means a unique opinion. Yet acknowledging that *Heart of Darkness* with all its virtues and its arguably controversial elements influences the view of Africa in the eyes of the rest of the world puts its message and effect into perspective. Being adapted several times through several different mediums serves to carry that message further.

Ellis (1982) in 'The Literary Adaptation' talks about the cultural memory of literary works. This phrase calls attention to a pattern that emerges through each adaptation of *Heart of Darkness* and indeed, broadly speaking, any extended universe based upon adapting and re-adapting literary or other narrative works. The novella's cultural memory can be interpreted to include all adaptations of it: from novels inspired by it to the deliberate rework of the narrative into a new setting, these leave footprints—impressions which add to the commonly understood concept of *Heart of Darkness*. In that, each adaptation has the potential to influence further rework of the novella, adding to this interlocking network of narratives the same way other iterations have previously done: the novella's setting and protagonist–antagonist relationship appear in *Apocalypse Now*, discussion around Conrad's work influences visual depictions of characters in the graphic novel, the film's visuals and military setting reflect in *Far Cry 2* and *Spec Ops: The Line*.

It is interesting to observe the evolution of Marlow from serving as a character argued to be the author's substitute through each of the novella's subsequent adaptations, both static and interactive. From his straightforward appearance in *Apocalypse Now* as Captain Willard through the emphasis Mairowitz and Anyango put on the connection between author and narrator to collapsing author, narrator, and antagonist into the player in *Far Cry 2*, these vary greatly in how they interpret Marlow in moral standing, contextual relevance and his function as 'protagonist' in an interactive setting.

Kurtz goes through a similar transformation visible especially in *Far Cry 2*, where the narrative reveals the player to be, in a sense, the moral successor to the game's Kurtz-character, the Jackal. By blurring the line between protagonist and antagonist, the game takes an unexpected approach to emphasise one of the novella's fundamental questions: what happens to a person when faced with the incomprehensible, relentless, and violent forces of nature and human beings?

Apocalypse Now and the graphic novel—although vastly different in approach and fidelity to the original material—stand as examples of straightforward linear adaptations that both view and respond to the novella in ways unique to them. While the film transplants the narrative to an entirely different setting, the graphic novel provides subtle commentary through its visuals while using the original work to recreate the story as accurately as possible within its format.

Games add another layer of depth to the retelling of Conrad's story by putting the narrative in a context in which the audience ceases to remain a passive observer and through interacting with the games, becomes complicit in how they unfold. Both games lean on this sense of shared responsibility. They offer choices to the player that come with serious consequences and through dialogue (*Far Cry 2*: e.g., the Jackal encounters) and in-game visual and textual cues (*Spec Ops*: e.g., loading screen taunts) makes the player aware of the active part they play in shaping the games' events. In this, interaction and the audience's expectations towards video games as a medium are used as tools to deliver the message.

In the field of postcolonial game studies, *Far Cry 2* and *Spec Ops: The Line* are part of a canon of games that portray—in one way or another—colonial spaces and narratives. Souvik Mukherjee (2018) in 'Playing Subaltern: Video Games and Postcolonialism' talks in some detail about identity tourism in *Far Cry 2*, the role of the coloniser and colonised in video games and the importance of meaningful representation that takes history and its meaning into consideration. Murray (2018) explores this in a wider context of video game criticism: she highlights the importance of video game analysis and critique that leads to meaningful change in thinking within the games industry.

While *Far Cry 2* and *Spec Ops: The Line* are successful examples of adapting a linear story to an interactive medium (both in a narrative delivery and in a commercial sense), what counts as traditional video games do not necessarily make a suitable vehicle for literary adaptations in general. Often the requirements of the market and the expectations of the players make it difficult to successfully transplant certain narratives into computer game form—sacrificing elements of story to the benefit of well-balanced mechanics and vice versa; marketability; intellectual property rights and other, often unexpected obstacles might make literary adaptations as games an unattractive decision for game developers and publishers. Yet interaction is a powerful tool that is capable of inserting audiences into stories in a way no other medium can: with due consideration, it could be a valuable platform to use in fields from education through academia to entertainment in preserving, reclaiming, and re-imagining classic and contemporary narratives through a new lens.

Looking past the boundaries of traditional game development, artworks, and interactive pieces on the borders of mediums and genres, pieces between comics and film, literary text and games, comics and games do not always meet with the same set of expectations games such as first-person military shooters do. Storytelling mediums that use techniques from literature, film, games, and art based on the unique requirements of the original literary work have the potential to be more flexible—breaking outside the set requirements of one medium can be a powerful tool to discover new means of effective storytelling (Jenkins 2003).

That *Heart of Darkness* still has such an effect on adventure stories that strive to explore the depth of human morality is not surprising. Stories of the wonders and horrors of newly discovered lands, faraway settings, and strange people have always had the power to pique curiosity in storytellers and audiences alike. Paired with themes of violence, the terrible force of nature and the fallible nature of human beings, Conrad's narrative sets the scene for an intriguing world. Using real places and real events as material to retell this story in new ways relevant to the audiences at the time (the Vietnam War, the futile interventions of America in West in African conflicts, the political situation in the Middle-East), these stories about human nature and its weakness against meaningless violence and the brutality of nature stay relevant and powerful even today.

Author Contributions: Conceptualization, F.P. and I.D.; Investigation, F.P. and I.D.; Supervision, I.D.; Writing—original draft, F.P.; Writing—review & editing, F.P. and I.D.

Funding: This research received no external funding.

References

Achebe, Chinua. 1977. An Image of Africa: Racism in Conrad's 'Heart of Darkness'. *Massachusetts Review* 18: 251–61. [CrossRef]

Anyango, Catherine, and Zane Mairowitz. 2010. *Heart of Darkness—A Graphic Novel*. London: SelfMadeHero, ISBN 978-1-906838-09-6.

Armstrong, Paul B. 2017. Introduction. In *Heart of Darkness: Authoritative Text Backgrounds and Context Criticism*, 5th ed. Edited by Paul B. Armstrong. New York: W. W. Norton & Company, pp. ix–xxi. ISBN 9780393264869.

Coker, Catherine. 2017. The margins of print? Fan fiction as book history. *Transformative Works and Cultures* 25. [CrossRef]

Conrad, Joseph. 2017. Heart of Darkness. In *Heart of Darkness: Authoritative Text Backgrounds and Context Criticism*, 5th ed. Edited by Paul B. Armstrong. New York: W. W. Norton & Company, pp. 3–78. ISBN 9780393264869. First published 1899.

Coppola, Francis Ford. 1979. *Apocalypse Now*. Beverly Hills: United Artists.

Crytek. 2004. *Far Cry*. Montreuil: Ubisoft.

Cutting, Andrew. 2011. Interiority, Affordances, and the Possibility of Adapting Henry James's The Turn of the Screw as a Video Game. *Adaptation* 5: 169–84. [CrossRef]

Ellis, John. 1982. The Literary Adaptation. *Screen* 23: 3–5. [CrossRef]

Faber, Michel. 2010. Heart of Darkness by Joseph Conrad, Adapted by Catherine Anyango and David Zane Mairowitz. *The Guardian*. Available online: https://theguardian.com/books/2010/sep/25/heart-darkness-conrad-anyango-mairowitz (accessed on 28 June 2018).

Fitzgerald, Francis Scott. 1994. *The Great Gatsby*. Harmondsworth: Penguin, ISBN 9780140620184. First published 1925.

Harrison, Rachel V. 2012. Up the Congo River into Cambodia: Literary and Cinematic Journeys to The Dark. *Asian Affairs* 43: 49–60. [CrossRef]

Hochschild, Adam. 2012. *King Leopold's Ghost: A Story of Greed, Terror and Heroism in Colonial Africa*. London: Pan, ISBN 9781447211358. First published 1998.

Hunicke, Robin, Mark LeBlanc, and Robert Zubek. 2004. MDA: A Formal Approach to Game Design and Game Research. Workshop on Challenges in Game AI 1–4. Available online: https://cs.northwestern.edu/~hunicke/pubs/MDA.pdf (accessed on 28 June 2018).

Jauss, Hans Robert. 1970. Literary History as a Challenge to Literary Theory. *New Literary History* 40: 7–37. [CrossRef]

Jeffries, L. B. 2009. Far Cry 2: The Heart of Darkness Game. *Popmatters*. Available online: https://popmatters.com/71590-far-cry-2-the-heart-of-darkness-game-2496045809.html (accessed on 28 June 2018).

Jenkins, Henry. 2003. Transmedia Storytelling. *MIT Technology Review*. Available online: https://technologyreview.com/s/401760/transmedia-storytelling/ (accessed on 28 June 2018).

Jenkins, Henry. 2017. Adaptation, Extension, Transmedia. *Literature/Film Quarterly* 45. Available online: http://salisbury.edu/lfq/_issues/first/adaptation_extension_transmedia.html (accessed on 28 June 2018).

Kinder, Marsha. 1979. The Power of Adaptation in Apocalypse Now. *Film Quarterly; Berkeley* 33: 12–20. [CrossRef]

Kwastek, Katja. 2013. *Aesthetics of Interaction in Digital Art*. Cambridge and London: MIT Press, ISBN 9780262019323.

Mukherjee, Souvik. 2018. Playing Subaltern: Video Games and Postcolonialism. *Games and Culture* 13: 504–20. [CrossRef]

Murray, Soraya. 2018. The Work of Postcolonial Game Studies in the Play of Culture. *Open Library of Humanities* 4: 13. [CrossRef]

Pakenham, Thomas. 1991. *The Scramble for Africa 1876–1912*. London: George Weidenfeld & Nicolson, ISBN 0297811304.

Raycevick. 2017. Spec Ops the Line … 5 Years Later. Available online: https://youtube.com/watch?v=8dzstxE_5Rc&t=741s (accessed on 28 June 2018).

Said, Edward W. 1993. Two Visions in Heart of Darkness. In *Heart of Darkness: Authoritative Text Backgrounds and Context Criticism*, 5th ed. Edited by Paul B. Armstrong. New York: W. W. Norton & Company, pp. 361–68. ISBN 9780393264869.

Ubisoft Montreal. 2008. *Far Cry 2*. Montreuil: Ubisoft.

Van Reybrouck, David. 2010. Congo under Leopold II, 1885–1908. In *Heart of Darkness: Authoritative Text Backgrounds and Context Criticism*, 5th ed. Edited by Paul B. Armstrong. New York: W. W. Norton & Company, pp. 107–23. ISBN 9780393264869.

Watt, Ian. 1979. Impressionism and Symbolism in Heart of Darkness. In *Heart of Darkness: Authoritative Text Backgrounds and Context Criticism*, 5th ed. Edited by Paul B. Armstrong. New York: W. W. Norton & Company, pp. 320–61. ISBN 9780393264869.

Whitlock, Gillian. 2007. Autobiographics: The Seeing 'I' of the Comics'. *Modern Fiction Studies* 52: 965–79. [CrossRef]

Yager Development. 2012. *Spec Ops: The Line*. Novato: 2K Games.

Article

Choice Poetics by Example

Peter Mawhorter [1,*], Carmen Zegura [2], Alex Gray [3], Arnav Jhala [3], Michael Mateas [4] and Noah Wardrip-Fruin [4]

[1] Computer Science & Artificial Intelligence Laboratory, Massachusetts Institute of Technology, Cambridge, MA 02139, USA

[2] Computer Science Department, Brown University, Providence, RI 02912, USA; carmen_zegura@brown.edu

[3] Computer Science Department, North Carolina State University, Raleigh, NC 27695, USA; magray2@ncsu.edu (A.G.); ahjhala@ncsu.edu (A.J.)

[4] Computational Media Department, University of California Santa Cruz, Santa Cruz, CA 95064, USA; michaelm@soe.ucsc.edu (M.M.); nwf@soe.ucsc.edu (N.W.-F.)

* Correspondence: pmawhorter@gmail.com

Received: 30 June 2018 ; Accepted: 27 August 2018; Published: 6 September 2018

Abstract: Choice poetics is a formalist framework that seeks to concretely describe the impacts choices have on player experiences within narrative games. Developed in part to support algorithmic generation of narrative choices, the theory includes a detailed analytical framework for understanding the impressions choice structures make by analyzing the relationships among options, outcomes, and player goals. The theory also emphasizes the need to account for players' various modes of engagement, which vary both during play and between players. In this work, we illustrate the non-computational application of choice poetics to the analysis of two different games to further develop the theory and make it more accessible to others. We focus first on using choice poetics to examine the central repeated choice in *"Undertale,"* and show how it can be used to contrast two different player types that will approach a choice differently. Finally, we give an example of fine-grained analysis using a choice from the game *"Papers, Please,"* which breaks down options and their outcomes to illustrate exactly how the choice pushes players towards complicity via the introduction of uncertainty. Through all of these examples, we hope to show the usefulness of choice poetics as a framework for understanding narrative choices, and to demonstrate concretely how one could productively apply it to choices "in the wild."

Keywords: choice poetics; poetics; narrative games; choices; player goals; roleplay; complicity

---

1. Introduction

Originally developed in some of our prior work (Mawhorter 2016; Mawhorter et al. (2014, 2015a, 2015b), choice poetics is a formalist framework for understanding the impact of narrative choices on the player experience via their options, their outcomes, and how those relate to player goals. Choice poetics was developed in order to be deployed in a generative system that produces narrative choices, as described in (Mawhorter 2016; Mawhorter et al. 2015a). However, the theory also supports human analysis, and the goal of this paper is to provide examples of that. We hope that these examples not only demonstrate the use of the framework, but also meaningfully contribute to existing discussions of the choices that we analyze.

The formal process of choice poetic analysis, having been designed with operationalization in mind, is quite detailed, but it can be summarized in four steps (concrete examples of these steps are provided below):

1. **Goal Analysis**: Consider the player's mode(s) of engagement (e.g., role play, power play, etc.), and observe or assume the set of goals that influences their decisions. For a specific analysis, defining one or more player models (as prioritized set(s) of goals) is often sufficient.

2. **Likelihood Analysis**: Review the options offered at the choice being analyzed, and note the full range of outcomes that those options might suggest to the player, as well as the outcomes they actually produce. In addition, note how likely each suggested outcome seems to be.

3. **Prospective Analysis**: Describe the impact of each suggested outcome on each player goal. This gives an overall impression of how the choice will appear to the player as they encounter it, known as their prospective impression. Option/outcome patterns are recognizable at this point.

4. **Retrospective Analysis**: Review the actual outcomes of each option, and describe their impacts on each player goal. This produces a picture of the retrospective impression that the choice will leave on the player once they observe an outcome. Pay close attention to any differences between suggested and actual outcomes. Again, specific patterns may be identifiable at this stage.

These four steps produce tables of prospective and retrospective impression labels for each option, which can usually be used to answer specific questions about a choice (e.g., "Which option will this type of player favor?" or "Will the player feel this is a difficult choice?"). In some cases, producing multiple contrasting analyses using different starting assumptions (such as about player goals or outcome likelihoods) can be used to answer design questions (e.g., "Will this choice tend to separate players according to player types?" or "Should the likelihood of this outcome be important for how players will perceive this choice?").

For prospective analysis, the valence and likelihood of outcomes can be summarized using concise labels. For each option × goal, labels can be assigned depending on whether that option has likely/unlikely outcomes that advance/hinder that goal. For likely outcomes, we assign the labels ○ advances and ∗ hinders, and for unlikely/unknown outcomes, we use the labels ○ enables and ∗ threatens. Note that most option/goal combinations will receive more than one label, e.g., an advantageous but not certain option could both ∗ threaten and ○ advance a goal. The assignment of prospective labels allows us to analyze the choice by comparing it to known choice structures, or just by observing patterns among the labels.

We start with an example of contrasting modes of engagement by looking at *Undertale*'s central repeated choice of how to interact with wandering monsters (Fox 2015). *Undertale*'s plot revolves around the player's aggression: does the player take their cue from other games and attack every "monster" they come across, or do they instead use the game's unusual "Mercy" option to avoid violence? Our analysis of *Undertale* examines both how that choice changes as the player learns about its outcomes, and how different goals might lead to different play styles. The game reinforces both aggressive and pacifist styles but gives those players different endings to encourage dialogue within the player community.

After exploring the importance of modes of engagement, we shift focus by deconstructing a repeated choice from *Papers, Please*: whether to approve the entry permit of someone who claims to be a refugee (Pope 2013). *Papers, Please* uses a carefully crafted choice structure to illustrate to the player how autocratic regimes instil complicity in their citizens by manipulating uncertainty. A detailed analysis of the options and outcomes involved reveals exactly how this choice structure operates, and how it would take a different form without the element of uncertainty. Choice poetics is useful here because it can show explicitly how important uncertainty is to the effect achieved by *Papers, Please*, illustrating not just that the game *does* encourage complicity, but the subtle psychological mechanism it uses to do so.

By providing examples of the application of choice poetics "by hand" as opposed to by computer, we hope to inspire others to use and eventually help refine this theory. Ideally, the formal structure of choice poetics can provide language to discuss choice structures precisely, and the exhaustive analysis of goals, options, and outcomes can help analysts uncover quirks and details not readily apparent from a more gestalt perspective. Although we do not believe in formalism as an ultimate goal of literary (or interactive) analysis, we do hope that this framework can become one useful tool among many for both designers and critics to better understand the impacts of narrative choices on their audiences.

2. Related Work

This work builds on our previous work on the theory of choice poetics. In particular, our paper "Towards a Theory of Choice Poetics" (Mawhorter et al. 2014) provides a concise summary of the aims of the theory and the phenomena that it attempts to explain, and Peter Mawhorter's dissertation (Mawhorter 2016) contains a chapter that provides a more detailed examination of the theory, including a walkthrough of the *Papers, Please* example that we also present here. It is worth acknowledging the lines of inquiry that choice poetics is in dialogue with, including formalist narratology from Aristotle (1917) to Barthes and Duisit (1975), the psychology of narrative Tversky and Kahneman (1981); Green and Brock (2000); Mar and Oatley (2008); Zunshine (2006), the psychology of decision-making Mellers et al. (1997); Schwartz et al. (2002), and of course other modern theories of interactive narrative (Aarseth 1997; Frasca 2003; Lindley 2005; Mateas 2001; Murray 1997; Ryan 1991; Tosca 2000). The specific ideas about modes of engagement and player motivations used here are based largely on the work of Yee (2006), along with other work summarized in (Hamari and Tuunanen 2014), although choice poetics can also incorporate non-standard modes of engagement such as critical play (Flanagan 2009) (see Chapter 3 of (Mawhorter 2016) for a more detailed explanation of these links). Other relevant studies provide insight into how engagement can be driven by multiple desires (Lindley 2005), can be affected by choices and their consequences (Mallon and Webb 2005), and can change over time (Lange 2014). The development of choice poetics was also informed by non-academic writing on choice design, such as design advice for authors of online interactive narratives (Fabulich 2010) or tabletop roleplaying game masters (Laws 2001). Finally, concurrent experimental work (including some of our own) around choices and outcomes in games has provided useful empirical data about choices and their consequences (Cardona-Rivera et al. 2014; Fendt et al. 2012; Iten et al. 2018; Mawhorter et al. 2015a).

2.1. Moral Choices

Our first analysis engages with the popular 2015 indie roleplaying game *Undertale* and how players with similar goals but different priorities can be steered towards different decisions. Existing scholarly literature on *Undertale* has examined its portrayal of morality and ethics through its primary choice of "kill" or "spare" (Müller 2017), the ways the game solidifies the significance of its choices through various mechanics (Day and Zhu 2017), and how its musical score changes from tonal and pleasant to atonal and eerie depending on the player's approach (Perez 2017). Notably, *Undertale* goes so far as to remember a player's decisions even after they ostensibly reset the game, encouraging the idea that its choices are meaningful (Hughes 2015). Although *Undertale*'s designer Toby Fox has been reticent about his intentions regarding the game's moral choices, he is clearly interested in aspects of game design beyond traditional roleplaying game mechanics (quoted in Feeld (2015)):

> The addictive quality of "numbers increasing" is what drives a lot of games. But some of the most important things in life can't be accurately represented by numbers.

As described by Müller, Undertale's various endings have encouraged the player community to discuss attitudes towards violence both in games and in real life (Müller 2017, sct. 2.2.1). The usefulness of choice poetics in this context is that is provides a concrete way of describing which aspects of Undertale's central kill/spare choice are mobilized to achieve this result, and by contrasting two different possible player perspectives, it illustrates how different players might naturally be encouraged to pursue different play styles and therefore observe different content, providing fodder for online discussion. Of course, a formalist analysis is not the only way to reach that conclusion, but it is a mechanical and reproducible way to do so, potentially making it accessible to novice critics (and as in our prior work, to automated systems).

Broader research on moral choices in games includes examinations of their implementation and studies of how players respond to them (Consalvo et al. 2016; Švelch 2010; Weaver and Lewis 2012). Of course, research on the psychological effects of games, especially violent games, is quite popular, but has come to largely mixed conclusions (Ellithorpe et al. 2015; Ferguson 2008). In fact, there is also interest in using video games to encourage better moral decision making (Katsarov et al. 2017).

2.2. Coercion and Complicity

In our second analysis, we discuss complicity in *Papers, Please*, and use a detailed breakdown of a single choice to illustrate how this moral issue is raised within the game. A version of this analysis appears in (Mawhorter 2016), but a more thorough analysis of the game and its themes has also been undertaken by Paul Formosa, Malcolm Ryan, and Dan Staines (Formosa et al. (2016)); for a critical perspective, see also Alexander (2013), which Formosa et al. cite themselves). Formosa, Ryan, and Staines' excellent analysis of the game and its moral dimension largely agrees with our conclusion that the game uses ambiguity as a mechanism to encourage complicity, and in fact they even quote personal correspondence with Lucas Pope, the game's designer, to the same effect: "On some level I want players to reach a point of self-realization—about how good people can be turned into uncaring cogs" (Pope quoted in Formosa et al. (2016)). We find these congruences encouraging, because they show that choice poetics can produce conclusions that are not only echoed by other analyses but which also seem to have been intended by the designer themselves. Of course, if existing analyses have reached these conclusions already, why use choice poetics at all? In this case, choice poetics provides a more detailed accounting of the importance of ambiguity in terms of the choices faced by the player, and is able to explain exactly why removing ambiguity would change a (hypothetical) player's perspective on the game. Such detailed accounting of the impact of outcomes could be useful for designers interested in tweaking their choices to best support desired narrative or persuasive goals, and in fact, at least for machine-designed choices, this has shown to be somewhat effective (see Mawhorter et al. (2015b)).

Other scholarly work dealing with complicity in games is also relevant here. Toby Smethurst and Stef Craps discussed the appearance of trauma in games, including a section on complicity (Smethurst and Craps 2015). In a similar vein, Holger Pötzsch discussed complicity in games, again in the context of more scripted narrative settings (Pötzsch 2017). Both of these analyses include *Spec Ops: The Line* (Yager Development 2012) as an example of a game that deals with complicity, but which does so in a completely different manner to *Papers, Please*, using a scripted narrative and being much more direct and extreme about the moral decisions being made (see also Murray (2016) on the game's failure to grapple with issues of racism and sexism even as it does address toxic masculinity).

3. Reinforcing Disparate Choices in *Undertale*

Undertale is an independently developed roleplaying game (Fox 2015) about a kid trying to get back home. The game appears at first to be a normal roleplaying game with some interesting mechanics, but the facade of standard RPG (role-playing game) mechanics hides a deeper morality-based storyline which challenges gamers to think more deeply about the random "monsters" they are fighting. Players face different challenges and receive different endings depending on whether they play the game passively or aggressively. These paths allow for the game to be a straightforward example of what happens when players with different play styles are forced to make the same choice.

Figure 1 shows the very first random encounter of the game, and illustrates the repeated central choice of whether to fight, flee, or "spare" each opponent ("Flee" and "Spare" are the options in the "Mercy" menu). With the exception of certain bosses, all "enemies" in the game must be dealt with in one of these three ways, where killing them awards gold and experience points, fleeing gives no reward, and sparing them awards just gold, which is only possible after taking a specific sequence of actions that pacify the opponent which the player must learn for each type of "monster." To understand how this repeated choice is set up to create dialogue within player communities, we can break it down using a formal analysis.

To simplify the analysis, we ignore concerns about player skill, which would provide an extra motive to select the "flee" option. Although contrasting approaches to this choice across players of

Figure 1. A screenshot from *Undertale* showing the first random encounter of the game, in which a "Froggit" "hops close" (note that aggression is implied via the convention of a random encounter but not by the text). The options are "fight," "act," "item," and "mercy," the last of which is unconventional. Screenshot by Peter Mawhorter, licensed under Creative Commons Attribution-ShareAlike 4.0 International License (CC BY SA).

different skill levels would also be an interesting approach, we consider here the perspective of players that have no trouble with the challenges involved in either attacking or pacifying the enemies.

The remaining subsections here describe the results of each of the analysis steps outlined in Section 1, and how they differ both for two different player models and between initial and subsequent encounters with the choice. Our first player model[1] (we call them the power player) is intended to model an experienced roleplaying game player, who is familiar with the conventions of the genre and who expects to be asked to fight their way to victory, collecting experience and gold along the way to gain power and overcome challenging bosses. This power player model is grounded in the "Achievement" dimension of player motivation identified in (Hamari and Tuunanen 2014), which corresponds to the idea of "power play" as a mode of engagement (Mawhorter et al. 2014). Our second player model (we call them the story player) attempts to approximate someone who has little experience with roleplaying games and is interested in experiencing the story of *Undertale*. This model is related to the dimension of player motivation that Hamari and Tuunanen identify as "Immersion," and the "avatar play" mode of engagement from (Mawhorter et al. 2014).

3.1. Goal Analysis

We use the following set of goals, with the listed power/story priorities for our respective player models (these prioritized goal sets are the player models):

---

[1] In choice poetics, a player model is defined as a specific set of prioritized goals, which makes it more specific than a "player type" as used in other literature, although our player models in this analysis roughly correspond to two popular "player types" identified in the literature (see below).

- Gain experience points (high/low)—The power player prioritizes experience points (XP), knowing that they may be necessary to accumulate power and beat the game. The story player understands them as a reward, but does not seek them out to the detriment of other goals.
- Gain gold (high/low)—Similar to XP, the power player seeks out gold while the story player welcomes it but does not prioritize it.
- Show mercy (none/high)—While the power player sees interactions with the monsters as instrumental and inconsequential, our hypothetical story player, swayed by the aesthetics of the game, finds them cute and feels bad being violent towards them (of course, not all story-focused players would have this outlook).
- Explore options (low/high)—Faced with a new game, both the power and story players are interested in figuring out what makes this game unique and what is possible within it, although for the power player this is secondary to other concerns. The "Mercy" menu especially, as an unconventional option, will attract interest.
- Behave consistently (low/low)—Both of our hypothetical players not only exhibit standard human biases towards consistent action (and justification of their past actions using future actions), but also recognize that, in most game systems, rewards are reserved for extreme behavioral profiles. This goal does not trump others, but influences ambiguous cases.

Although these exact goal sets might not be those of any actual player, they do approximate common aspects of player psychology described within existing literature (e.g., the "Achievement" and "Immersion" dimensions from Hamari and Tuunanen (2014)). Any concerns about particular goals or their prioritization could always be investigated by contrasting results with yet another player model that differed from one of these in terms of the goal in question, and of course, were data on actual player goals available in some form, they could be used to define detailed player models for personalized or aggregate analysis. Examples of blind playthroughs uploaded to YouTube (e.g., fuandon (2015) for the story player model and TheRPGMinx (2015) for the power player model) also support the idea that these profiles might model some actual players.

3.2. Likelihood Analysis

The next task is to decide which options suggest what outcomes, which can be tricky, as there is a wide range of possible outcomes to consider. Luckily, our choice of player goals can narrow that range somewhat—for example, in this analysis, we have assumed our players are skilled enough that they will always succeed, so we ignore outcomes related to player injury or death.

Table 1. Likelihood analysis for the player's initial encounter with the choice shown in Figure 1. The "new option" "outcome" reflects the player goal of exploring unknown options, whereas the "repeated" "outcome" reflects the player goal of behaving consistently (both are the same for all three options the first time the player encounters this choice).

Fight	Flee	Spare
(likely) Froggit dies	(likely) Froggit lives	(likely) Froggit lives
(likely) XP reward	(likely) no XP	(unlikely) XP reward
(likely) Gold reward	(likely) no Gold	(unlikely) Gold reward
(known) New option	(known) New option	(known) New option
(known) Not repeated	(known) Not repeated	(known) Not repeated

Table 1 shows likelihood analysis results for the player's first encounter with this choice (which are the same for both player models), including extradiegetic outcomes relating to exploration and consistency goals.

Once the player learns the actual outcomes of each choice, these likelihoods will be simplified: the player will know the true outcomes (all "likely" outcomes become "known"), and the two unlikely outcomes will be revealed (sparing rewards gold, but no XP). For the extra-diegetic outcomes, players who have explored all the options will view none of them as novel, and depending on which option they picked most, they will view one as more consistent with their past behavior.

3.3. Prospective Analysis

Having listed a set of suggested outcomes and their likelihoods, the analysis can proceed to evaluate the prospective impressions created by this choice (as described in Section 1). The results are shown in Table 2, which includes two versions: the block on the left shows evaluations using the initial likelihoods, while the block on the right shows the evaluations after all outcomes are known. The subsequent results also use (P) and (S) to show labels that differ between the power (P) and story (S) player models (mostly, the two models just have different priorities for the different goals). The post-hoc evaluations from the right side of Table 2 are further summarized in Table 3 which shows at a high level how many goals are advanced or hindered by each option for the two player models.

Table 2. Option analysis for the example choice shown in Figure 1. The results for initial and subsequent encounters are shown separately in the left and right halves of the table. All of the labels apply to both of our player models, except the be-consistent labels for the subsequent analysis, where the power (P) and story (S) player models each view either "fight" or "spare" as consistent and the other options as inconsistent (elsewhere stacked labels indicate that multiple labels apply for both models).

	Initial			Subsequent		
Goal	**Fight**	**Flee**	**Spare**	**Fight**	**Flee**	**Spare**
gain-XP	○ enables ○ advances	∗ hinders ∗ threatens	○ enables ∗ threatens	○ advances	∗ hinders	∗ hinders
gain-gold	○ enables ○ advances	∗ hinders ∗ threatens	○ enables ∗ threatens	○ advances	∗ hinders	○ advances
show-mercy	∗ hinders ∗ threatens	○ enables ○ advances	○ enables ○ advances	∗ hinders	○ advances	○ advances
explore-options	○ advances	○ advances	○ advances	<none>	<none>	<none>
be-consistent	<none>	<none>	<none>	○ advances (P) ∗ hinders (S)	∗ hinders	○ advances (S) ∗ hinders (P)

In this case, we can see that, for both player models, the fight and spare options are more attractive than the flee option, and in fact the spare option dominates the flee option for this goal set in all cases, making it mostly irrelevant (of course, this is because we are ignoring player skill as a factor). Comparing just the fight and spare options for the initial decision, we can see that the spare option is seen as a bit dubious in terms of the power-related goals, but clearly superior in terms of the mercy goal.

Considering the power and story players, the power player is most likely to pick "fight," because they ignore the show-mercy goal, so from their perspective, fight is the only option without downsides (of course considering player skill would have complicated that). Meanwhile, the story player, whose highest-priority goals are to explore and show mercy, will likely pick "spare," as it is best for those goals while not entirely sacrificing their low-priority goals. As both of these players encounter this choice again, their explore-options goal will now favor the options they did not choose at first, and the story player may now attempt fighting, and will probably attempt fleeing, because their high-level goals of exploration and mercy are now in conflict. Ultimately, the story player will find sparing most rewarding after all options have been explored. In contrast, the power player, with a lower priority on exploration, may eventually try spare and/or flee out of boredom, but upon learning that those options do not award XP, they will continue to fight most enemies.

As these patterns are established, biases that promote consistency (see e.g., Brehm 1956; Mather et al. 2000; Hall et al. 2012) will be reinforced, and the power and story players will in all likelihood settle for picking fight and spare, respectively. As we can see, the key factor that separates these models is their relative prioritization of the mercy goal, in conjunction with their priorities for gaining XP and gold. Importantly, beyond the immediate rewards shown here, sparing monsters also leads to a number of other acknowledgements and ultimately rewards the player with the ability to befriend some of the more important characters, which is a reward well-suited to players interested in exploring a deeper story. Given an audience of players with a spectrum of preferences, the game prompts different initial choices, and then encourages sticking to those choices (via consistent gold and XP rewards for fighting, and via gold and story rewards for sparing).

3.4. Retrospective Analysis

After making each decision, the immediate rewards are as expected. However, as the game progresses, there are longer-term consequences for both systematic approaches that we consider here. In particular, towards the end of the game, the story line diverges sharply, in the aggressive case throwing the player into brutal battles against several bosses, and in the passive case allowing the player to befriend some of those characters and not fight them at all (although other bosses appear).[2]

The long-term consequences of these individual decisions are not simply rewards or punishments, although sparing monsters leads to a happier story outcome. Instead, they represent divergent worlds, which gives the player a strong sense of agency, but also causes players who take different paths and then compare notes to surprise each other. By reinforcing each path separately and letting content diverge significantly, *Undertale* fosters dialogue between its players, because once they learn of each others' disparate experiences, they will naturally be curious as to how those experiences were unlocked. Had the game simply punished players for fighting the enemies, this would have delivered a fairly simplistic moral message, but instead, the game lets that message unfold via dialogue with other players, and as previously mentioned, uses some extra-diegetic mechanics to give its choices extra permanence.

3.5. Discussion

This analysis set out with the goal of understanding how two different player models could be encouraged to routinely deal with *Undertale*'s randomly-encountered "monsters" in different ways. After understanding the prospective option impressions involved for both initial and repeated iterations of this choice, we can see that the reward structure does indeed encourage power-focused and story-focused players to take different paths, and rewards them for doing so in different ways. By deconstructing *Undertale*'s repeated kill/spare choice using two generic player models, we have gotten some insight into how different players might be encouraged to explore the game differently, but of course there are other important choices and mechanics in the game that help push players down one path or the other.

As explored in Hughes' review of the game and Müller's thesis (Hughes 2015; Müller 2017), part of the message of *Undertale* is not merely about violence itself, but about the player's willingness to callously manipulate the lives of the characters in the game. The moral dichotomy that it sets up through a carefully crafted choice that will separate its audience into opposing camps serves to underline this point and get players to think deeply about it as they attempt to justify their decisions to each other (see, e.g., oh (2016) for an example of discussion within the player community).

The value of choice poetics here lies in explaining the mechanisms behind such narrative choices with specificity. For example, in Table 3, we can see that for our story player model, both the fight and

---

[2]   Note that these divergences still happen even if the player does not reach one of the special endings to the game, which
       typically require extensive forethought and would not be reached by first-time players who do not consult a guide.

spare options are not purely good or bad: the fight option advances some low-priority goals, while the spare option hinders one. As a designer, if we wanted to tweak this choice to more strongly reinforce sparing the monsters, we could consider rewarding some XP for sparing monsters, which would cause the spare choice to dominate the fight choice for players interested in showing mercy. By the same token, the choice not to do so makes the spare option more meaningful: the player actually has to make a sacrifice in order to access it, which potentially increases psychological attachment to that choice, and which might also heighten the player's sense of agency.

These kinds of detailed observations about individual outcomes are something that choice poetics enables naturally. In fact, choice poetics offers a mechanism whereby approaching a choice with a specific question (e.g., "How do power and story players approach this choice differently?") leads to formal descriptions of that choice that can be used to answer other questions (e.g., "How would awarding XP for sparing monsters change this choice?"). In the best case, those formal descriptions or the process of their production raise further questions that highlight as-yet-unconsidered issues with the design of a choice. For example, in this analysis, we noted in passing that the flee option is always dominated by one of the other options assuming the player has a certain level of skill. That observation prompts the question: how do different levels of difficulty affect the player's perception of this choice, which could be answered using further comparative analysis that introduced goals related to self-preservation and player models with different skill levels (which could be modeled using outcome likelihoods for taking damage and/or dying). Although there is not room here to carry out that analysis, the fact that our initial analysis suggests it is a good sign that choice poetics as a formal system can be a productive tool for these kinds of analytical projects.

Table 3. Option analysis results from the right-hand (post-hoc) side of Table 2, grouped according to player models, options, and goal priorities. This illustrates at a high level how (after exploring each option) the power player is encouraged to fight "monsters" while the story player is encouraged to spare them.

	Power Player		
Priority	**Fight**	**Flee**	**Spare**
High	○ advances × 2	* hinders × 2	○ advances × 1, * hinders × 1
Low	○ advances × 1	* hinders × 1	* hinders × 1
	Story Player		
Priority	**Fight**	**Flee**	**Spare**
High	* hinders × 1	○ advances × 1	○ advances × 1
Low	○ advances × 2, * hinders × 1	* hinders × 3	○ advances × 2, * hinders × 1

4. Uncertainty and Complicity in *Papers, Please*

Papers, Please (Pope 2013) gives the player the role of a border inspector in the fictional autocratic regime of Arstotzka. Struggling to support their family at home, they are challenged to quickly inspect passports, visas, and eventually travel permits and vaccination records to either permit or deny entry for a stream of hopeful immigrants and travelers, earning money for each applicant correctly approved or denied. A central part of the game is unresolved ambiguity, both about the identities and claims of those seeking entry and about the motives and legitimacy of the government and opposing revolutionary forces. Alexander (2013) gives a nice overview of the game from a critical perspective, and Formosa et al. (2016) provides a detailed analysis of its systemic engagement with a variety of moral issues.

Of interest to this analysis is the choice shown in Figure 2, and similar choices with higher stakes which come up at several points in the game. In each case, the player must decide whether to take someone at their word that, despite a missing or incorrect document, they still deserve admission. This decision is complicated by the fact that the game also presents situations where applicants attempt to bribe or threaten the player, implying that not all of their claims can be taken at face value. This decision about the fate of an ostensible refugee (or similar person) embodies one of the central themes of the game: how the uncertainty of information from unreliable sources can be pitted against the certain plight of one's family to turn a moral dilemma into a choice with a reluctant "better" option. In the rest of this section, we show the results of each step of a choice poetic analysis (see Section 1) for the choice described in Figure 2.

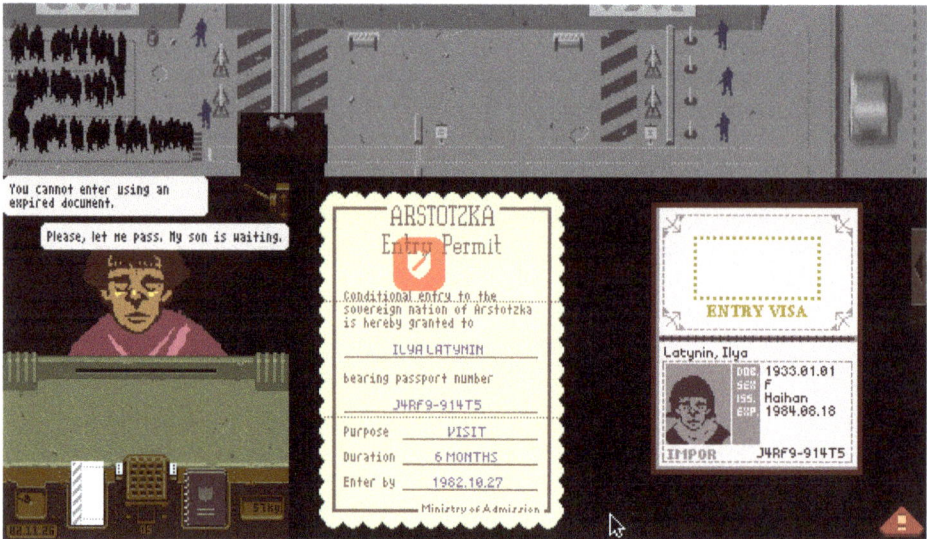

Figure 2. A screenshot from *Papers, Please* showing the interface as the player decides whether to admit a traveler. The traveler in question previously stated that she was coming to visit her son, who she has not seen in 6 years. Although her entry permit is slightly out-of-date, she is asking for leniency. At this point, the player must decide to either approve or deny her visa. Screenshot by Peter Mawhorter, licensed under CC BY SA.

4.1. Goal Analysis

For the purposes of understanding this choice, it is sufficient to use a single player model with the following prioritized goals:

- (high-priority) Provide for your family—the player wants to earn credits and avoid penalties to be able to pay for food and shelter at the end of the day.
- (high-priority) Act ethically—as much as possible, the player wants to treat applicants ethically and avoid acting in ways that would harm them without a proportionate justification, even when this goes against the government's dictates.
- (medium-priority) Apprehend criminals—separate from their desire to earn credits, the player actively wants to identify applicants who might be attempting to gain entry to the country deceitfully and reject their applications.
- (low-priority) Admit approved travellers—all else being equal, the player seeks to treat applicants fairly and admit those that have everything in order.

If we were concerned about differences between players, we could repeat this analysis with another set of player goals and contrast the results, as we did with *Undertale*. Note that, especially in this case, the results of the analysis inform and justify the player model used. If results differ significantly from what we know about a choice, there are two possibilities: either one or more of our assumptions (about goals, goal priorities, and/or the perception of outcomes) was wrong, in which case we can revise or extend our assumptions and re-do the analysis, or what we thought we knew was wrong, and we should be able to use our analysis to demonstrate why. In this case, we think, based on other analyses and interviews with the game designer, that *Papers, Please* uses ambiguity to encourage complicity, and through a formal analysis, we should be able to either back up that intuition or demonstrate why things do not actually work that way.

Because choice poetics makes its assumptions about player motivations and perceived outcome likelihoods explicit, these aspects of the analysis can be easily examined and criticized. In many cases, the most efficient means of dealing with such criticism is to expand the analysis or contrast it with a proposed alternative. When an analysis disagrees with other sources, the source of that disagreement is often differing assumptions about how players will perceive a choice or about how they will respond to the options offered. Making those assumptions explicit thus helps ground potential disagreements, and not only allows for stating disagreements clearly (e.g., "I don't think that most players will place a high priority on acting ethically.") but allows for alternative assumptions to be tested using an identical analytical process.

When an analysis agrees with other sources in its conclusions, the burden is on the critic to argue why a specific choice of goal priorities or outcome likelihoods is unrealistic, and demonstrate how that affects the overall argument put forward. Ideally, of course, such questions might also be settled by gathering real data about player perceptions of goals and outcomes, and choice poetics provides a framework for doing so (see Mawhorter et al. (2015b)).

4.2. Likelihood Analysis

Table 4 shows a breakdown of outcomes and their likelihoods for both possible decisions; relevant outcomes have been essentially intuited from player goals. Note in particular the outcomes with unknown likelihood that represent competing possible worlds with respect to the trustworthiness of the applicant: if they are telling the truth about their plight, admitting them realizes a different outcome than if they are just making up their story to gain entrance, and the player does not have enough information to make an informed judgement either way.

Table 4. Likelihood analysis for the choice shown in Figure 2.

Approve	Deny
(likely) Do not earn a credit	(likely) Earn a credit
(likely) Get punished	(likely) No punishment
(unknown) Refugee is saved	(unknown) Refugee is condemned
(unknown) Scam is rewarded	(unknown) Scam is thwarted

4.3. Prospective Analysis

The prospective analysis results are shown on the left side of Table 5; note that one of the goals (that of admitting approved applicants) is irrelevant here. From these results, we can immediately see that, although both options threaten some goals, the deny option is clearly better with regards to the high-priority goal of feeding your family. In fact, although approving the applicant might be an ethical action, that is not certain, and denying the applicant might also be in line with our player model's ethical standards if in fact they are making up their story.

While this choice does not contain any well-known outcome patterns (cf. Mawhorter et al. (2014)), it does involve some moral concerns, pitting one's desire to help one's family against concerns about turning away a refugee. The structure is clarified further if we consider the same analysis under the assumption that the applicant is telling the truth, which is shown on the right side of Table 5. This new analysis has the structure of a classic dilemma: Two options, each of which * hinders an equally important goal. Compared to the left side of Table 5, concerns about apprehending criminals are gone, and the refugee-related outcomes, now believed to be likely, make the moral weight of the decision unambiguous.

This comparison thus illustrates exactly how *Papers, Please* (and governments) can manufacture complicity: by introducing doubts about the motives of strangers while emphasizing the certainty of outcomes for loved ones, a dilemma that clearly warrants serious moral concern can be transformed into an uneven choice where multiple avenues of justification are available. Note in particular that the player model's goal of apprehending criminals was not a deciding factor in this case. Regardless of the existence of that goal, uncertainty about the applicant's situation still eliminates any o advances labels from the "Approve" column while leaving the "Deny" column * hinders-free. The ambiguous decision is still not an easy one, as evidenced by the fact that it * threatens a top-priority goal (behaving ethically). This leaves the player feeling uneasy about the decision, and potentially helps prompt more reflection on the decision, but ultimately our player model will still view denying the application as the better choice once uncertainty is introduced.

Table 5. Option analysis for the example choice shown in Figure 2. The default analysis is shown on the left ("With Suspicion"), and a revised analysis assuming that the player trusts the applicant ("Without Suspicion") is shown on the right. See Section 1 for how the labels were applied.

Goal	With Suspicion		Without Suspicion	
	Approve	Deny	Approve	Deny
provide-for-family	* threatens * hinders	o enables o advances	* threatens * hinders	o enables o advances
act-ethically	o enables	* threatens	o enables o advances	* threatens * hinders
apprehend-criminals	* threatens	o enables	\<none\>	\<none\>
admit-approved	\<none\>	\<none\>	\<none\>	\<none\>

4.4. Retrospective Analysis

At the end of each day in *Papers, Please*, the player is paid based on the number of applicants they processed "correctly," and then must decide how much money to allocate for family needs, such as food, heating, and eventually, medicine. However, except in a few special cases, there is no information provided about the subsequent outcomes for the applicants who have entered the country that day. In cases where information is available, it is as likely to raise more suspicions as assuage them: The player is eventually asked to participate in a plot to overthrow the Arstotzkan government, and both sides of the conflict are presented as having questionable motives. The player is thus not given many chances to justify their beliefs about the truth of applicants' statements, and in some cases, is given extra reasons to doubt them. Of course, such blanket beliefs about future applicants based on past applicants are simple biases, not rational conclusions, because the applicants are independent of each other, but they would help assuage the player's conscience (or potentially inflame it if the evidence contradicted the player's assumptions). However, by denying even such a false sense of closure, the game encourages the player to feel vaguely uneasy about their role.

At the same time, by emphasizing the outcomes for the player's family, the game pushes the player away from the dilemma mindset and towards an obvious justification for complicity: the player "had" to act in the state's interests because their family's welfare was at stake. From a choice poetic perspective, this choice thus has two interesting properties: First, certain outcomes remain hidden from the player indefinitely, and second, the outcomes that are apparent are emphasized in the course of continued play. The withholding of information serves the purpose of introducing and even emphasizing the uncertainty about outcomes that tilts the choice as discussed above, while the emphasis on the relatively certain outcomes gives the player an extra push towards viewing the choice not as a moral dilemma but as a situation where there is only one "correct" choice.

4.5. Discussion

As with our *Undertale* analysis, the conclusions we reach are the same as those of other analysts (Alexander 2013; Formosa et al. 2016), which is encouraging, because it validates our methodology. At the same time, the level of detail we achieve enables us to answer further questions: how exactly does ambiguity play a role in encouraging complicity in *Papers, Please*, and what changes in player mindset or choice specifics might lead to a different outcome?

Having set out to understand how exactly *Papers, Please* uses ambiguity to encourage complicity, we have used choice poetics to provide a detailed explanation of the mechanisms behind this effect. The comparison presented in Table 5 shows that suspicion about the motives of petitioners is key to turning a dilemma into a more murky and lopsided choice. From this detailed analysis, we can also see which aspects of the player's mindset are necessary for this effect to occur: The player model's goal of apprehending criminals is surprisingly irrelevant to the deconstruction of the dilemma, because the goal of providing for one's family pushes in the same direction and is more clearly established by the context of the decision. What is important instead is the player's willingness to be persuaded that some applicants do not deserve entry, and that denying them entry would be a good thing. An anarchist player who believed that denying anyone entry was immoral (or at least, that some balance of honest and dishonest applicants should always be resolved to favor the honest applicants) would resist the technique used here and face a clear dilemma between feeding their family and obeying their conscience.

5. Conclusions

Through our analyses of choices from *Undertale* and *Papers, Please*, we have demonstrated the concrete application of choice poetics to two very different choices. As already mentioned, the conclusions drawn here about both games have already been reached by others, which confirms that our analytical approach leads to sound conclusions. Relative to a typical close reading approach, choice poetics provides extra formal structure that encourages detailed observation and which can lead to secondary observations about the choice being analyzed. In addition, where a close reading uses the author's experience to stand in for the experience of players, choice poetics forces the analyst to create explicit player models, thus reifying their assumptions about how choices will be perceived and opening them up for examination. The assumptions that choice poetics makes about player goals are thus both a weakness (they might be wrong) and a strength (errors can be identified exactly, and contrasting analyses can test hypotheses about player goals).

Besides encouraging more explicit examination of choices, we also hope that a formalist framework can make analysis more accessible to novice critics, allowing them to systematically identify interesting aspects of a choice, and that it can provide precise language for describing narrative choices and their poetic effects. Ideally, choice poetics should support discussions about why and how a choice achieves its poetic effect, and should enable those discussions to be more detailed and specific.

To explore modes of engagement, we gave an example of paired choice analysis with a central and recurring choice from *Undertale*, showing how choice poetics can be used to contrast different play styles. The benefit in this case was a detailed look at how *Undertale* separates players with different priorities into different choice patterns to encourage dialogue between players who experience the game differently, including how divergence is encouraged at both initial and subsequent encounters with a repeated choice. Choice poetics helps pinpoint exactly which outcomes drive that separation, and what sets of priorities are necessary for it to happen.

We then went into depth with *Papers, Please*, using prospective and retrospective analysis to pin down subtle characteristics of a common choice in that game. Noting how uncertainty undermined a dilemma configuration for that choice, we were able to describe in detail how that choice tilts players towards complicity with the game's fictional regime, and what other aspects of the choice design help contribute to this outcome. In fact, our analysis reveals several simple changes that could have been implemented had the author wished to create a different narrative. For example, revealing after-the-fact that most applicants begging for asylum were in fact refugees would be enough to permit a story where the player bravely resists their regime's authoritarian tendencies by turning the present ambiguous choice into a clear moral dilemma. The utility of choice poetics here then is to identify exactly how a choice creates a certain feeling, and which elements of the choice might be changed to create a different one.

In all of the analyses presented here, we engage with choice poetics as human scholars, using only those pieces of the theory that are relevant to the specific choices at hand and glossing over details that seem evident from common sense. Although choice poetics was designed with operationalization in mind, our analyses show that it can also be of use to human critics as a framework for discussion. We also expect that the framework's systematic steps will be useful when confronted with choices that are difficult to understand, and that the notion of different player models will help illuminate choices that leave different actual players feeling different things.

As we continue to develop this theory, we plan to explore further computational models and collect and analyze play traces to demonstrate the theory's utility in the domain of automated analysis, with the eventual goal of using it for on-line player modeling to enable responsive stories. Additionally, we hope to remain in dialogue with critics and games scholars who seek to understand narrative choices, and hope that our framework can at least provide useful language to this community for discussing poetic choices. Of course, we will also continue examining games, and may come up with more examples of how choice poetics can be productively applied to understanding how their choices fit into their narratives.

Author Contributions: Conceptualization, all authors; Investigation, P.M., C.Z., A.G. and A.J.; Writing–Original Draft Preparation, P.M., C.Z. and A.G.; and Writing–Review and Editing, P.M. and N.W.-F.

Funding: The authors would like to acknowledge the support of National Science Foundation grant IIS-1409992, which supported some of the initial development of choice poetics.

Conflicts of Interest: The authors declare no conflict of interest.

References

Aarseth, Espen J. 1997. *Cybertext: Perspectives on Ergodic Literature*. Baltimore: JHU Press.

Alexander, Leigh. 2013. Designing the Bleak Genius of *Papers, Please*. Available online: http://www.gamasutra. com/view/news/199383/Designing_the_bleak_genius_of_Papers_Please.php (accessed on 22 May 2018).

Aristotle. 1917. *The Poetics of Aristotle*. London: Macmillan.

Barthes, Roland, and Lionel Duisit. 1975. An introduction to the structural analysis of narrative. *New Literary History* 6: 237–72. [CrossRef]

Brehm, Jack W. 1956. Postdecision changes in the desirability of alternatives. *The Journal of Abnormal and Social Psychology* 52: 384. [CrossRef]

Cardona-Rivera, Rogelio Enrique, Justus Robertson, Stephen G. Ware, Brent E. Harrison, David L. Roberts, and Robert Michael Young. 2014. Foreseeing meaningful choices. Paper presented at the 10th Artificial Intelligence and Interactive Digital Entertainment Conference, Raleigh, NC, USA, October 3–7.

Consalvo, Mia, Thorsten Busch, and Carolyn Jong. 2016. Playing a better me: How players rehearse their ethos via moral choices. *Games and Culture* 11: 1–20. [CrossRef]

Day, Timothy, and Jichen Zhu. 2017. Agency informing techniques: Communicating player agency in interactive narratives. Paper presented at the 12th International Conference on the Foundations of Digital Games (FDG '17), New York, NY, USA, August 14–17. New York: ACM, pp. 56:1–56:4. [CrossRef]

Ellithorpe, Morgan E., Carlos Cruz, John A. Velez, David R. Ewoldsen, and Adam K. Bogert. 2015. Moral license in video games: When being right can mean doing wrong. *Cyberpsychology, Behavior, and Social Networking* 18: 203–207. [CrossRef] [PubMed]

Fabulich, Dan. 2010. 5 Rules for Writing Interesting Choices in Multiple Choice Games. Available online: http://www.choiceofgames.com/2010/03/5-rules-for-writing-interesting-choices-in-multiple-choice-games/ (accessed on 22 June 2018).

Feeld, Julian. 2015. Interview: Toby Fox of Undertale. Available online: http://outermode.com/interview-toby-fox-undertale (accessed on 22 June 2018).

Fendt, Matthew William, Brent Harrison, Stephen G. Ware, Rogelio E. Cardona-Rivera, and David L. Roberts. 2012. Achieving the illusion of agency. In *Interactive Storytelling*. Berlin: Springer, pp. 114–25.

Ferguson, Christopher J. 2008. The school shooting/violent video game link: Causal relationship or moral panic? *Journal of Investigative Psychology and Offender Profiling* 5: 25–37. [CrossRef]

Flanagan, Mary. 2009. *Critical Play: Radical Game Design*. Cambridge: The MIT Press.

Formosa, Paul, Malcolm Ryan, and Dan Staines. 2016. *Papers, Please* and the systemic approach to engaging ethical expertise in videogames. *Ethics and Information Technology* 18: 211–25. [CrossRef]

Fox, Toby. 2015. *Undertale*. Self-Published. Various platforms.

Frasca, Gonzalo. 2003. Ludologists love stories, too: Notes from a debate that never took place. In *Level up Conference Proceedings*. JE Utrecht: University of Utrecht.

fuandon. 2015. Let's Play Undertale! [BLIND] Part 1: Hello, Mom. Available online: https://www.youtube.com/watch?v=plvjJx-ERWY (accessed on 16 August 2018).

Green, Melanie C., and Timothy C. Brock. 2000. The role of transportation in the persuasiveness of public narratives. *Journal of Personality and Social Psychology* 79: 701. [CrossRef] [PubMed]

Hall, Lars, Petter Johansson, and Thomas Strandberg. 2012. Lifting the veil of morality: Choice blindness and attitude reversals on a self-transforming survey. *PLoS ONE* 7: 1–8. [CrossRef]

Hamari, Juho, and Janne Tuunanen. 2014. Player types: A meta-synthesis. *Transactions of the Digital Games Research Association* 1: 29–53. [CrossRef]

Hughes, William. 2015. Undertale Dares Players to Make a Mistake They Can Never Take Back. Available online: https://games.avclub.com/undertale-dares-players-to-make-a-mistake-they-can-neve-1798287299 (accessed on 22 June 2018).

Iten, Glena H., Sharon T. Steinemann, and Klaus Opwis. 2018. Choosing to help monsters: A mixed-method examination of meaningful choices in narrative-rich games and interactive narratives. Paper presented at the 2018 ACM CHI Conference on Human Factors in Computing Systems, Montreal, QC, Canada, April 21–26.

Katsarov, Johannes, Markus Christen, Ralf Mauerhofer, David Schmocker, and Carmen Tanner. 2017. Training moral sensitivity through video games: A review of suitable game mechanisms. *Games and Culture* 12: 1–23. doi:10.1177/1555412017719344. [CrossRef]

Lange, Amanda. 2014. "you're just gonna be nice:" How players engage with moral choice systems. *Journal of Games Criticism* 1: 1–16.

Laws, Robin. 2001. *Robin's Laws of Good Game Mastering*. Austin: Steve Jackson Games.

Lindley, Craig A. 2005. Story and narrative structures in computer games. In *Developing Interactive Narrative Content: Sagas/Sagasnet Reader*. Edited by Brunhild Bushoff. Munich: High Text Verlag.

Mallon, Bride, and Brian Webb. 2005. Stand up and take your place: Identifying narrative elements in narrative adventure and role-play games. *Computers in Entertainment* 3: 6. [CrossRef]

Mar, Raymond A., and Keith Oatley. 2008. The function of fiction is the abstraction and simulation of social experience. *Perspectives on Psychological Science* 3: 173–92. [CrossRef] [PubMed]

Mateas, Michael. 2001. A preliminary poetics for interactive drama and games. *Digital Creativity* 12: 140–52. [CrossRef]

Mather, Mara, Eldar Shafir, and Marcia K. Johnson. 2000. Misremembrance of options past: Source monitoring and choice. *Psychological Science* 11: 132–38. [CrossRef] [PubMed]

Mawhorter, Peter. 2016. Artificial Intelligence as a Tool for Understanding Narrative Choices. Ph.D. dissertation, University of California Santa Cruz, Santa Cruz, CA, USA.

Mawhorter, Peter, Michael Mateas, and Noah Wardrip-Fruin. 2015a. Generating relaxed, obvious, and dilemma choices with dunyazad. Paper presented at the 11th Annual AAAI Conference on Artificial Intelligence and Interactive Digital Entertainment (AIIDE '15), Santa Cruz, CA, USA, November 14–18. pp. 58–64.

Mawhorter, Peter, Michael Mateas, and Noah Wardrip-Fruin. 2015b. Intentionally generating choices in interactive narratives. Paper presented at the 6th International Conference on Computational Creativity (ICCC '15), Park City, UT, USA, June 29–July 2. pp. 292–99.

Mawhorter, Peter, Michael Mateas, Noah Wardrip-Fruin, and Arnav Jhala. 2014. Towards a theory of choice poetics. Paper presented at the International Conference on the Foundations of Digital Games (FDG '14), Liberty of the Seas, Caribbean, April 3–7.

Mellers, Barbara A., Alan Schwartz, Katty Ho, and Ilana Ritov. 1997. Decision affect theory: Emotional reactions to the outcomes of risky options. *Psychological Science* 8: 423–29. [CrossRef]

Murray, Janet H. 1997. *Hamlet on the Holodeck: The Future of Narrative in Cyberspace*. New York: Free Press.

Murray, Soraya. 2016. Race, gender, and genre in Spec Ops: The Line. *Film Quarterly* 70: 38–48. [CrossRef]

Müller, Alexandra Karin. 2017. Undertale: Violence in Context. Ph.D. dissertation, Simon Fraser University, Burnaby, BC, Canada. Available online: http://summit.sfu.ca/item/17572 (accessed on 22 June 2018).

oh. 2016. "Genocide the Best Ending?" Steam Community Thread. Available online: https://steamcommunity.com/app/391540/discussions/0/392185054118254079/ (accessed on 16 August 2018).

Perez, Matthew. 2017. Undertale: A Case Study in Ludomusicology. Ph.D. dissertation, Queens College of the City University of New York, New York, NY, USA.

Pope, Lucas. 2013. *Papers Please*. 3909 LLC. Various platforms.

Pötzsch, Holger. 2017. Selective realism: Filtering experiences of war and violence in first- and third-person shooters. *Games and Culture* 12: 156–78. [CrossRef]

Ryan, Marie-Laure. 1991. *Possible Worlds, Artificial Intelligence, and Narrative Theory*. Bloomington: Indiana University Press.

Schwartz, Barry, Andrew Ward, John Monterosso, Sonja Lyubomirsky, Katherine White, and Darrin R. Lehman. 2002. Maximizing versus satisficing: Happiness is a matter of choice. *Journal of Personality and Social Psychology* 83: 1178. [CrossRef] [PubMed]

Smethurst, Toby, and Stef Craps. 2015. Playing with trauma: Interreactivity, empathy, and complicity in the walking dead video game. *Games and Culture* 10: 269–90. [CrossRef]

TheRPGMinx. 2015. LET'S GO DEEPER UNDERGROUND | Undertale | 01. Available online: https://www.youtube.com/watch?v=DDLmmljliy0&list=PLQLck4CGSUpt4rFlbspHGNKg31Z9cKJpY (accessed on 16 August 2018).

Tosca, Susana Pajares. 2000. A pragmatics of links. Paper presented at the 11th ACM Conference on Hypertext and Hypermedia, San Antonio, TX, USA, May 30–June 3. New York: ACM, pp. 77–84.

Tversky, Amos, and Daniel Kahneman. 1981. The framing of decisions and the psychology of choice. *Science* 211: 453–58. [CrossRef] [PubMed]

Švelch, Jaroslav. 2010. The good, the bad, and the player: The challenges to moral engagement in single-player avatar-based video games. In *Ethics and Game Design: Teaching Values through Play*. Edited by Karen Schrier and David Gibson. Hershey: IGI Glboal, pp. 52–68. [CrossRef]

Weaver, Andrew J., and Nicky Lewis. 2012. Mirrored morality: An exploration of moral choice in video games. *Cyberpsychology, Behavior, and Social Networking* 15: 610–14. [CrossRef] [PubMed]

Yager Development. 2012. *Spec Ops: The Line*. Novato: 2K Games. Various Platforms.

Yee, Nick. 2006. Motivations for play in online games. *CyberPsychology & Behavior* 9: 772–75.

Zunshine, Lisa. 2006. *Why We Read Fiction: Theory of Mind and the Novel*. Columbus: Ohio State University Press.

arts

MDPI

Article

Expansion, Excess and the Uncanny: *Deadly Premonition* and *Twin Peaks*

Julian Novitz

Faculty of Health, Arts and Design, Swinburne University of Technology, P.O. Box 218, Hawthorn, Victoria 3122, Australia; jnovitz@swin.edu.au

Received: 29 June 2018; Accepted: 3 September 2018; Published: 7 September 2018

Abstract: The influence of the cult television series *Twin Peaks* (1990–1991) can be detected in a wide range of videogames, from adventure, to roleplaying to survival horror titles. While many games variously draw upon the narrative, setting and imagery of the series for inspiration, certain elements of the distinctive uncanniness of *Twin Peaks* are difficult to translate into gameplay, particularly its ability consistently disrupt the expectations and emotional responses of its audience. This paper examines the ways in which the 2010 survival horror title *Deadly Premonition* replicates the uncanniness of *Twin Peaks* in both its narrative and gameplay, noting how it expands upon conceptualizations of the gamerly uncanny. It contends that *Deadly Premonition*'s awkward recombination of seemingly inconsistent and excessive gameplay features mirrors the ways in which David Lynch and Mark Frost draw upon and subvert audience expectations for police procedurals and soap operas in the original *Twin Peaks* in order to generate an uncanny effect. Furthermore, *Deadly Premonition* uses the theme of possession—a central element of the television series—to offer a diegetic exploration of the uncanny relationship between the player and their onscreen avatar. In these regards, *Deadly Premonition* provides a rare example of how the subversive uncanniness of *Twin Peaks* can be addressed through gameplay, rather than solely through the game's narrative or representational elements.

Keywords: the uncanny; *Deadly Premonition*; *Twin Peaks*; survival horror

1. Introduction: The Uncanny in Survival Horror Video Games

The contemporary idea of the uncanny first emerges in a 1906 essay by Ernst Jentsch, in which he characterizes as the psychological state that results from unsettling experiences of uncertainty, particularly in relation to the status of inanimate objects (Jentsch 1995). Jentsch's definition of the uncanny is famously cited and quoted by Sigmund Freud, who rejects Jentsch's conceptualization of the uncanny as intellectual uncertainty, suggesting rather that the inanimate objects that Jentsch identifies as distinctly uncanny—"wax-work figures, ingeniously constructed dolls and automata" (Freud [1919] 1955, p. 226) are such because they combine familiarity and strangeness. In working to transform the familiar into something strange, Freud argues that uncanny objects, narratives and phenomena challenge our sense of reality through the evocation of repressed memories, images and fears. Encounters with doppelgangers, reflections and corpses are also given as examples of potentially uncanny experiences.

The uncanny evokes a dual sense of fascination and repulsion, which made it a common feature of horror and suspense narratives long before the term was first defined. The popular Gothic literature of the nineteenth century often delivers uncanny an uncanny reading experience by encouraging readers to speculate on whether their central mysteries have mundane or supernatural causes, leaving them uncertain as whether the narratives are realistic or fantastical for as long as possible (Botting 2008). Uncanny images, characters and aesthetics have long been a feature of horror cinema, with living characters being frequently contrasted with blank-faced, lurching automata. Dread is powerfully evoked on screen by imbuing the familiar and recognizable human form with a fascinating strangeness (Royle 2003). In *the Powers of Horror* Kristeva (1982) locates the abject within the realm of the uncanny, suggesting that it is represented by border figures that are not quite right and must be cast out in order to survive. Furthermore, both horror literature and cinema frequently evoke a sense of the uncanny through the use of both literal doppelgangers and doubling effects in their narrative structures and imagery (Schneider 2004). These uncanny aesthetics have been translated into video games, particularly those situated within the survival horror sub-category.

Many different varieties of videogames (from action to horror to roleplaying and more) draw upon these traditions in order to deliver uncanny visual effects, frequently confronting the player with human-like yet deformed monsters, and distortions of seemingly familiar environments, like the archetypical abandoned town or haunted house (Holmes 2010). However, uncanniness in a video game can also manifest itself simply through the designers' attempts at representation. The increasingly realistic, yet still strange, representations found in videogames can have an uncanny effect on both players and observers, entering what robotics scientist Masahiro Mori famously defined as "the uncanny valley", where an artificial representation or duplicate becomes increasingly unsettling once it is sophisticated enough to cross a certain level of resemblance (Mori [1970] 2012). The uncanny can also manifest itself through glitches and bugs in the game's design, where distorted images and animations can result in uncanny experiences for the player (Holmes 2010).

Beyond its intentional and unintentional evocations through representational strategies in videogames, uncanniness can emerge as a feature of the gameplay itself when gameplay mechanics and operations that should feel familiar to the player are made to feel strange and unwieldly (Kirkland 2009b). As Holmes (2010) notes, this may occur due to errors or bugs in the game's design, but when this uncanniness is intentionally introduced into the gameplay it is usually used to emphasize a particular movement in the game's narrative, often a change or shift in the physical or mental state of the video game protagonist that the player is controlling. Examples might include the slowed responses to controller inputs that occur when the player enters a hallucinatory dream sequence in *Grand Theft Auto 5* (Rockstar North 2013) or the sudden inversion of the player's control scheme that occurs at the climax of *Beyond Good and Evil* (Ubisoft 2003), when the protagonist is subjected to a psychic assault. In most games, these moments of uncanny gameplay will only occur briefly, so as to avoid frustrating their players. Survival horror games, however, arguably tend to offer more prolonged experiences of uncanny gameplay as their principal aim is to unsettle and destabilize their players, and therefore much of the scholarly discussion of the uncanny in videogames has tended to focus on this category. Gameplay in survival horror titles can easily be understood as uncanny because the games often use controls that are awkward when compared to other titles, so as to create a sense of vulnerability for the player (Perron 2018). Because players are unable to function as effectively as they would in games outside of the survival horror category, actions that would be routine and familiar (e.g., walking or turning) are transformed into tense and nerve-wracking activities. As Thomas Grip puts it: "It (survival horror) is the only genre where it is okay to sacrifice gameplay in order to create emotions and build atmosphere" (quoted in Thomsen 2010). The typical third-person perspective of survival horror games is important in creating an uncanny experience for the player, with their avatar operating as their on-screen double, under their control yet uncomfortably separate from them, extending the frequent doubling effects that Schneider (2004) locates in horror fiction and cinema into gameplay. Tanya Krzywinska argues that the player's third-person control over their onscreen avatar (and the frequent moments when this control is disrupted through the movement to a non-interactive cut scene) can operate as an expression of a recurrent theme in horror fiction and cinema "in which supernatural forces act on, and regularly threaten, the sphere of human agency" (Krzywinska 2002, p. 207). Kirkland (2009b) observes that this relationship between the player and their avatar creates an uncanny space, which "unsettles the boundaries between dead object and living person" and that this is accentuated through the slow and disorienting navigation of threatening, maze-like environments in survival horror titles. Perron (2018) notes that the less immediately responsive third person controls and fixed camera angles of classic survival horror work to unsettle the typically close relationship between the player and their avatar in videogames, blurring the subjectivity and objectivity of the player's perspective. Hoeger and Huber (2007) focus on this customarily uneasy relationship between the player and their onscreen avatar in survival horror titles in their discussion of what they define as the "gamerly uncanny", this being the uncanniness that is created through player-directed movement and navigation, and which has its basis in the particular mode of attention that videogames demand.

> The gamer is obligated to actively decode and navigate a genre-constructed space of threats and secrets. This navigation is performed by a surrogate-body in that fictive space: the avatar-character whose activities depend on the player's activities. The effort to overcome incoherence takes on a specific kind of urgency, one based on a possibility of death (Hoeger and Huber 2007, p. 153).

While the uncanny hyper-awareness around movement is feature of all videogames, Hoeger and Huber argue that it is particularly important to the evocation of dread in survival horror game, which "thematises and foregrounds the complicated relationship between these virtual bodies and the immersed situation of the player" (2007, p. 153). Conventional video game design would usually attempt to avoid distancing or detaching the player from their onscreen avatar, but survival horror games can evoke tension, dread and anxiety through an avatar that appears incomplete and not wholly human (Tinwell and Grimshaw 2009), or by using narrative and visual strategies that disrupt the player's identification with the onscreen character (Perron 2012).

This common feature of survival horror titles creates a tension between the player's tendency to identify with their avatar and the limitations that survival horror games place on their perception, agency and control. Thus, within games in the survival horror category, the uncanny experience is often generated through the defining features of survival horror gameplay itself rather than just the representational qualities of the setting, visuals and narrative.

However, the "gamerly uncanny" that Hoeger and Huber (2007) define as essential to survival horror can be perceived as limited, or even predictable, in some respects, and this becomes particularly apparent when considering the frequent attempts of various video games (and certain survival horror titles in particular) to reference and homage the cult television series *Twin Peaks* (1990–1991). The expansive and consistently subversive nature of the uncanny aesthetic of *Twin Peaks* has been difficult to replicate in gameplay (if not in narrative and representational content), and cannot be easily accommodated by the type of "gamerly uncanny" identified by Huber and Hoeger, which develops out of the strict minimalism of survival horror titles.

2. Twin Peaks and Video Games

Frost and Lynch (1990–1991)'s cult television series *Twin Peaks* is considered a distinctively and unusually uncanny television series (Weinstock 2016), which likely contributes to its continuing influence on a wide variety of media, including videogames, and in particular, survival horror titles. Many of the most memorable scenes and images from *Twin Peaks* stray into uncanny territory, particularly in the sequences that most closely align with horror or supernatural genres of storytelling. The backwards speech and jerky, distorted movements of the inhabitants of the Red Room serve as an example, as does the leering, malevolent image of Killer BOB, which appears in dreams and reflections. Furthermore, *Twin Peaks* abounds with both overt and subtle doublings and duplications, which contributes to the uncanniness of its narrative, atmosphere and overall viewing experience.

However, the uncanniness of *Twin Peaks* also operates at a more sophisticated and subversive level in its approach to familiar film and television genres. Jowett (2016) argues that *Twin Peaks* is unsettling not just because its uncanniness disturbs its viewers in the manner of a classic horror or supernatural narrative but because it frequently disrupts their expectations as to what they are about to see or experience in any given moment. Jowett (2016) contends that *Twin Peaks* develops its most distinctively uncanny effect through the combination of television genres/storytelling traditions that would have been highly familiar to audiences at the time of its first broadcast: the police procedural and the soap opera. The typically self-contained or episodic murder mystery or police procedural is expanded to an unwieldly and perplexing length through its integration into a soap opera, with the usually linear and logical accumulation of detail and evidence being diverted into a tapestry of side narratives, red herrings and dead ends. Similarly, the soap opera-like romances, schemes and conflicts of *Twin Peaks'* supporting cast take on unusually sinister undertones when they are united by the narrative thread of Laura Palmer's murder. As the series progresses it draws in a range of other genres: supernatural horror, hardboiled noir, melodrama, teen rebel movies and more. The excess of influences and references in *Twin Peaks* can have a disorienting effect, making it challenging to predict the flow of the narrative or to understand and interpret key events.

The influence of *Twin Peaks* on video games is arguably felt most strongly in narrative-focused adventure games, such as *Life is Strange* (Dontnod Entertainment 2015), *Virginia* (Variable State 2016), *Thimbleweed Park* (Terrible Toybox 2017), *Kathy Rain* (Clifftop Games 2016) and other titles, though homages and references to the series can be also be detected in the role-playing series *Persona*, in particular *Persona 4* (Atlus 2008) and the action/horror title *Alan Wake* (Remedy Entertainment 2010). In so far as these games replicate or draw upon elements of the distinctive uncanniness of *Twin Peaks*, they do in terms of their representational content—their narratives, characters, settings, and their visual and audio aesthetics—rather than through their gameplay. Videogames typically require their audiences to engage with a limited set of mechanics which are generally determined by the broad category that the game falls into (e.g., role-playing, action, etc.). While the narrative or visual imagery found in the game may work to destabilize the player, the gameplay itself, once mastered, will typically remain familiar.

The influence of *Twin Peaks* can be detected in survival horror titles as well. Developers of the seminal *Silent Hill* series have acknowledged its influence on the setting, narrative and visual aesthetic of their games, particularly the highly regarded *Silent Hill 2* (Konami 2001) (Perron 2012). However, while survival horror games certainly deliver an uncanny style of gameplay relative to other titles, this "gamerly uncanny" identified by Hoeger and Huber (2007) is incapable of replicating the subversive component of the uncanniness of Twin Peaks—where familiar genres and categories of storytelling are combined in ways that render them strange and subvert audience expectations and responses—due to its own internal consistency and the focused, minimalist aesthetic that classic survival horror encourages through its emphasis on restriction and limitation. As Krzywinska (2015b) notes, survival horror games are defined in large part by the restrictions that they place upon the player relative to other types of games, in terms of movement, in-game resources, field of view and other affordances. Perron (2018) notes that popular discussion of survival horror often tends to focus on its "purity" as a video game category, with the titles that deviate from this minimalist aesthetic (for example *Resident Evil 4* [2007] and *Silent Hill Homecoming* (Konami 2008) which both introduced a greater variety of combat options for players) having their status as "true" survival horror games questioned. While the way in which survival horror foregrounds and complicates the relationship between the player and their avatar can certainly produce an unsettling uncanny effect, it is an effect that will probably be expected, anticipated and appreciated by the player, due to their familiarity with the survival horror category itself and/or their growing familiarity with the systems and mechanics of a specific survival horror title. The spare, stripped-back focus of classic survival horror titles has proven effective in scaring and unsettling players, but it also reveals the limitations of the "gamerly uncanny" that players encounter in these titles, as the minimalism of classic survival horror games makes their features and objectives immediately recognizable. In this sense, the "gamerly uncanny" that is frequently encountered in survival horror is only uncanny due to the contrast that it presents with the gameplay of titles outside of the category, but can become, paradoxically, familiar within it. It works to unsettle the player—but only within strictly defined parameters.

The cult videogame title *Deadly Premonition* (Access Games 2010) provides a rare example of how the subversive elements of the uncanniness of a show like *Twin Peaks* can be incorporated into uncanny play. Where Hoeger and Huber (2007) principally explore the ways in which the "gamerly uncanny" develops out of the player's relationship with their onscreen avatar, an examination of *Deadly Premonition* reveals that uncanniness can also be evoked through the destabilizing combination of familiar modes of gameplay. *Deadly Premonition* replicates the distinctive uncanniness of *Twin Peaks* by expanding upon some of the gameplay features traditionally associated with survival horror titles. It does so by incorporating elements from other categories of gameplay in ways that render them strange and unfamiliar to experienced players, and also by self-consciously foregrounding the uncanny relationship between the player and their onscreen avatar in its narrative.

3. Expansion and Excess: Uncanny Play in *Deadly Premonition*

Deadly Premonition is a third person survival horror/adventure game in which the player takes the role of an FBI agent, Francis "York" Morgan, who has been sent to investigate the murder of a young woman in the small rural town of Greenvale. Upon arrival, York and the player discover that supernatural forces to be at work as their investigation takes them into a nightmarish otherworld inhabited by hostile ghosts and spirits. Reviews (for example, Sterling 2010; VanOrd 2010; Wales 2010), popular articles (Carmicheal 2013; Green 2017) and scholarly texts (Perron 2018) have all noted the strong influence of *Twin Peaks* on *Deadly Premonition*, particularly with regard to its narrative, its small-town setting, the eccentricities of its detective protagonist, and the quirky behavior of Greenvale's residents. While this commentary has identified the parallels between the game and the television series in terms characters, locations, story beats and imagery, it generally overlooks the ways in which *Deadly Premonition* is able to translate the subversive uncanniness of *Twin Peaks* into its novel style of play, which combines survival horror traditions with a free-roaming open world and life-simulation elements. Both the positive and negative reviews of *Deadly Premonition* have tended to be critical of its gameplay mechanics, viewing them either as fatally flawed (Brudvig 2010) or as poorly implemented systems that could be endured for the sake of an entertaining narrative (Sterling 2010). These assessments overlook the way in which *Deadly Premonition*'s seemingly discordant and inconsistent combination of gameplay features creates an uncanny effect that is similar to that of the contradictory juxtaposition of genres and styles in *Twin Peaks*.

Upon its release, *Deadly Premonition* was generally received and evaluated as a survival horror title and this categorization is understandable, given that it shares many of the gameplay features and representational elements commonly associated with this category. In the game's combat focused sections, the player is trapped in the dark, maze-like environments common to survival horror (Kirkland 2005), and the awkward movement and aiming mechanics (reminiscent of *Resident Evil* (Capcom 1996) work to both highlight the uncanny relationship between the player and their onscreen double (Hoeger and Huber 2007) and to restrict the player's control and field of view in the manner described by Krzywinska, who notes that survival horror games typically position the player as being "unable to act as efficiently as would be expected" (2015b, p. 296). These sections pit the player against the types of uncanny monstrous adversaries that are typical of survival horror games (Perron 2018). As Pruett (2011) notes, player characters in survival horror titles tend to be presented as relatively ordinary in their physical attributes and fighting abilities when compared to the protagonists of more action-oriented video games, and this is true of Francis York Morgan in *Deadly Premonition*, who has a slow walking and running speed, and limited health in combat. Furthermore, Agent York is frequently presented as overwhelmed by the foes that he faces, being forced to run and hide at various points in game, providing the sense of vulnerability that Hand (2004) identifies as being essential to the success of survival horror.

Despite the presence of these elements, few, if any, reviews suggest that *Deadly Premonition* is particularly scary to play, which has led to it being received as a flawed or failed survival horror title (Brudvig 2010; Clarkson 2010). *Deadly Premonition*'s general inability to scare the player could be taken as a result of its outdated technology and graphics, which were noted in a number of highly critical reviews, most notably IGN's withering appraisal at the time of its release (Brudvig 2010). In particular, the game has a limited number of enemy types when compared to most survival horror titles, and their predictable artificial intelligence resulted in the game's combat sections lacking the sense of surprise and uncertainty that is often considered essential to survival horror (Perron 2012). Furthermore, many players and critics found the game's poor animations unintentionally hilarious, which works to further undermine the scariness of the experience (Sterling 2010). While *Deadly Premonition* certainly possesses the comparatively awkward third person controls that Hoeger and Huber (2007) identify as contributing to the development of a "gamerly uncanny" in survival horror, its technical limitations mean that this is more likely to result in frustration rather than fear.

However, technical limitations and shortcomings are not the only reason that *Deadly Premonition* fails to unsettle players in the ways that are expected from a survival horror title. Some conscious design choices work to disrupt and undermine the expected rhythms of survival horror gameplay in interesting ways. In contrast to the minimalism of classic survival horror, *Deadly Premonition* features an excess and combination of seemingly contradictory gameplay features. Of these, the one that is perhaps most antithetical to the agenda of survival horror, is the open world nature of the game, which allows the player to explore the town of Greenvale in a manner reminiscent of *Grand Theft Auto 4* (Rockstar North 2008). While backtracking between previously explored locations is a common feature of survival horror titles, relatively few games within this category provide a genuinely open world for players to freely explore at their leisure. The oppressive, terrifying atmosphere of survival horror games is often linked to the restrictive and claustrophobic environments that they force the player to traverse (Stienmetz 2018; Kirkland 2005), and is generally developed at the expense of player preference or choice, with horror games tending to favor a predetermined or 'on rails' structure (Kirkland 2009a). Girard (2011) goes as far as to argue that it would be impossible to develop the mounting terror that defines survival horror gameplay in a free roaming environment. The relatively few survival horror titles that do provide open worlds usually maintain their tension by surprising the players with aggressive enemies (for example *Silent Hill: Downpour* [Vatra Games 2012] or *The Evil Within 2* [Tango Gameworks 2017]), but this is not the case in *Deadly Premonition* where the player can explore the town and its surroundings in complete safety between story missions. The player can drive cars, talk to non-player-characters (NPCs), and complete supplementary activities, like darts and fishing mini-games, in a manner reminiscent of adventure/role-playing titles like *Shenmue* (Sega 1999) and *Yakuza* (Sega 2005), as well as engaging in life-simulation activities like eating, bathing and sleeping. The populated and welcoming small-town environment that the player explores offers a prolonged relief from the sense of isolation that is often vital to the development of discomfort and terror in survival horror titles (Hand 2004), and the rewards and extra resources accumulated in the open world work to undermine the more conventional survival horror sequences. Survival horror titles tend to place strict limits on the in-game resources that that the player can accumulate to aid them in combat encounters (Perron 2009; Kirkland 2005). This typically forces players to inhabit a "survival space" within the game (Browning 2011), where the decisions they make in regard to exploration and combat are unusually fraught. The open world sections of *Deadly Premonition*, however, allow them to easily accumulate enough resources to act confidently in most instances, removing this expected tension. Conversely, as the game retains the awkward movement, perspective and navigation controls associated with survival horror titles, the open world exploration in *Deadly Premonition* does not feel as free and or as fluid as players might expect from games like *Grand Theft Auto 4* and its various derivatives.

The deliberate combination of these contradictory modes of gameplay creates an experience that does not feel quite right to the player: a mode of uncanny play that makes the player uncomfortably aware of their movement and mediation of their onscreen avatar, but which does not result in the sense of fear and trepidation that Hoeger and Huber (2007) identify as the purpose of the "gamerly uncanny". Furthermore, the experience that it offers is quite distinct from the "hybridised" forms of survival horror discussed by Perron (2018), where survival horror conventions are combined with other forms of gameplay, such as the actionized survival horror of *Resident Evil 4* (Capcom 2005), or the light role-playing mechanics incorporated into the character customization in *Dead Space* (EA Redwood Shore 2008), or the fusion of survival horror with first person shooter found in games like *Call of Cthulhu: Dark Corners of the Earth* (Headfirst Productions 2005), *Pathologic* (Ice Pick Lodge 2005) or *Alien Isolation* (Creative Assembly 2014). In these hybrid games the mechanics and rhythms of the different gaming categories are more-or-less fluidly combined with intention of delivering a terrifying experience. In *Deadly Premonition*, gameplay features are brought together in a way that contradicts and confuses their usual intentions and pleasures. Its uncanny gameplay does not deliver the terror of the "gamerly uncanny" typically found in survival horror titles, but when coupled with the equally sudden and contradictory shifts in the game's narrative (from horror to surreal comedy to character-focused drama to tragedy) it arguably replicates some elements of the subversive uncanniness of *Twin Peaks* in a ludic form.

The combination of different and seemingly incompatible gameplay styles (survival horror, open-world adventure, life-simulation and more) in *Deadly Premonition* mirrors the combinations and juxtapositions of different genres and modes of television storytelling found in *Twin Peaks*. In both cases, the uncanny experience that results from these combinations works to make the viewer/player intimately aware of the constructed nature of the forms of viewing/gameplay that are being referenced and confounds their expectations, complicating or challenging the audience's immersion. This is further demonstrated through the ways in which both the series and the game integrate seemingly "realistic" elements into their plot/narrative (in the case of the former) and gameplay (in the case of the latter) in ways that make them feel strange and unnatural when placed within the context of television and videogame genres they are drawing upon. Todd McGowan argues that *Twin Peaks* "often seems unrealistic because of its excess of realism" (McGowan 2016, p. 145)—the show's tendency to focus on mundane exchanges and details that would normally be ignored in television narratives will seem strange to audiences familiar with the rhythms of police procedurals and soap operas. This persists through the typical Lynchian visual fixation on objects and locations in the series—the lingering shots and close-ups of numbered doors, corridors and staircases, curtains, machinery, etc. noted by Molodvan (2015)—where mundane features become strange through the unfamiliar focus and emphasis that is applied to them. A similar uncanniness is generated through the approach to "realistic" detail found in *Deadly Premonition*. In survival horror games, seemingly realistic objects and settings are traditionally important to deepening the player's immersion in the terrifying experience (Holmes 2010), but some of the excessively realistic elements of *Deadly Premonition* run counter to this, disrupting the player's immersion due to their lack of practical gameplay utility and their destabilizing contrast with more overtly game-like features. For example, the player has the option to view the interior of the car in first person, with a functioning gas gauge, speedometer, windscreen wipers and turn signals. All of the NPCs in the town follow complex daily schedules, and the player even has the ability to peer through their bedroom windows to watch them sleep at night. These excessively realistic features clash awkwardly with the game's frequent reminders of its own artificiality. These include the cash rewards which appear on screen like points or scores in arcade games; the flashing and rotating icons used to represent health supplies and ammunition; and the names that float above the heads of NPCs in a manner reminiscent of older Japanese role-playing games. In this sense, the excessive realism found in certain aspects of *Deadly Premonition*'s setting and gameplay works to create an uncanny effect in a manner similar to the focus on mundane objects and exchanges in *Twin Peaks*. In both cases they do not work to heighten the player's immersion in a realistic fictional world but rather deliver an alienating uncanniness due to the sense of strangeness that is created through their seemingly unnecessary presence.

The uncanny excess of both realistic detail and gameplay features found in *Deadly Premonition* connects it both to *Twin Peaks*, and the tradition of the Gothic that the series draws upon. In Gothic literature (and its successor the 'Weird' tale) a wealth of detail, description and incident is used prolong rather than resolve the uncertainties of the reader (Krzywinska 2015a), and Gothic narratives are usually set against a background of excess (like castles and manors of rich elites), which provides a symbolic frame for the transgressive themes of their narratives (Chess 2015). While survival horror games often indulgence in Gothic sensibilities via some of their representational qualities, particularly their settings and the macabre and transgressive histories that underpin their narratives (Taylor 2009), the expansive and destabilizing excess of the genre is not typically reflected through their minimalist gameplay.

Deadly Premonition's expansion of uncanny play beyond the typical parameters and objectives of survival horror allows it a space to engage with the recurrent focus on doubles and duality that is also found in *Twin Peaks*. The double is one of the principle areas for the experience of the uncanny (Royle 2003) and in both its narrative and visual imagery, *Twin Peaks* explores dual or contrasting worlds, characters and identities. *Deadly Premonition* parallels this fixation in the way it overtly narrativizes the gameplay relationship between the player and their onscreen avatar, Agent York. In doing so it uses the principle mechanism of the "gamerly uncanny" as described to Hoeger and Huber (2007) not to create a sense of terror for the player, but rather to comment upon one of the most powerful expressions of duality in *Twin Peaks*: the recurrent theme of possession.

4. Possession in *Twin Peaks* and *Deadly Premonition*

Like Freud, Lacan emphasized the importance of the double or reflection in encounters with or experiences of the uncanny. Where Freud identifies the double as the "uncanny harbinger of death" (Freud [1919] 1955, p. 235), in that the uneasiness it evokes is due to the idea of immortality it implies or creates—a duplicate or repetition that can survive the original—Lacan argues that uncanniness results from the way in which a double or duplicate blurs the boundaries of interiority and exteriority. Lacan defined the territory of the uncanny as *extimite*, a point where the most intimate interiority of a subject is somehow externalised and separated from them, becoming unfamiliar, threatening or horrifying (Dolar 1991). For Lacan the double or reflection is profoundly uncanny not only because it conveys an intimation of death, but because it transforms what should be the most familiar territory of all—the interior self—into something strange and disconnected.

As Weinstock (2016) notes, possession is the uncanny horror at the heart of *Twin Peaks*—where the interior self is revealed as an alien duplicate or consciousness. In the series the malevolent spirit Killer BOB is able to inhabit both the bodies and identities of others. Savoy (2016) argues that BOB operates as a literalization of Lacan's model of the uncanny, observing that BOB is often depicted as appearing in mirrors, eerily mimicking the movements and expressions of those he has possessed, an exposure of the interior self that, in a Lacanian sense, transforms it into an alien and menacing countenance. BOB is arguably presented as the ultimate evil in *Twin Peaks*, the "dark passenger" (Savoy 2016, p. 124) concealed within seemingly benign individuals and the traces of his hidden presence within the show work to transform the familiar tropes and rhythms of the soap opera and the police procedural into something unsettling and sinister.

The preoccupation with possession in *Twin Peaks* is interesting to consider alongside the ways in which third-person survival horror titles typically foreground and complicate the relationship between the player and their onscreen avatar as a means of producing tension and fear (Kirkland 2009b; Hoeger and Huber 2007). The onscreen avatar serves, at one level, as the player's point of entry and orientation, the game's most familiar and accessible feature. At another level, the disconnection between the player and their avatar, where the player's inputs and commands have delayed, cumbersome or unexpected outcomes, is undeniably uncanny. Hoeger and Huber (2007) suggest that this can be akin to a battle between the player and an unknown intelligence for possession of the onscreen avatar. This uncanniness is occasionally accentuated by games with dialogue and narratives that emphasize the separation of the player and their avatar. In *Silent Hill 2* the player is initially unaware of the true history of the protagonist they are controlling and advancing through the game works to alienate the player from their onscreen avatar rather than deepening their identification (Perron 2012). The protagonist of *Silent Hill 3* (Konami 2003), Heather, will occasionally address the player directly or refuse to perform an action in ways that make the player uncomfortably aware of the control they are exerting over her in a narrative that revolves around the themes of possession and exploitation (Kirkland 2007). In some other titles outside of the survival horror category (for example, *Metal Gear Solid* [Konami 1998] and *The Bureau: XCOM Declassified* [2K Marin 2013) moments in the narrative that call overt attention to the player's control and manipulation of their avatar can be likened to Brechtian alienation in that they suddenly expose the system that has been used to produce and prolong the player's immersion and potentially open it to critique (Dunne 2014). In all of these examples the sudden or gradual disruption of the player's identification with their onscreen avatar is presented as an unsettling moment, where the fictional conceit that the player is operating as the interior consciousness of the character is broken.

Conway (2010) argues that these self-aware moments in videogame play do not break the fourth wall in the way that that they do in non-interactive media, where they momentarily or permanently disrupt the suspension of disbelief that allows the audience to emotionally invest themselves in a fictional world or narrative. Rather they have the potential to extend the game's "magic circle" (Huizinga [1938] 1949) to encompass the player themselves, giving traditionally non-diegetic actions diegetic meaning. *Deadly Premonition* is novel in that it uses this extension to explore the idea of the player as a possessing consciousness in a sustained and consistent way through both narrative and gameplay. As previously noted, the awkward navigation and perspective controls in *Deadly Premonition* make the player uncannily aware of their distant and mediated relationship with their onscreen avatar. At the same time, however, the narrative of *Deadly Premonition* works to normalize the duality of player and player character rather than using it to produce moments of discomfort or alienation in the manner of the games mentioned above. Throughout *Deadly Premonition*, the player character, Agent York, delivers a series of monologues to his apparently imaginary friend named Zach (this is very similar to Agent Cooper's tape-recorded reflections in *Twin Peaks*, which are directed towards his never-seen secretary Diane). As *Deadly Premonition* develops, it becomes clear that when York is talking to Zach, he is actually talking directly to the player, and that York seems aware that the player, as Zach, is directing the action. For example, when enemies are approaching in the opening level, York quips "Looks like we've got company, Zach. I'll let you handle the meet and greet", acknowledging that the player is taking control as the game moves from cut-scene to combat. Throughout the game, York regularly congratulates Zach for finding objects and items, and completing in-game tasks and activities. The moments of shock or disruption in the player/avatar relationship described in other games rely heavily on an assumption of direct identification between the player and their avatar in order to have their desired effect. *Deadly Premonition*, by contrast, emphasizes that the player and the onscreen personality are separate and distinct from the outset, using York's monologues and comments to Zach (which in other narrative games might be explained as the protagonist talking to "themself") to constantly remind the audience of this division. In this sense, the narrative of the game uses the theme of possession to diegetically address the player's constant awareness of their mediated relationship with their onscreen avatar, which has been prompted through *Deadly Premonition*'s uncanny combination of contradictory gameplay.

While the control scheme throughout the game remains uncannily awkward, Zach's control over York's body is presented as natural—when the player chooses to diverge from the critical path to pause or explore, York will typically make an encouraging or accepting comment (e.g., "Seen something Zach? It's okay, we have time."). The final movements of the game's plot reveal that York was an alternative personality created by Zach in response to an acute childhood trauma: the protagonist's true identity has been concealed behind the façade of York all along. While the overt acknowledgement that the player is possessing the protagonist is uncanny, due to its contrast with familiar video game player/avatar relationships, this uncanniness is not used to accentuate the terrifying or alienating atmosphere of typical survival horror titles. The dual identities are presented as working in tandem, with York providing observation and commentary and Zach determining movement and direction. In this sense, *Deadly Premonition* presents an inversion of the approach to possession found in *Twin Peaks*. In the series, the "passenger" that resides within and asserts control over a number of the characters is something alien and other, in *Deadly Premonition* it is presented as a welcome presence—the player themselves. By the end of the game, once the true nature of the York/Zach duality has been revealed, York's commentary can be understood as encouragement—prompting Zach/the player to emerge and take direct control and agency. Tellingly, the final moments of the game see the player exploring Greenvale as Zach, who has been stripped of his alternative York personality. The NPCs remaining in the town identify and address the player as Zach, suggesting that the video game character that the players have inhabited or possessed throughout the game has always been a protective fiction and that they have been the true protagonist all along. In this sense, *Deadly Premonition* reflects or inverts the preoccupation with duality and possession in *Twin Peaks* to explore the ways in which the player may possess or inhabit a video game protagonist—where the hidden passenger is revealed is revealed not as dangerous or unknowable other but as the true self. The uncanny effect that is created through the York/Zach meta-commentary is distinct from the "gamerly uncanny" that is typically present in survival horror titles. As Hoeger and Huber (2007) note, the "gamerly uncanny" in survival horror is usually created through the disruption or complication of the player's control over their avatar, but this is dependent on a strong sense of identification with the avatar, or at least the desire for it. The exploration of the player/avatar relationship in *Deadly Premonition* lacks the terrifying or alienating dimensions that might be expected from survival horror titles, but it is nonetheless distinctly and provocatively uncanny, as it works to dispute this need for the familiar illusion of a singular identification, rather engaging with (and exposing) the player/avatar relationship as a possessive duality.

5. Conclusions: The Uncanniness of *Deadly Premonition*

While it can be understood simply as a flawed or failed video game title, an appreciation of the unusual uncanniness of *Deadly Premonition* helps to explain its niche appeal and divided critical reception. Hoeger and Huber (2007) define the "gamerly uncanny" as an uncanniness that develops not just out of a game's representational elements, but also from the ways in which it renders familiar videogame actions and relationships as strange. They argue that the "gamerly uncanny" develops principally out of the ways in which games, and in particular survival horror titles, disrupt or complicate the player's relationship with their onscreen avatar. *Deadly Premonition* serves to demonstrate how this idea of the "gamerly uncanny" can be expanded upon and explored more deeply in order to deliver a novel gameplay experience. It's distinctly uncanny character results from a number of interconnected elements. In contrast to typical survival horror design, which is usually defined by the limitations it places on the player and a minimalist aesthetic, *Deadly Premonition* offers expansion and excess, combining a range of gameplay styles and experiences. This has the effect of rendering familiar gameplay features strange and uncanny to the player due to their apparent incompatibility and contradictory outcomes. *Deadly Premonition* disrupts not just the familiar player/avatar relationship, but the familiarity of the survival horror category of gameplay itself in order to deliver a distinctly uncanny effect. In this sense, it is very similar to the genre-bending elements of its source material *Twin Peaks*, which used the juxtaposition of different styles of familiar television narratives to subvert the expectations of its audience. It should be noted that it is difficult to establish the extent to which these outcomes align with the original intentions of the game's developers. The director, Hidetaka "SWERY" Suehiro, is reportedly unwilling to directly acknowledge the influence of Twin Peaks on *Deadly Premonition* despite the many obvious parallels between the series and the game (Kumar 2011). Furthermore, it is by no means certain that the uncanny elements of its gameplay which result from conscious design decisions, such as the deliberate combination of seemingly contradictory categories and styles of play, were intended to have a subversive effect. However, *Deadly Premonition* has been largely received and understood as a homage, parody or quasi-adaptation of *Twin Peaks*, and intentionally or not, its uniquely uncanny aesthetic and atmosphere parallels that of the series and has a similarly effect on its audience. A significant number of games demonstrate the clear influence of *Twin Peaks* in their narrative and visuals, but the destabilizing uncanniness of *Deadly Premonition* connects it to the themes of the series through both its representational and gameplay elements. Its foregrounding of the themes of duality and possession leads to a provocative commentary on the player/avatar relationship, which is expressed through its both its narrative and gameplay. *Deadly Premonition* ultimately works to demonstrate the ways in which uncanny play can be used not just to create a sense of fear or alienation, but also a sophisticated self-awareness in relation to familiar and accepted relationships between videogame narrative and gameplay features.

Funding: This research received no external funding.

Conflicts of Interest: The author declares no conflict of interest.

References

2K Marin. 2013. *The Bureau: XCOM Declassified*. PC, PlayStation 3, Xbox 360. Novato: 2K Games.

Access Games. 2010. *Deadly Premonition*. PlayStation 3, Xbox 360. Tokyo: Marvellous Entertainment.

Atlus. 2008. *Persona 4*. PlayStation 2, PlayStation Vita. Tokyo: Atlus.

Botting, Fred. 2008. *Limits of Horror: Technology, Bodies, Gothic*. Manchester and New York: Manchester University Press.

Browning, John Edgar. 2011. Survival Horrors, Survival Spaces: Tracing the Modern Zombie (cine) Myth. *Horror Stories* 2: 41–59. Available online: https://www.academia.edu/6697551/_Survival_Horrors_Survival_Spaces_Tracing_the_Modern_Zombie_Cine_Myth_HORROR_STUDIES_2011_uncorrected_proof_ (accessed on 29 June 2018).

Brudvig, Erik. 2010. Deadly Premonition Review. *IGN*, February 22. Available online: http://au.ign.com/articles/2010/02/23/deadly-premonition-review (accessed on 22 June 2018).

Capcom. 1996. *Resident Evil*. Playstation. Osaka: Capcom.

Capcom. 2005. *Resident Evil 4*. Gamecube. PC. PlayStation 2. Osaka: Capcom.

Carmicheal, Stephanie. 2013. How Twin Peaks Finds New Life in the World of Deadly Premonition. *Kill Screen*, April 30. Available online: https://killscreen.com/articles/how-twin-peaks-finds-new-life-world-deadly-premonition/ (accessed on 29 June 2018).

Chess, Shira. 2015. Uncanny Gaming: The Ravenhearst Videogames and Gothic Appropriation. *Feminist Media Studies* 15: 382–96. [CrossRef]

Clarkson, Sparky. 2010. Deadly Premonition Review. *Game Critics*, March 14. Available online: https://gamecritics.com/sparky-clarkson/deadly-premonition-review/ (accessed on 29 June 2018).

Clifftop Games. 2016. *Kathy Rain*. PC. Stockholm: Raw Fury.

Conway, Steven. 2010. A Circular Wall? Reformulating the Fourth Wall for Videogames. *Journal of Gaming and Virtual Worlds* 2: 145–55. [CrossRef]

Creative Assembly. 2014. *Alien Isolation*. PC, PlayStation 3, PlayStation 4, Xbox 360, Xbox One. Tokyo: Sega.

Dolar, Mladen. 1991. "I Shall Be with You on Your Wedding-Night": Lacan and the Uncanny. *October* 58: 5–23. Available online: https://www.jstor.org/stable/778795 (accessed on 29 June 2018).

Dontnod Entertainment. 2015. *Life is Strange*. PC, PlayStation 3, PlayStation 4, Xbox 360, Xbox One. Tokyo: Square Enix.

Dunne, Daniel. 2014. Brechtian Alienation in Videogames. *Press Start* 1: 79–99. Available online: https://press-start.gla.ac.uk/index.php/press-start/article/view/8/7 (accessed on 29 June 2018).

EA Redwood Shore. 2008. *Dead Space*. PC, PlayStation 3, Xbox 360. Redwood City: EA.

Freud, Sigmund. 1955. The Uncanny. In *The Standard Edition of the Complete Psychological Works of Sigmund Freud, Volume XVII (1917–1919): An Infantile Neurosis and Other Works*. Translated by James Strachey. London: The Hogarth Press. First published 1919. pp. 213–56.

Frost, Mark, and David Lynch. 1990–1991. *Twin Peaks*. Performed by Kyle MacLachlan, Michael Ontkean, Mädchen Amick, Dana Ashbrook, Richard Beymer, Lara Flynn Boyle, Sherilyn Fenn, Warren Frost, Peggy Lipton, James Marshall, and et al. Los Angeles: Lynch/Frost Productions and Spelling Television Inc.

Girard, Pavel. 2011. *"The Fear System"—Triggering Tension in Survival Horror Videogames*. Norderstedt: GRIN Verlag.

Green, Holly. 2017. 9 Games to Play if you love Twin Peaks. *Paste Magazine*, May 21. Available online: https://www.pastemagazine.com/articles/2017/05/9-games-to-play-if-you-loved-twin-peaks.html (accessed on 29 June 2018).

Hand, Richard J. 2004. Proliferating Horrors: Survival Horror and the Resident Evil Franchise. In *Horror Film: Creating and Marketing Fear*. Edited by Steffan Hantke. Jackson: University Press of Mississippi, pp. 117–34.

Headfirst Productions. 2005. *Call of Cthulhu: Dark Corners of the Earth*. PC, Xbox. Rockville: Bethesda Softworks.

Hoeger, Lauren, and William Huber. 2007. Ghastly multiplication: Fatal Frame II and the Videogame Uncanny. Paper presented at the 2007 DiGRA International Conference: Situated Play, Tokyo, Japan, September 24–28; Edited by Akira Baba. pp. 152–56. Available online: http://www.digra.org/wp-content/uploads/digital-library/07313.12302.pdf (accessed on 29 June 2018).

Holmes, Eben. 2010. Strange Reality: Glitches and Uncanny Play. *Eludamos. Journal for Computer Game Culture* 4: 255–76. Available online: http://eludamos.org/index.php/eludamos/article/view/vol4no2-9/188 (accessed on 29 June 2018).

Huizinga, Johan. 1949. *Homo Ludens: A Study of the Play-Element in Culture*. London: Routledge. First published 1938.

Ice Pick Lodge. 2005. *Pathologic*. PC. Moscow: Ice Pick Lodge.

Jentsch, Ernst. 1995. On the Psychology of the Uncanny. Translated by Roy Sellars. *Angelaki* 2: 7–16. [CrossRef]

Jowett, Lorna. 2016. Nightmare in red: Twin Peaks parody, homage and mashup. In *Return to Twin Peaks: New Approaches to Materiality, Theory, and Genre on Television*. Edited by Jeffery Andrew Weinstock and Catherine Spooner. New York: Palgrave Macmillan, pp. 211–27.

Kirkland, Ewan. 2005. Restless Dreams in Silent Hill: Approaches to Videogame analysis. *The Journal of Media Practice* 6: 183–95. [CrossRef]

Kirkland, Ewan. 2007. The Self-Reflexive Funhouse of Silent Hill. *Convergence* 3: 403–15. [CrossRef]

Kirkland, Ewan. 2009a. Storytelling and Survival Horror. In *Horror Video Games*. Edited by Bernard Perron. Jefferson: McFarland & Company, Inc., pp. 26–45.

Kirkland, Ewan. 2009b. Horror Videogames and the Uncanny. Paper presented at the 2009 DiGRA International Conference: Breaking New Ground: Innovation in Games, Play, Practice and Theory (DiGRA '09), London, UK, September 1–4. Available online: http://www.digra.org/wp-content/uploads/digital-library/09287.25453.pdf (accessed on 29 June 2018).

Konami. 1998. *Metal Gear Solid*. PC, PlayStation. Tokyo: Konami.

Konami. 2001. *Silent Hill 2*. PlayStation 2, Xbox. Tokyo: Konami.

Konami. 2003. *Silent Hill 3*. PlayStation 2. Tokyo: Konami.

Konami. 2008. *Silent Hill Homecoming*. PC, PlayStation 3, Xbox 360. Tokyo: Konami.

Kristeva, Julia. 1982. *Powers of Horror: An Essay on Abjection*. Translated by Leon S. Roudiez. New York: Columbia University Press.

Krzywinska, Tanya. 2002. Hands-On Horror. In *Screenplay: Cinema/Videogames/Interfaces*. Edited by Geoff King and Tanya Krzywinska. London: Wallflower Press, pp. 206–23.

Krzywinska, Tanya. 2015a. Conspiracy Hermeneutics: The Secret World as Weird Tale. *Well Played* 3: 119–38.

Krzywinska, Tanya. 2015b. Gaming Horror's Horror: Representation, Regulation, and Affect in Survival Horror Video Games. *Journal of Visual Culture* 14: 293–97. Available online: http://vcu.sagepub.com/content/14/3/293.abstract?rss=1 (accessed on 29 June 2018).

Kumar, Matthew. 2011. The 'Swery Game': Hidetaka Suehiro on Deadly Premonition. *Gamasutra*, June 3. Available online: https://www.gamasutra.com/view/feature/134764/the_swery_game_hidetaka_suehiro_.php (accessed on 29 June 2018).

McGowan, Todd. 2016. Lodged in a Fantasy Space: Twin Peaks and Hidden Obscenities. In *Return to Twin Peaks: New Approaches to Materiality, Theory, and Genre on Television*. Edited by Jeffery Andrew Weinstock and Catherine Spooner. New York: Palgrave Macmillan, pp. 143–57.

Molodvan, Raluca. 2015. "That Show You Like Might Be Coming Back in Style": How Twin Peaks Changed the Face of Contemporary Television. *American, British and Canadian Studies* 24: 44–68. [CrossRef]

Mori, Masahiro. 2012. The Uncanny Valley. *IEEE Spectrum*, June 12. Translated by Karl F. MacDorman and Norri Kageki. First published 1970. Available online: https://spectrum.ieee.org/automaton/robotics/humanoids/the-uncanny-valley (accessed on 29 June 2018).

Perron, Bernard. 2009. Introduction: Gaming after Dark. In *Horror Video Games*. Edited by Bernard Perron. Jefferson: McFarland & Company, Inc., pp. 13–14.

Perron, Bernard. 2012. *Silent Hill: The Terror Engine*. Ann Arbor: University of Michigan Press.

Perron, Bernard. 2018. *The World of Scary Videogames: A Study in Videoludic Horror*. New York: Bloomsbury Academic.

Pruett, Chris. 2011. "Designing Characters to Be Scared For", Chris's Survival Horror Quest [blog]. June 12. Available online: http://horror.dreamdawn.com/?p=60990 (accessed on 29 June 2018).

Remedy Entertainment. 2010. *Alan Wake*. Xbox 360. Redmond: Microsoft Game Studios.

Rockstar North. 2008. *Grand Theft Auto 4*. PC, PlayStation 3, Xbox 360. New York: Rockstar Games.

Rockstar North. 2013. *Grand Theft Auto 5*. PC, PlayStation 3, Xbox 360. New York: Rockstar Games.

Royle, Nicholas. 2003. *The Uncanny*. New York: Routledge.

Savoy, Eric. 2016. Jacques Lacan, Walk with Me: On the Letter. In *Return to Twin Peaks: New Approaches to Materiality, Theory, and Genre on Television*. Edited by Jeffery Andrew Weinstock and Catherine Spooner. New York: Palgrave Macmillan, pp. 123–41.

Schneider, Steven Jay. 2004. Manifestations of the Literary Double in Modern Horror Cinema. In *Horror Film and Psychoanalysis: Freud's Worst Nightmare*. Edited by Steven Jay Schneider, William Rothman and Dudley Andrew. Cambridge: Cambridge University Press, pp. 106–21.

Sega. 1999. *Shenmue*. Nintendo Gamecube. Tokyo: Sega.

Sega. 2005. *Yakuza*. PlayStation 2. Tokyo: Sega.

Sterling, Jim. 2010. Review: Deadly Premonition. *Destructoid*, February 27. Available online: https://www. destructoid.com/review-deadly-premonition-165168.phtml (accessed on 29 June 2018).

Stienmetz, Kevin F. 2018. Carceral horror: Punishment and control in *Silent Hill*. *Crime, Media Culture: An International Journal* 14: 265–87. [CrossRef]

Tango Gameworks. 2017. *The Evil within 2*. PC, PlayStation 4, Xbox One. Rockville: Bethseda Softworks.

Taylor, Laurie. 2009. Gothic Bloodlines in Survival Horror Gaming. In *Horror Video Games*. Edited by Bernard Perron. Jefferson: McFarland & Company, Inc., pp. 46–61.

Terrible Toybox. 2017. *Thimbleweed Park*. Terrible Toybox.

Thomsen, Michael. 2010. Revival Horror: New Ideas in Fear-Making. *Gamasutra*, June 1. Available online: http:// www.gamasutra.com/view/feature/134160/revival_horror_new_ideas_in_.php (accessed on 29 June 2018).

Tinwell, Angela, and Mark Grimshaw. 2009. Survival Horror Games—An Uncanny Modality. Paper presented at the Thinking after Dark Conference, Montreal, QC, Canada, April 23–25. Available online: http://www. academia.edu/1358775/Tinwell_A._and_Grimshaw_M._2009_Survival_horror_games_-_an_uncanny_ modality_paper_presented_at_the_Thinking_After_Dark_Conference_Montreal_Canada_23-25_April (accessed on 29 June 2018).

Ubisoft. 2003. *Beyond Good and Evil*. Gamecube, PC, PlayStation 2, Xbox. Montreuil: Ubisoft.

VanOrd, Kevin. 2010. Deadly Premonition Review. *Gamespot*, April 19. Available online: https://www.gamespot. com/reviews/deadly-premonition-review/1900-6258973/ (accessed on 29 June 2018).

Variable State. 2016. *Virginia*. Mac, PC, PlayStation 4, Xbox One. Milan: 505 Games.

Vatra Games. 2012. *Silent Hill: Downpour*. PlayStation 3, Xbox 360. Tokyo: Konami.

Wales, Matt. 2010. Deadly Premonition UK Review. *IGN*, November 8. Available online: http://au.ign.com/ articles/2010/11/08/deadly-premonition-uk-review (accessed on 29 June 2018).

Weinstock, Andrew. 2016. Wondrous and Strange: The Matter of Twin Peaks. In *Return to Twin Peaks: New Approaches to Materiality, Theory, and Genre on Television*. Edited by Jeffery Andrew Weinstock and Catherine Spooner. New York: Palgrave Macmillan, pp. 29–46.

arts

MDPI

Article

"Game Over, Man. Game Over": Looking at the Alien in Film and Videogames

Brendan Keogh [1,*] **and Darshana Jayemanne** [2]

[1] School of Communication, Queensland University of Technology, Queensland 4001, Australia
[2] School of Design and Informatics, Abertay University, DD1 1HG Dundee, UK; d.jayemanne@abertay.ac.uk
* Correspondence: brendan.keogh@qut.edu.au

Received: 2 July 2018; Accepted: 15 August 2018; Published: 24 August 2018

Abstract: In this article we discuss videogame adaptations of the *Alien* series of films, in particular *Alien: Colonial Marines* (2013) and *Alien: Isolation* (2014). In comparing critical responses and developer commentary across these texts, we read the very different affective, aesthetic and socio-political readings of the titular alien character in each case. The significant differences in what it means to 'look' at this figure can be analyzed in terms of wider storytelling techniques that stratify remediation between film and games. Differing accounts of how storytelling techniques create intensely 'immersive' experiences such as horror and identification—as well as how these experiences are valued—become legible across this set of critical contexts. The concept of the 'look' is developed as a comparative series that enables the analysis of the affective dynamics of film and game texts in terms of gender-normative 'technicity', moving from the 'mother monster' of the original film to the 'short controlled burst' of the colonial marines and finally to the 'psychopathic serendipity' of *Alien: Isolation*.

Keywords: Alien; videogames; film; fifth look; remediation

1. Introduction

Ridley Scott's 1979 film *Alien* and James Cameron's 1986 sequel *Aliens* are foundational reference points for action videogames. *Aliens* in particular has remarkable tenacity across the history of blockbuster science-fiction videogames, most notably through its squad of memorable marines and their equally memorable hardware. Tough-guy soldiers have hosed down hordes of aliens in multitudinous videogame homages to these marines. First-person shooter franchise *Halo* pays direct homage to *Aliens'* gruff, cigar-chomping Sergeant Apone with its own Sergeant Johnson; Midway's 1980 arcade game *Xenophobe* directly adapts H. R. Giger's now-ubiquitous "razor-toothed phallic monster" (Kavanaugh 1980, p. 94) to an extent that verges on plagiarism; Nintendo's *Metroid* series makes a direct nod to *Alien* with an alien antagonist adopting the name 'Ripley'. Official adaptations or extensions of the film franchise include beat-em-ups, arcade shooters, and first-person titles. These include *Alien* (Atari, 1982), *Aliens versus Predator* (Jorudan, 1993) and its many sequels, *Alien 3: The Gun* (Sega, 1993), *Aliens Infestation* (Sega, 2011), *Aliens: Colonial Marines* (Gearbox, 2013), and *Alien: Isolation* (Sega, 2014).

The films' visual motifs thus recur "explicitly through games adapted from the film franchise and implicitly through games which mimic it" (Weise and Jenkins 2009, p. 111). However, just as many of the themes of *Alien* are somewhat muted when filtered through the tonal shift of the second film ("This time, it's war" the sequel's marketing material assured us), so too have videogames drawn a very selective set of inspirations from the *Alien* series. Mainstream videogames are bedazzled by the colonial marines and their impressive military hardware, yet remain relatively disinterested in the gender politics or critiques of technological corporate culture that film theorists have long noted as being so prevalent to the films (Bundtzen 1987; Creed 1986; Doherty 2015; Greven 2011; Kavanaugh 1980; Sloan 2016).

Here, we will make a comparative study of storytelling techniques utilised by *Aliens: Colonial Marines* (hereafter *Colonial Marines*) and *Alien: Isolation* (hereafter *Isolation*), situating these two titles as a way to explore the complexities of remediated storytelling across film and videogame forms. *Colonial Marines* sought to remediate the feel of Cameron's sequel film in the action-FPS (First Person Shooter) genre, and in many ways exemplifies the tendencies in game design identified by Weise and Jenkins. Conversely, *Isolation* explicitly rejects many of the typical design mechanisms that games draw from *Aliens* and reintroduces feminist themes of techno-pessimism from Scott's first film.

In comparing these texts, we will focus on what it means to *look* at the titular alien monster, beginning with Creed's (1986) discussion of maternal monstrosity and the 'fifth look' of horror film. Second, through Weise and Jenkins' analysis, we examine how the alien reverses its valency in FPS games such as *Colonial Marines*: rather than looking away from the horrific mother monster, players instead *focus* their gaze in order to eliminate multiple aliens in 'short controlled bursts'. Finally, we discuss how *Isolation* reintroduces the critique of technicity present in the original films, thematised through its design of 'psychopathic serendipity'.

2. The Mother Monster and the 'Fifth Look'

Alien is a landmark of sci-fi horror, and has long been read in terms of psychoanalysis. Here we will focus on the important reading by Creed (1986) and the notion of the 'abject'. For Kristeva (1982), the abject represents the ambiguous maternal body as the site of conflicting desires. The subject desires both union with the maternal body as a source of plentitude and comfort, as well as the differentiation and individuation from that same body that is the precondition of entry into the paternal symbolic order (in the film, represented by the quiet and logical rhythms of spaceship life).

The individuated subject is, however, never free of the tension it locates in the maternal body: expulsion of the abject is not a discrete event so much as a ritual repetition (Creed 1986, p. 48). Horror films are a key site in which this expulsion of the abject is 'staged and re-staged': the awful monsters of horror cinema may be defeated, but are often liable to return and wreak more havoc. *Alien* is exemplary: the creature, which through Geiger's design invokes viscera and excreta, must be literally abjected into space for the peaceful and controlled routines of the spaceship to return to normal.

Creed argues that the xenomorph's maternal monstrosity is more radical than the theory of abjection, theorising an 'archaic' mother-figure that precedes any relation to the patriarchal order. Kristeva's psychoanalytic notion of the abject, Creed argues, still places the maternal body in relation to the father as the signifier and guarantor of the symbolic order. Unlike this pre-Oedipal mother, the archaic mother is not simply the opposite of the father in a relationship of lack, but a truly different and autonomous psychical function. The archaic mother works outside the symbolic order entirely as the black, gaping womb or maternal body, as a pure generative force: "The womb is not the site of castration anxiety. Rather, the womb signifies 'fullness' or 'emptiness' but always as its *own point of reference*" (Creed 1986).

This procreative force is often coded negatively, as the terrible goddess or Medusa, a devouring mother asserting sovereign claims over her offspring. While Creed argues that the archaic mother is so remote that it can be difficult to fraction out within the complex of the 'monstrous-feminine', the threat here is less a crippling or numbing dismemberment (as in the castration complex) than a swallowing-whole that completely de-individuates the subject: death, the fade to black. The elongated form of the creature, pharyngeal jaws, and lack of facial features and organs of sense give prominence to the fangs, "the most living part ... the most terrifying for neighbouring animals" (Bataille 1985, p. 59).

Alien is a key example. Creed associates the creature in *Alien* with the Medusa myth, pointing towards the stunned transfixion exhibited by characters when they first catch sight of the creature in the film. The archaic mother is operative here as "the voracious maw, the mysterious black hole which ... threatens to give birth to equally horrific offspring as well as threatening to incorporate everything in its path" (Creed 1986, p. 63). Certainly, the alien is extremely toothy—often the first thing that is recognised through the darkness is the gleam of its fearsome dentition. Horror film has often made use of the returned gaze—the sudden realisation, which shocks audience and character alike, that eyes are staring back—but here, the returned 'gaze' is not one of recognition (however sudden and horrid), but of pure hunger; not an exchange over a void but a one-way trip down the gullet. Characters often doomed once the camera cuts between their horrified face and the drooling creature in *Alien*; but this trope is further reinforced by the literal incorporation of human crew members into the alien reproductive matrix. Creed's association of the creature in *Alien* with the Medusa myth is echoed in *Isolation* with the player's knowledge that once the alien is spotted, it can often be too late to do anything other than wait for death and reload the game (a point expanded below).[1]

The key point for our discussion is the account of how the 'sighting' of the Medusa-mother-monster has the power of transfixing the viewer—both diegetic character and extra-diegetic audience member—with shock (Jayemanne 2017). This relates to a crucial element of how Creed understands the operation of horror film. As a medium, film utilises strategies and processes of identification (such as montage) through which it 'sutures' viewers in a kind of 'immersion' in cinematic space and time. Horror film both makes use of and challenges these strategies of identification:

> In contrast to the conventional viewing structures working within other variants of the classic text, the horror film does not constantly work to suture the spectator into the viewing processes. Instead, an unusual phenomenon arises whereby the suturing processes are momentarily undone while the horrific image on the screen challenges the viewer to run the risk of continuing to look ... strategies of identification are temporarily broken, as the spectator is constructed in the place of horror Geiger. (Creed 1986, p. 64)

Creed argues that this relation be considered a 'fifth look' that can take its place among the suturing techniques of cinema. In particular, it can be seen as an expansion of Willemen's 'fourth look' (Willemen 1980), which itself draws on Mulvey's (1975) discussion of three cinematic looks. While this is not the context to review these accounts in detail, we want to highlight the increasingly 'interactive' or 'immersive' quality through which key critics have described the fourth and fifth looks—indicated by the importance of affective states such as shame and horror in these critical accounts. There is also a *punctual* element: as Creed writes, the suturing processes are undone 'momentarily' in the horrific shot.

Willemen notes that, in describing the three types of 'look' she discerns in cinema (such as the camera lingering on a character's face, or two characters exchanging a glance), Mulvey focuses on intra-diegetic phenomena. He suggests a 'fourth look', analogous to Lacan's mirror stage insofar as it is a moment of self-consciousness arising from a fragmented field that reflects the piecemeal nature of subjectivity itself: 'an imagined look experienced by the audience as a sense that is seen in the process of seeing' (Freedman 1991, p. 69). This look is the sense that the cinematic apparatus itself has powers of agency and judgment and thus has a potential for generating surprise, self-critique and shame in audiences—an incorporation of the viewer as not simply passive but as in some sense *responsible* for their continued looking. Scopophilia, typically considered an attribute of subjects, is refigured as an *activity*. As such, the fourth look's extra-diegetic dimension can be seen as a forerunner of the feedback loops by which players are woven into videogame space and time (Jayemanne 2005) and come to experience a different kind of immersion than that prompted by classic processes of cinematic suture. Similarly, Creed's fifth look operates as a meta-cognition of the self's relation to the text: a certain 'looking back'; only here the effect is maximally intensive. The fifth look is perhaps most evident in

---

[1] The xenomorph's capability of incorporating both victims and environment into its hive to use as raw materials for more monsters is only magnified by the rest of the film series. For example, Cameron's *Aliens* introduced the Alien Queen as the ultimate mother-monster, while also exploring Ellen Ripley's own maternal impulses (in her case, coded positively) through the character of Newt. This is further emphasised in the extended cut through the loss of her daughter (that we play in *Isolation*) to old age while Ellen drifted through space. Later films continued the use of themes and imagery that are evocative of both the pre-Oedipal and the archaic mother, indicating the acumen of Creed's (along with other scholars such as Bundtzen 1987) analysis of the original film.

the technique of the jump-scare, where sudden montage creates suture and identification in the same moment as repulsion and fear.

In violently halting the process of identification through the shocking appearance of the monstrous and abject, then, horror film in general—and the alien in particular—puts the spectator's sense of a unified self into crisis: "By not-looking, the spectator is able momentarily to withdraw identification from the image on the screen in order to reconstruct the boundary between self and screen and reconstitute the 'self' which is threatened with disintegration" (Creed 1986, p. 65). Looking in the face of a shocking appearance becomes gruelling labour and risk. Horror film derives some of its most powerful effects through the fifth looks' 'jamming' of the very technical-psychological mechanisms and feedback loops that the cinematic text has worked so hard to perfect.

3. 'Short Controlled Bursts' and 'Para-Social' Camaraderie

The above discussion of the reception and remediation of *Alien* is admittedly very brisk, but our goal here is not to engage with the detail of psychoanalytic film theory or its critiques (see for example Shaviro 2010) so much as to identify key characteristics of Creed's highly influential reading as basis for a comparative method. We will proceed by comparing Creed's 'fifth look' with another perceptive critical response to looking at the alien: Weise and Jenkins' praise of the videogame *Alien vs Predator 2* (hereafter *AvP2*). This will serve as a means to triangulate some of the complexities of remediation between film and the normative conventions of blockbuster videogames. Weise and Jenkins' piece is explicitly responding to Steven Spielberg's 2000s foray into gaming: i.e., they are posing the question of what a film director is liable to overlook when making a videogame.

Where for Creed the horror film's fifth look works through a traumatic risk or labour of 'looking away' from an abject scene or object that jams the suturing codes of cinema, the action videogame demands a constant and unwavering gaze (or what Chesher (2004) conceives of as videogame's sticky 'glaze'). This association is powerfully affirmed in the marquee genre of the First-Person Shooter, which integrally relates scopophilia and militarist dominance over space: the look is sutured to the fetish of the firearm. In *AvP2*, this requires 'riding' the weapon in what Weise and Jenkins term "short controlled bursts" following the advice given in the film by the level-headed Corporal Hicks. Key to the videogame player's successful sortie against the swarm of aliens is the *need to keep looking* that is necessary to effectively control the marine's weapon. Far from looking away from the alien appearance, first-person shooter players repetitively perform the expulsion of the abject by keeping their eyes (and their crosshairs) firmly fixed on the target. Weise and Jenkins thus articulate the visual and identificatory logics of the first-person shooter in *completely inverse terms* to Creed's account of what it means to look at the alien. Between these two responses, as Shaviro notes in another context, "something has happened to the act of looking" (Shaviro 1993).

The short controlled burst is as far as can be from the Medusa-like transfixion of *Alien*'s fifth look. However, it is also the exact opposite of the blind-fire panic of the marines in the latter half of Cameron's sequel film, in which the marines are overwhelmed by the alien swarm as Lieutenant Gorman loses control of the situation in spite of his videogame-like command apparatus. Weise and Jenkins marshal psychological and social insights in their characterization of why the 'affective dynamics' of *AvP2* make it an exemplary videogame adaptation of *Aliens*. They praise *Aliens* for its "high affective intensity", but attribute this intensity primarily not to the horror of the aliens nor to the character arc of the film's protagonist, Ripley, but to the "para-social" (Weise and Jenkins 2009, p. 115) camaraderie between the team-members of the marine squad. Exposure to the personality and mannerisms of each squad member in the earlier parts of the film feeds into the audience's investment in the team during the frenetic combat scenarios.

This intensity also resonates with the marines' ritualistic military argot. The iconic high-tech weapons (pulse rifle, sentry and smart guns) and equipment (shoulder lamps, IR goggles, dropships, motion-trackers) of the film are critical to the experience of space in the first-person shooter.

These technological devices have their own specific properties that train players in the "embodied literacy" (Keogh 2018) and "tactile habituation" (Jayemanne 2017) needed to succeed at the game:

> The possibility space of *Aliens versus Predator 2* is derived most directly from the moment-to-moment experience, seen repeatedly in the film [*Aliens*], of being a marine trapped in close corridors with aliens. This may sound like a generic scenario from many videogames, but its uniqueness comes from the specific player tools, enemy behaviour, and level design derived from Cameron's film. (Weise and Jenkins 2009, p. 114)

The role of the technological paraphernalia from the film is key to transitioning fully to the game situation: "Once the player has mastered most of these tools, she has become, in essence, a good colonial marine" (Weise and Jenkins 2009, p. 115).

Weise and Jenkins synthesise their reading in a key passage as an attenuation of the multi-character 'para-social' ethos of the film into the individualist and technophilic design of a successful videogame—giving the individual to fulfil the promise of the many:

> The affective mechanics of the game might better be described as ego-centric, restricted to what can be known and experienced by a single character ... the game designers shape our affective experience through procedural design, through the properties they program into our weapons ... When these devices are deployed effectively, they can yield a satisfying emotional experience; they can make us cry, experience fear, shock and horror, or feel exhilaration depending on the choices we make and their outcomes.

This transition from cinematic para-social to ludic ego-centric engagement manifests in what it means to look at the alien in this context. Where the player character condenses the affective dynamics of the marine squad, the singular creature conversely becomes the dispersed and unthreatening pop-up targets of the skeet-shoot. The occasional jump-scare notwithstanding, *Alien*-adapted first-person shooter videogames consist of acquiring and eliminating multiple targets, rather than desperately avoiding the petrifying gaze of one invincible monster. There seems little point in debating whether the alien in *Colonial Marines* represents a pre-Oedipal or archaic mother monster—numbing shock or complete oblivion. Instead, the key question becomes how efficiently the player's short controlled bursts—the look-firearm complex—can remove it from play. Failure to do so efficiently just means a reload and perhaps a visit to the 'difficulty' toggle.

The creature thus has inverted both its storytelling function and its role in generating an experience of immersion, becoming something that *presents* itself to players. The alien's pliant 'defeatability' is ramified at every level of design. Where the monstrous appearance in *Alien* halted the cinema's characteristic 'strategies of identification', in the first-person shooter the monster aids and abets those of the videogame. Both cinematic and videogame experience could be described as 'immersive', but very different affective infrastructures are operative in each case. Rather than being constructed in the space of horror through the fifth look, looking at the alien through the short controlled burst constructs videogame players as ego-centric subjects who dominate fictional space through mastering multiple feedback loops. These loops are painstakingly calibrated through playtesting so that players with normative ability can both experience affective intensities and win the game through 'colluding' with the apparatus. The affective camaraderie that Weise and Jenkins argue is central to the para-social dynamics of Cameron's *Aliens*, then, is transferred onto the ego-centric relation of empowerment and collusion between player and videogame as represented by the fictional and fantastical military hardware.

4. Videogame Technicities and Techno-Masculine Anxiety

It is important to recognise that Weise and Jenkins' reading of *AvP2* is partial: they explicitly focus on the single-player rather than the multiplayer aspects of the game, as well as the alternate modes which allow play as alien and Predator characters. We shall argue that what is left out of their analysis—including these alien 'looks' and of course Ellen Ripley—are potentials that are in some sense seized upon in *Isolation* through its design of 'psychopathic serendipity'. However, Weise and Jenkins' articulation of the affective dynamics of looking at the alien through the short controlled burst is acute as a metonym for widespread design philosophies and approaches to videogame storytelling in the mainstream industry and its occasionally ornery but reliably lucrative consumer culture: the notion of player empowerment as collusive, ego-centric 'technicity'.

Along with the psychoanalytic tradition represented by Creed, many scholars have noted the reversal (and convergence) of traditional science-fiction gender roles in *Alien* and its sequels (Bundtzen 1987; Kavanaugh 1980; Doherty 2015). Criticism has also focused on the pessimistic attitudes of the films towards technology and capital:

> *Alien* offers a pessimistic vision of humanity dominated by a technological empire. Programmed by an unethical corporation . . . , technology emerges as a ubiquitous, insidious, and totalitarian force. The human victims of the technological system have been so conditioned to its rule that they perceive its stranglehold as the natural state of things, not even recognizing their enslavement. (Dinello 2013, p. 193)

These themes are intertwined in *Aliens* as the traditional male heroes are satirically shown as completely incapable of dealing with the alien creature. Hudson's iconic line "Game over, man. Game over!" in *Aliens* is, despite being an explicit reference to a videogame phrase, rarely remembered by those games that celebrate the dominating power of the colonial marines through ego-centric design, and this is the ethos that Weise and Jenkins articulate for the apparent benefit of Spielberg.[2]

Numerous authors have traced how patriarchal values have influenced understandings of both videogames specifically and digital technology more broadly through their symbiotic development across the 20th Century. Lister et al. (2009, p. 290). Observe that "if computers and video games have made computer technology accessible and popular, they have, in doing so, effectively commodified computer technology, turning the radical hacker ethic into consumerist entertainment". Hackers birthed the videogame form, and imbued an ethos, attitude, and culture "that is produced by the conjunction of particular kinds of young men, technology and the mathematical systems of coding that are the language of computing" (Dovey and Kennedy 2006, p. 38). Directly influenced by a neoliberal subjectivity through their ancestry in the hacker mythos (see Chun 2011, p. 7; Keogh 2018), the videogame works historically most often valued by videogame critics, enthusiasts, and scholars alike are those that allow players to express an individualistic sense of freedom, agency, autonomy, power, and control. Players take on powerful roles like commander, mayor, god, soldier, gangster, and indeed colonial marine to both save the world and, fairly routinely, 'save the girl'. It is here that the ego-centric underpinnings of blockbuster videogame design highlighted above find their center of gravity. Weise and Jenkins' reading of *AvP2* as a 'great' videogame adaptation of *Aliens* must *necessarily* elide the feminist critique of technicity found in that film in the course of valorising the transition from para-social affect to ego-centric design. Ripley cannot reprise her role as protagonist in this schema because in her survivalist strategy the short controlled burst is at best a means and not an end in itself.

As a consequence of videogames' historical alignment with a hacker mythos that favours technological competency, formal virtuosity, and systems literacy, discourses around videogames (both scholarly and popular) have produced what Dovey and Kennedy note is "an 'ideal' player subject that is naturalised as 'white', 'male' and 'heterosexual'" (Dovey and Kennedy 2006, p. 63;

---

2   There is considerable evidence that Spielberg was already across these issues, given that he wrote the introduction to Martin Amis' *Invasion of the Space Invaders* (1982): 'The aliens have landed, and the world can never be the same again . . . I speak as one who knows. I have actually exceeded 500,000 at Missile Command . . . the Invaders, far from confining their activities to public places and consenting adults, have established themselves in our homes in various shapes and forms, to the extent that there's really nowhere left to go to avoid them. Well—that's if you really want to. I don't want to be accused of collaboration, but some of them are really quite friendly when you get to know them . . . ' (Amis 1982, p. 7). The director's return to filmmaking after a hiatus with 2018's *Ready Player One* also speaks to conversance with the medium.

see also Kirkpatrick 2012). Ego-centric design often facilitates a highly gendered and conservatively formalist notion of videogame play: a set of "anterior motives" (Jayemanne 2017) that both push players forward and reliably gratify them should they 'ride the weapon' just so. Those videogames that have goals to achieve, complex systems to master, and surmountable challenges to overcome become exemplary of a videogame form perceived as primarily about gaining skill and exerting power through conscious choices or the cybernetic gratifications of the short controlled burst. At the same time, those videogames deemed to be too easy (not enough challenge), too challenging (not enough fairness), too cinematic (not enough agency), or too 'linear' (not enough complexity) are commonly marginalised as lesser examples of the form (Dovey and Kennedy 2006, p. 37), as 'walking sims' or 'notgames'.

The notion of 'technicity' is useful here to unpack this interplay of gender and technology. We draw on Tomas's coining of this term in his exploration of William Gibson's *Sprawl* novels. Tomas (1989, p. 123) advances the notion of technicity to account for the "different systems of identity composition" that emerge in "cyborg-dominated culture". Dovey and Kennedy (2006) productively build on Tomas's outline in the context of videogame culture. The concept of technicity brings concerns of gender, ethnicity, and class to account for how particular socio-cultural power dynamics both form and are formed through technological competency, access, and literacy. Further, technicity designates how certain modes of identifying with technology become hegemonic and obscure myriad other "marginal, subaltern or oppositional identities which define themselves in reference to the dominant group" (Dovey and Kennedy 2006, p. 64). Through technicity, the complex critiques of technology and gender present in *Alien* can be seen as intimately connected.

What we can now identify as a normatively masculine technicity can be traced across conventional blockbuster videogame design in its focus on individualistic and empowered player positions that echo those of dominant Western masculinity and neoliberalism: a privileged individual given all the right tools so that every challenge faced is surmountable through just the right amount of effort. The individual in the end finds themselves in a position of great power (and often just as importantly, universal acclaim) that they obtained through what seems like hard work but what was, in reality, a world in which even the most alien being appears as a slippage between para-social and ego-centric affective dynamics: a guarantor that players were and always will have been capable to succeed. Boredom is never the consumer's fault.

This dominant technicity is a powerful influence on videogame storytelling in the form of what Boluk and LeMieux (2017) have incisively termed the 'Standard Metagame'. The influence of this standard metagame is reflected in numerous studies into gender and videogame culture. These critiques of ego-centric design range from the dominance of particular action genres at the expense of other genres that focus on emotions or empathy (Dovey and Kennedy 2006), to the systemic sexism of online videogame communities (Harper 2014; Shaw 2014), to the dramatic gender inequality of the videogame industry (Dyer-Witheford and de Peuter 2009). Blockbuster videogames typically promise experiences of technology-aided mastery and concomitant domination of both opponents and space (Wajcman 1991; Keogh 2015; Giddings and Kennedy 2008).

These dynamics are most legible in the storytelling techniques of the game that most stridently attempted to actualise Weise and Jenkins' notion of realising para-social dynamics through ego-centric design. When Gearbox released the first-person shooter *Aliens: Colonial Marines* in 2013, it was met with derision, critical panning, and even a lawsuit from disgruntled fans. The oppressive atmosphere and intimidating aliens of the films were diluted by the game as bored players sprayed waves of groggy creatures with machine-gun fire. A scathing review from game journalism outlet *Polygon* claims the game "fails to grasp the functional core of the series" and accuses the developers of "just checking off the list of 'Stuff that should probably be in an *Alien* game'" (Gies 2013)—that is, the very criteria that Weise and Jenkins attribute to a successful ego-centric game design.

Tellingly, "stuff that should probably be in an *Alien* game" does not include Ellen Ripley, who remains absent from *Colonial Marines*. Instead, the story of *Alien 3* is retconned to revive the marine Hicks: the guiding figure of the 'short controlled burst'. Significant efforts are made to evoke the para-social dynamics of *Aliens*, with Lance Henriksen and Michael Biehn reprising their roles as the voices and likenesses of Bishop and Hicks respectively. Marines bark orders, banter, callsigns, waypoints and hardware designations as players move their PC behind his gun and blast away countless alien creatures. All seems set for another ego-centric design. Yet the negative reception of the game shows it could not provide the affective intensities its marketing material had promised: it failed at both maternal monstrosity and short controlled burst. *Colonial Marines* marks a catastrophic breakdown of the collusive relationship between what is expected of a first-person shooter (action, powerful technology, hordes of defeatable foes), and what is expected of *Alien* (terror, untrustworthy technology, a small number of invincible foes).

This is not to say that the game does not display, at one level, a healthy skepticism of corporate power, figured through the rapacious Weyland–Yutani corporation. The ending of *Colonial Marines* sees the vengeful marines vowing to eliminate the head of a corporation that views them as expendable. However, the result of the corporate malfeasance forms the pretext for another moment of para-social camaraderie—a far cry from the claustrophobic Mother computer in *Alien* or the betrayal by Burke in *Aliens*. In *Colonial Marines*, the critique of technology is recouped within the family-like structure of the marine unit itself. It is also subordinate to the affective camaraderie players like to imagine they have with the game industry itself: the promise of a sequel with more pulse rifles, more smart guns, more defeatable aliens and more nostalgic design (Sloan 2016). The largely male marine fraternity is freed from the failure of *Aliens* not just by the ego-centric design noted by Weise and Jenkins but also by the para-social consumerist ethos that such design fosters at scale.

The intensity of the fan backlash shows that this transfer was botched but potent. The animus against the game was sufficient that it would re-surface in 2018 after a story emerged that *Colonial Marines'* A.I. deficiencies were due to a simple typo rather than some arcane technological slipup (Machkovech 2018). In this light, the sidelining in *Alien* videogames of Ripley—who so often has to deal with ego-centric men—in favour of techno-fetishist marines exemplifies the gender dynamics that have historically conditioned the videogame form. This backlash is also one early forerunner of later movements that show how the ego-centric and para-social affects cultivated by blockbuster videogames can be mirrored in society at large through targeted use of communications technologies; a kind of 'hacking the social' (Milner 2013).

5. Isolation

Creative Assembly's 2014 title *Alien: Isolation* here marks a significant intervention, explicitly engaging with the thematic anxieties of the *Alien* films through complications of ego-centric videogame storytelling. As Creative Lead Alistair Hope (2015) notes in a lecture on the game's design process, the developers were less interested in *Isolation* feeling like an *Alien* videogame than in feeling like *Alien*. That is, the conventions and norms of blockbuster videogame design that are mulishly rehearsed by *Colonial Marines* become incidental in *Isolation*, and in fact are shown up as ripe for subversion.

Taking place in the decades between *Alien* and *Aliens* (while Ellen Ripley drifts through space in stasis as a sole human survivor of the events of the first film), *Isolation* follows the story of Ripley's daughter, Amanda. When the flight recorder of the doomed *Nostromo* ship finds its way to the Seegson corporation's space station Sevastopol, Amanda Ripley travels with representatives of Weyland–Yutani in the hope of learning her mother's fate. Instead of finding her mother, Amanda is caught up in her own nightmare encounter with the alien creatures that echoes many of the story beats that her mother endured in the original film *Alien*.

The game begins on a ship that just happens to be the same model as the *Nostromo*. Reinforcing the sense of re-enactment, other characters regularly refer to Amanda simply as 'Ripley'. Once on the Sevastopol station, Ripley survives malfunctioning androids, malignant corporate agendas, cowardly and incompetent men, and, of course, the horrific alien itself. Through Amanda Ripley, *Isolation* pays homage to *Alien*, allowing the player to walk in Ellen Ripley's footsteps both literally and figuratively.

Immediately, then, *Isolation* engages with a mother/daughter complex central to the films but typically ignored by videogame adaptations. As Bundtzen (1987, p. 14) notes: "the major confrontation of [*Aliens*] will not be impotent male marines vs. Alien Big Mama, but between Ripley, a woman who practices the maternal as compassionate care vs. biological-maternal principle of monstrous proportions, embodied in the Alien other". *Isolation* engages with this paradigm from the inverse perspective: not the mother protecting her daughter, but the daughter searching for her mother.

Ego-centric ways of conceptualising how players engage with videogames see player-consumers held in a privileged position: *using* the technology to do what they want it to do, to make the choices they want to make, to beat the inhuman aliens in the same gesture as they beat the inhuman videogame machine; to get the high score, to win. Such conceptions of ego-centric design ignore the coercive and inequitable aspects of how such desires are generated in the first place—to some degree, this is supposedly the 'natural' orientation of videogame consumers. *Isolation*, on the other hand, draws on the tradition of survival horror games to powerfully reject the ego-centric paradigm of *Alien* videogame adaptations and re-thematise the critical elements of the films. Where ego-centric design sees players as exceptional and privileged, *Isolation* instead works to place them at the whim of both game and alien in a literal convergence of the alien creature's "organic machinery" (Dinello 2013, p. 197). Just as *Alien* presents a "pessimistic vision of humanity dominated by a technological empire" (Dinello 2013, p. 193), *Isolation* places players in a space saturated with this techno-pessimism. Survival horror stages not just the fulfilment of desire but its *production* in a maximally intensive form, decentering the assumption of collusion between player and game.

This skepticism towards technology is carried into *Isolation*'s world through the Seegson corporation. Weyland–Yutani is high-tech, sleek and wealthy; Seegson is incompetent, dilapidated and in financial trouble. Weyland–Yutani has lifelike androids that can pass as humans; Seegson's are 'future-retrospective' robotic, unreliable, malfunctioning beings whose front-loaded artificiality brings corporate callousness into a far future that still advertises a yearning for the posthuman. While *Isolation* is one of the most technologically competent videogames of its contemporaries (nominated for numerous awards for its sound and visual design, as well as the creature's convincing intelligence), it is not celebratory of technology as a source of liberating, cathartic empowerment.

Through parodic corporate aesthetics, retro-futurism and inhuman androids, *Isolation* expresses what Dinello calls the "techno-totalitarianism" of the original film. Where titles such as *Colonial Marines* embrace the advanced technology and weaponry of the marines in order to defeat the creature, *Isolation* embraces retro-futurism, presenting not a far future but the future of the late 1970s that produced *Alien*. Machines are clunky and analogue; computers blurt out DOS-like text onto cathode-ray monitors and trill like old school modems. The clunkiness of *Isolation*'s retro-futurist technologies, the claustrophobia of room-sized computers and whirring machines, and the eerie hum of fluorescent lights each reinforce that cutting-edge technology is not the solution to defeating the alien beast—players are much more likely to find a cassette tape than a laser cannon. Likewise, the cutting-edge technology that allows this videogame to exist will not provide the typical, ego-centric sense of empowerment typically promised by blockbuster videogames.

This pessimism contradicts the celebratory ways in which empowerment through technology is commonly marketed to videogame players—typically as an extension of the ego-centric empowerment afforded *by* videogame technologies themselves. Where Weise and Jenkins suggest a worthy *Aliens* game would be one where players are reliably given the tools and know-how to defeat the alien and thereby vindicate the 'para-social' affects set up by the movie's early scenes, Dinello's observations suggest that a worthy *Alien* videogame is one that *rejects* players' ability to dominate either the virtual space or the alien creature; it would instead be one where the player is *dominated by* both alien and corporate technologies.

6. Psychopathic Serendipity

The most powerful element of *Isolation* is players' encounters with the alien itself. The creature that stalks the halls of Sevastopol cannot be defeated nor can it be easily predicted. Bullets or explosives or hits will not kill this creature and if the alien sees Ripley, it is already too late for players to do anything other than freeze like a transfixed character in the films and wait for death. Looking at the alien becomes a game of hoping that the alien doesn't ever look at you. In this way the game recreates the *affect* of *Alien* within the blockbuster first-person space, and it achieves this in part by stripping out the 'shooter'. Firearms are limited and even then they are counter-productive: firing one connotes not domination over space but a fatal error in which the alien becomes aware of where the player character is. This gameplay restores Ellen Ripley's survivalist tactics to prominence—which, after all, were far more successful than the gunplay of the marines in *Aliens*.

As innumerable online videos will attest, the alien of *Isolation* well and truly regained the powers of horror that were so dulled by repetition and ego-centric design in *Colonial Marines*. However, while the alien's power of transfixion is once more in evidence, it would be inadequate to suggest that this is merely the return of Creed's fifth look. Instead, we suggest a final type of 'look' to characterise the affective dynamics of *Isolation*. To do this we draw on a term suggested by the game's artificial intelligence director Andy Bray: 'psychopathic serendipity'. This refers to the A.I. design such that the 'alien will always find itself in the right place at the right time' (Thompson 2017): a set of techniques used to modulate tension in players. This potential for the alien to burst forth from the environment at any moment means that the short, controlled burst is not merely inadequate: it is an invitation to a hideous death.

Psychopathic serendipity indicates that the creature is guided by its own procedural intelligence rather than the canned foreknowledge of a game designer: it is the *alien's* look that is important. The creature may lurk in the one corridor for long minutes, forcing players to hold their breath in a locker only to unfairly turn back around the moment players think they are safe. If players too often rely on throwing flares to distract the creature, it might begin to inspect where the flare was thrown *from*. The biological and technological fears that the creature embodies in the films are dramatically collusive in *Isolation* through the fear of an alien programmed to be both unstoppable and unpredictable.

As the players attempt to navigate Sevastopol's hallways to their goal (ultimately: escape from Sevastopol), *Isolation*'s alien feels less like a ludic challenge to learn, overcome and enjoy, and more like an intentional, unpredictable and malicious glitch in the system to be avoided at all cost. *Isolation* fosters an explicit need to compromise and adapt to situations, insisting through design on Ripley's survivalist ethos. In this way *Isolation* not only adapts many of the original *Alien* film's anxieties towards gender (Kavanaugh 1980; Bundtzen 1987; Doherty 2015), technology (Dinello 2013), and corporate-inflected imagery of totalitarianism (Dinello 2013), but *converges* them through the many procedural, artistic and narrative techniques of the videogame form.

Through 'psychopathic serendipity', *Isolation* disturbs the affective camaraderie between player and game not only by reintroducing a female protagonist and neutering gunplay but also through the creature's superior adaptation to the dilapidated industrial space station. The level designs and environmental art conspire to emphasise that industrial environments are better suited to the alien than to the worker, bringing back the films' theme of a para-social relation between creature and corporation (which from the point of view of Amanda Ripley is decidedly *anti-social*). Furthermore, the soldier's advantage of choosing their battlefield—so often a core assumption of ego-centric videogame design through notions such as 'balance' or 'fairness'—is subverted. Compared to most videogame 'boss monsters' which are encountered in arena-like locales in which their spectacular designs make sense but can also be predictably exploited, *Isolation*'s creature could potentially be staring back at players as they creep through any of the game's depressing environments. Ripley's survivalist approach is the only successful response to the collusion between alien and environment, but rarely does it allow the player to feel powerful or in control.

Psychopathic serendipity is a pointedly subversive 'look' that, analogous to the fifth look before it, jams the strategies of the ego-centric style of videogame storytelling: both the retro-futuristic technologies of the Sevastopol space station and those of the videogame that give the creature its procedural intelligence are at the service of the creature's empowerment, not that of players. It is *Isolation*'s mutual *subversion of* the collusiveslippage between para-social and ego-centric looks, fusing corporate and biological antagonisms while still leveraging powerful contemporary videogame graphics technology, that reintroduces a fundamental aspect of what it means to look at the alien: the power to terrify.

7. Conclusions

The alien character has been subjected to intensive critical analysis amidst consistent popular appeal, making it a fruitful locus for comparative analysis. In tracing what it means to 'look' at the alien across these manifestations, we have highlighted the complex ways that affective dynamics work across very different storytelling functions and media forms to create differential forms of immersive experience. From 'fifth look' to 'short controlled burst' and finally to 'psychopathic serendipity': all are powerfully 'immersive', but very different in their aesthetic underpinnings. Each look is a moment in which the text returns the gaze and seeks to construct us through powerful effects of attraction and repulsion. Each acts as a locus for discussing the set of artistic techniques and critical responses that are operative in a series of alien appearances—and also the breadth of issues that can confront critics in trying to describe storytelling and varieties of immersive experience across media even within the very limited domain of a single, if alien, character.

Isolation's auto-critique of gaming's technicity highlights the game's canny reversal of the approach crystallised in Weise and Jenkins' reading: in remediating *Alien*, the game moves not from para-social to ego-centric dynamics but from ego-centrism to wider aesthetic, social and political issues. This reading shows why the powerful affective storytelling techniques identified by Creed have lain fallow in gaming for so long; only to emerge when the ideologies of tech platforms come to a rolling boil. The centrality of ego-centric design imperatives guides assumptions about 'what gamers want'—and hence processes of development and investment that mean that the alien is present in and conditional of our very desires.

Recent years have seen a wider range of fringe videogame creators pushing back against the ego-centric design norms favoured by the blockbuster videogame industry. *Isolation*'s commitment to a look of psychopathic serendipity shows up the hidebound nature of videogame adaptations of *Alien* and thereby points towards the imaginative inertia which has led blockbuster videogames' palette of theme, subject matter, character and so on to be so impoverished, even amidst constant technical innovation. Although it does itself end with a conventional narrative resolution and the seeming promise of more consumer-friendly storytelling, our reading valorises *Isolation*'s brilliant revivification of the immersive powers of *Alien* through very different technical means, and points to other unrealised potentials latent in the videogame form.

Author Contributions: Both authors contributed equally to the research, writing, and editing of this article.

Funding: Keogh is funded by an Australian Research Council Discovery Early Career Research Award, grant number (DE180100973). Jayemanne was funded by the Arts and Humanities Research Council, grant number (AH/R009368/1).

Acknowledgments: We thank Helen Berents for invaluable feedback on an earlier draft of this article.

Conflicts of Interest: The authors declare no conflict of interest.

References

Amis, Martin. 1982. *Invasion of the Space Invaders*. New York: Hutchinson.
Bataille, Georges. 1985. *Visions of Excess*. Minneapolis: University of Minnesota Press.

Bundtzen, Lynda K. 1987. Monstrous Mothers: Medusa, Grendel and Now Alien. *Film Quarterly* 40: 11–17. [CrossRef]

Boluk, Stephanie, and Patrick LeMieux. 2017. *Metagaming: Playing, Competing, Spectating, Cheating, Trading, Making, and Breaking Videogames*. Minneapolis: University of Minnesota Press.

Chesher, Chris. 2004. Neither gaze nor glance, but glaze: Relating to console game screens. *SCAN: Journal of Media Arts Culture* 1: 98–117.

Chun, Wendy Hui-Kyung. 2011. *Programmed Visions: Software and Memory*. Cambridge: The MIT Press.

Creed, Barbara. 1986. Horror and the monstrous-feminine: An imaginary abjection. *Screen* 27: 44–71. [CrossRef]

Dinello, Dan. 2013. Techno-totalitarianism in Alien. In *The Culture and Philosophy of Ridley Scott*. Edited by Adam Barkman, Nancy Kang and Ashley Barkman. Plymouth: Lexington Books, pp. 193–200.

Doherty, Thomas. 2015. Genre, gender, and the Aliens trilogy. In *Gender and the Horror Film*. Edited by Barry Keith Grant. Austin: University of Texas Press, pp. 209–27.

Dovey, Jon, and Helen Kennedy. 2006. *Game Cultures: Computer Games as New Media*. Berkshire: Open University Press.

Dyer-Witheford, Nick, and Greig de Peuter. 2009. *Games of Empire: Global Capitalism and Video Games*. Minneapolis: University of Minnesota Press.

Freedman, Barbara. 1991. *Staging the Gaze: Postmodernism, Psychoanalysis, and Shakespearean Comedy*. Ithaca: Cornell University Press.

Giddings, Seth, and Helen Kennedy. 2008. Little Jesuses and fuck-off robots: On aesthetics, cybernetics and not being very good at Lego Star Wars. In *The Pleasures of Computer Gaming*. Edited by Melanie Swalwell and Jason Wilson. Jefferson: McFarland, pp. 13–32.

Gies, Arthur. 2013. Aliens: Colonial Marines Review: The worst species. *Polygon*. February 12. Available online: https://www.polygon.com/2013/2/12/3978652/aliens-colonial-marines-review-the-worse-species (accessed on 2 July 2018).

Greven, David. 2011. *Representations of Femininity in American Genre Cinema*. New York: Palgrave Macmillan.

Harper, Todd. 2014. *The Culture of Digital Fighting Games: Performance and Practice*. New York: Routledge.

Jayemanne, Darshana. 2005. The nip and the bite. Paper presented at the the 2005 DiGRA International Conference, Vancouver, BC, Canada, June 16–20; pp. 1–10.

Jayemanne, Darshana. 2017. *Performativity in Art, Literature and Videogames*. New York: Palgrave Macmillan.

Kavanaugh, James H. 1980. "Son of a Bitch": Feminism, humanism, and science in "Alien". *October* 13: 90–100. [CrossRef]

Keogh, Brendan. 2015. Hackers and cyborgs: Binary Domain and two formative videogame technicities. Paper presented at the 2015 DiGRA International Conference, Luneburg, Germany, May 14–17; pp. 1–15.

Keogh, Brendan. 2018. *A Play of Bodies: How We Perceive Videogames*. Cambridge: MIT Press.

Kirkpatrick, Graeme. 2012. Tensions of gaming's field: UL gaming magazines and the formation of gaming culture 1981–1995. *Game Studies* 12.

Kristeva, Julia. 1982. *Powers of Horror*. New York: Columbia University Press.

Lister, Martin, Jon Dovey, Seth Giddings, Iain Grant, and Kieran Kelly. 2009. *New Media: A Critical Introduction*, 2nd ed. New York: Routledge.

Machkovech, Sam. 2018. A Years-Old, One Letter Typo Led to *Aliens: Colonial Marines'* Weird AI. *Wired Magazine*. Available online: https://arstechnica.com/gaming/2018/07/a-years-old-one-letter-typo-led-to-aliens-colonial-marines-awful-ai/ (accessed on 2 July 2018).

Milner, Ryan. 2013. Hacking the social: Internet memes, identity antagonism, and the logic of lulz. *Fibreculture* 22: 62–92.

Mulvey, Laura. 1975. Visual Pleasures and narrative cinema. *Screen* 16: 6–18. [CrossRef]

Shaviro, Steven. 1993. *The Cinematic Body*. Minneapolis: University of Minnesota Press.

Shaviro, Steven. 2010. *Post Cinematic Affect*. Winchester: Zer0 Books.

Shaw, Adrienne. 2014. *Gaming at the Edge: Sexuality and Gender at the Margins of Gamer Culture*. Minneapolis: University of Minnesota Press.

Sloan, Robin. 2016. Homesick for the Unheimlich: Back to the uncanny future in *Alien: Isolation*. *Journal of Gaming and Virtual Worlds* 8: 211–30. [CrossRef]

Thompson, Tommy. 2017. The Perfect Organism: The AI of *Alien:Isolation*. Gamasutra. Available online: https://gamasutra.com/blogs/TommyThompson/20171031/308027/The_Perfect_Organism_The_AI_of_Alien_Isolation.php (accessed on 2 July 2018).

Tomas, David. 1989. The technophilic body: On technicity in William Gibson's cyborg culture. *New Formations* 8: 113–129.

Wajcman, Judy. 1991. *Feminism Confronts Technology*. Pennsylvania: Pennsylvania State University Press.

Weise, Matthew, and Henry Jenkins. 2009. Short controlled bursts: Affect and Aliens. *Cinema Journal* 48: 111–16. [CrossRef]

Willemen, P. 1980. Letter to John. *Screen* 21: 53–66. [CrossRef]

arts
MDPI

Article

Walter Benjamin on the Video Screen: Storytelling and Game Narratives

Carly A. Kocurek

Department of Humanities, Illinois Institute of Technology, Siegel Hall, 3301 South Dearborn, Suite 218, Chicago, IL 60616, USA; ckocurek@iit.edu; Tel.: +1-(312)-567-3474

Received: 29 June 2018; Accepted: 19 October 2018; Published: 23 October 2018

Abstract: Walter Benjamin's 1936 essay, "The Storyteller" (2006) defines storytelling as a mode of communication that is defined in part by its ability to offer listeners "counsel", or meaningful wisdom or advice. This article considers the earmarks of storytelling as defined by Benjamin and by contemporary writer Larry McMurtry and argues this type of narrative experience can be offered via interactive media and, in particular, video games. After identifying the key characteristics of storytelling as set forth by Benjamin, the article proposes and advocates for a set of key characteristics of video game storytelling. In doing so, the article argues that effective narrative immersion can offer what Benjamin calls counsel, or wisdom, by refusing to provide pat answers or neat conclusions and suggests these as strategies for game writers and developers who want to provide educational or transformative experiences. Throughout, the article invokes historic and contemporary video games, asking for careful consideration of the ways in which games focused on sometimes highly personal narratives rely on storytelling techniques that instruct and transform and that can provide a rich framework for the design and writing of narrative games.

Keywords: storytelling; narrative theory; empathy games; Walter Benjamin; interactive storytelling; transmedia; Larry McMurtry; video games

1. Introduction

> In every case the storyteller is a man who has counsel for his readers. But if today 'having counsel' is beginning to have an old-fashioned ring to it is because the communicability of experience is decreasing.
>
> Benjamin (2006)

In Larry McMurtry's quasi-memoir *Walter Benjamin at the Dairy Queen*, the iconic Texas writer ruminates on the Texas he has lived and the one he has recounted for his readers, a landscape that is at turns both intoxicating and brutal. The book begins with McMurtry's own reading of Walter Benjamin's "The Storyteller" in his hometown Dairy Queen in Archer City, Texas (McMurtry 1999). In the essay, quoted above, Benjamin mourns the decline of storytelling in the period leading up to the first World War; McMurtry maps a similar fading during his own lifetime as Texas has shifted from a state of small towns to one of bustling global cities. Both Benjamin's essay and McMurtry's book are driven in part by a sense of nostalgia, the belief that something has been lost, which is unlikely to be recovered. However, in claiming personal experience of Benjamin-style storytelling, McMurtry is also offering a corrective: After all, Benjamin's piece first appeared in print in 1936, the year of McMurtry's birth, which means that the decline McMurtry notes comes decades after the one that Benjamin laments.

I begin with Benjamin and McMurtry not to take issue with either of their works, but rather to introduce a broader argument about the power and potential of a certain type of storytelling. This argument emanates from Benjamin's "The Storyteller", but draws, too, on McMurtry's relatively modern invocation. After all, if McMurtry can find evidence of this endangered, yet deeply satisfying style of storytelling in the late 1960s, so might we find more recent evidence in our own places and practices. In this article, I consider the earmarks of storytelling as defined by Benjamin and McMurtry and argue this type of narrative experience can be offered via interactive media and, in particular, video games. In doing so, I ultimately suggest that effective narrative immersion can offer what Benjamin calls counsel, or wisdom, by refusing to provide pat answers or neat conclusions. This type of storytelling is not, as I frame it, dependent on the technological wizardry that drives many games, but rather on a careful engagement of the audience through the deliberate construction of meaningful narrative. Its ultimate goal is a kind of transformative experience, one by which profound types of experiences and knowledge—counsel—are imparted to audience members.

I turn now to a consideration of Benjamin's definition of storytelling in a wider context of play theory and narrative theory (Callois 2006; Huizinga 1971; Juul 2005; Ryan 2001). Play, as I invoke it here, occupies an uneasy space between the real and the fictional and is deeply enmeshed with narrative strategies. Using this context, I consider the work of recent independent games. The games selected here tend to deal with emotional and/or highly personal experience as a primary concern. For example, in *Depression Quest* (Independent, 2013), the player takes the role of a depressed young adult, attempting to navigate a life in which choices are steadily eliminated by worsening symptoms. Through this, the game attempts to model the experience of depression for players who may not have the kind of first-hand experience the game draws from. Richard Hofmeier's *Cart Life* (Independent, 2011) uses time and resource management mechanics to force players to confront the difficulty and stress of operating a small food or coffee cart. These games, and others like them, aspire to convey or form shared experiences and produce deep emotional responses; they move by providing familiarity with the stories and experiences of other. In this, they resonate with Walter Benjamin's longing for storytelling as a means of conveying what he calls counsel or wisdom. I focus on these kinds of games because they are distinctly invested in the acquisition and circulation of experiential knowledge, a type of knowledge that seems particularly difficult to quantify or to convey through designed experiences. However, Benjamin holds, and McMurtry reiterates, that proper storytelling does just this; I forward that well-designed narrative games, games invested in personal stories (or at least, stories that seem personal) and experiential knowledge, too, can achieve this.

In this article, I outline a rubric for crafting successful storytelling games broadly defined; because storytelling structures are used across game forms and genres, I draw examples from a diversity of styles of game design and production. Utilizing methods proposed by theorists including Stuart Hall, Antonio Gramsci, Chantal Mouffe, and other experts in articulation theory, first, I review Benjamin's definition of storytelling and show examples of how his key characteristics are evident in narrative media forms; then, I turn to the use of narrative in games before discussing how Benjamin's style of storytelling might be evidenced in games and why this might be useful (Grossberg 1986; Mouffe 1979). Ultimately, I propose a list of key characteristics for storytelling games that could be used by developers, arguing that this approach could be used as a framework for effective transformative games.

2. Storytelling Things

The value of information does not survive the moment in which it was new. It lives only at that moment; it has to surrender to it completely and explain itself to it without losing any time. A story is different. It does not expend itself.

Benjamin (2006)

The storyteller, as Benjamin defines him, is part historian, part performer, part fabulist. Storytellers pass on local scandals and lore, but they do not provide information; rather, they transform facts into meaningful, engaging narratives. To tell a story, then, is not merely to tell what happened but to offer a means of making sense of it. Stories, for Benjamin, demand interpretation while information refuses it. Some key characteristics of a storyteller, as carefully defined by Benjamin, are shown in Table 1.

What becomes apparent in listing these characteristics is that storytelling is a craft, a creative art, and an idiosyncratic instructional strategy; we are entertained by storytellers, we admire their artistry, but we also learn from them and from the lived experiences they convey. In this way, the most skillful storytellers are not unlike the most skilled game designers, and there is a meaningful overlap between storytelling and play. Storytelling, as Benjamin describes it, is fanciful in that it is less interested in factual information and explanations than it is in the imparting of wisdom, morals, and deeper truths; in this way, it is a bit like the documentaries of filmmaker Werner Herzog, who introduces visually compelling and fabricated metaphor to his ostensible nonfiction, as in *Little Dieter Needs to Fly*, where he shows the titular character locking and unlocking doors to emphasize the lingering effects of his previous imprisonment. Storytelling is also fanciful because it is, in most cases, both improvisational and playful. As envisioned by both Benjamin and McMurtry, storytelling is a kind of performance, but it is also a kind of play, not in the sense of a theatrical performance, although it can be this, but in the sense of the types of fiction-driven games described by Roger Callois. There are games, according to Callois, "which presuppose free improvisation, and the chief attraction of which lies in the pleasure of playing a role, of acting *as if* one were someone or something else, a machine for example" (Callois 2006; Juul 2005). In these, the fiction, the acting *as if*, takes the role of a rule set. Storytelling has its own rules and principles. Benjamin identifies some of them, but I would highlight that the guidelines Benjamin lays out require their own acting *as if*. Those listening to a storyteller often accept that the tale they are told may be nonfactual even as it is true; these inaccuracies are accepted in the service of the broader narrative point. Further, in engaging with the storyteller, the audience necessarily enters a state of suspended disbelief, which is a prerequisite of immersion and of truly experiencing the work of a storyteller.

Table 1. Benjamin's key characteristics of storytellers.

Benjamin's Key Characteristics of Storytellers
Relies on experiential knowledge, both his own and that of others
Tends toward useful knowledge in the form of morals, practical advice, or proverbs or maxims
Connects to oral tradition—either looking backward to it or goes forward into it
Refuses to explain stories in their telling
Leaves his own imprint on his stories, is artisanal in his form of communication
Shares companionship with audience by providing a place for audience members to recognize themselves and feel less alone
Uses hands for storytelling in a skillful way, as "storytelling … is by no means a job for the voice alone"
Engages an audience

The storyteller may break this suspension through ineptitude or they may subtly adjust their tale to lure the audience back. Storytellers may alter their performance to best engage their current audience or insert humor as a hook. They may draw on their knowledge of audience members to tease and cajole. These interactions with the audience provide a type of multisensory experience and heighten immersion; audience members don't just listen to a storyteller, they also watch them, and may find themselves engaged in prompted callbacks.

The storyteller is not a lecturer or a finger-wagger; they provide a framework in which people may learn for themselves. The storyteller draws audiences into moral instruction. Stories are often parables or warnings, imparting fairytale knowledge or practical reminders. Many of us know these lessons from fairy tales—it is easy, after all, to get lost or injured in the woods alone after dark, and such folly can end in humiliation as easily as physical harm—or from fables—the tortoise's steady pace is more successful if less glamorous than the rabbit's. These lessons are old, sometimes ancient, but they are easier to learn with a thrill or a laugh than they are through nagging reminders. In providing a fanciful framework for imparting necessary knowledge, too, the storyteller is playful. Play is well documented as a means through which children develop and learn (Broadhead et al. 2010; Cook 2000; Elkind 2007; Singer et al. 2006). In addition, it is also key for adults' well-being and satisfaction

(Proyer 2013; Magnuson and Barnett 2013). Play is not only an action, but an approach to the world, a means of interacting.

Fables, and storytelling too, as described by Benjamin, provide a means of inviting audience members to participate in their own education, since they require interpretation and application. Research suggests that storytelling can play a key role in education in a diversity of subjects (Brown 1997; Rodgers 1980; Short and Ketchen 2005; Whyte 1995). Again, these types of stories are rarely explained directly, but rather impart knowledge indirectly by providing the audience with a story to mull over and make sense of.

Storytelling is a kind of fiction game as described by Callois, not only because a fiction is relayed, but also because the audience is asked if not to *act* as if, at least to *imagine* as if. Imagine as if the story is factual or real even when it defies other known information; imagine as if you are one of the characters in the story. What might you have done differently? How will you, in future, avoid the fate of some unfortunate? I reference Callois here in part to move this discussion towards games, but also because Callois' elastic definition of games and of play allows room for considering as playful many types of social interactions and narrative forms. As Johan Huizinga implies and Callois makes explicit, rules generate their own kinds of fictions as well. These rule-based fictions are, in the words of Jesper Juul, half-real in that their rules are treated as real even as they are effectively laid over a fabricated reality (Juul 2005).

The storyteller Benjamin describes is one who, like the designers of the games Juul references, creates a half-real place, one governed by real rules even as it creates a fictionalized reality that can deliver greater truths. While expressing his distaste for novels as lacking in counsel, Benjamin allows that stories of the kind propagated by storytellers can be written down; in this, he suggests that storytelling can be mediated and that, in the absence of a human storyteller, the story can be carried forward by other recorded means. There is a danger in this, however; while some such efforts retain the story's punch and purpose, others effectively sanitize the story, closing down its possibilities and robbing it of counsel. In transitioning to a consideration of mediated stories, I would like to turn to the idea of storytelling things, or, more specifically, storytelling games.

3. Storytelling Games

> The more self-forgetful the listener is, the more deeply is what he listens to impressed upon his memory.
>
> Benjamin (2006)

The audience member's willingness to suspend their sense of self and their own sense of the world makes it easier for them to remember the lessons imparted in the story and to place themselves in the narrative. This is a fundamental requirement for immersion; it is also a reminder that audience members are often making choices of their own—they are choosing to go along with the story, to forget themselves. The person listening to a Benjamin-style storyteller is an active participant. Researchers like Zunshine (2006) and Vermeule (2009) have shown the similarities in how we process and interpret real and fictional events; we become immersed in stories much as we become immersed in our own daily lives. This type of immersion, this possibility of forgetting the self, of finding ourselves in the experiences of others, is why games are so well suited to storytelling. It is also why one of the key questions raised in the arena of serious and learning games over the past few decades has been the question of whether or not games can teach, and if so, what they can teach. James Paul Gee, for example, has called games "learning machines", and numerous other scholars have argued for the application of games as educational tools (Gee 2003; Mayo 2007; McGonigal 2011; Prensky 2006; Rieber 1996; Shaffer et al. 2005). More recent work, often undertaken by scholars working in learning science, has shifted from the question of whether games can be educational and moved into more specific questions about efficacy and design (Schrier 2016; Trujillo et al. 2016).

Callois (2006) argues that play requires consent. It is an opting in; forced play ceases to be play and becomes something else. While learning games are often, to their detriment, made compulsory, as in the case of games used to train employees, the appeal and true potential of learning games and most serious games lies in the possibility that players will choose them of their own accord (deWinter et al. 2014). In this, too, they echo Benjamin's storytelling. After all, children submit to lectures, but beg to hear stories. Stories offer an immersive experience, while often lectures provide only a pedantic one. Immersion and voluntary participation are not explicated as such in either Benjamin's original essay or McMurtry's later revisiting of it, but they are implied in the key characteristics of a storyteller that Benjamin identifies. The storyteller is a performer who draws the audience in.

In this way, Benjamin's proposed storyteller is again somewhat like a gamemaster. His storytelling draws people in, immersing them in the world and lessons of the tale to be told. As Marie-Laure Ryan points out, advocates of virtual reality frequently tout the possibilities for immersion; however, peculiarly, in doing so they frequently summon the metaphor of a literary text (Ryan 2001). To be immersed in a virtual reality is similar to being immersed in a good book. The world presented is not necessarily real, but real enough. Similarly, the world of a story is real enough, a frame in which we are willing to act as if. Ryan ultimately argues that narrative is itself a kind of virtual reality. So, too, are stories. But, in all cases, for these virtual realities to be effective, they have to provide an experience of immersion. There are well-known enemies to immersion—games that are too easy or too difficult readily lose players who grow bored or frustrated and many games require strenuous effort from players wishing to occupy the fictional world (Linderoth 2012). Ultimately, I suggest that Benjamin's storytelling model offers a potentially powerful model for the development of effective storytelling games that offer players not just information, but counsel—and, because of this, Benjamin's classic essay is a useful resource for game designers and writers who strive to produce meaningful experiences in new media.

4. Putting Benjamin on Screen

It has seldom been realized that the listener's naive relationship to the storyteller is controlled by his interest in retaining what he is told.

Benjamin (2006)

In this section, I turn to an examination of how principles from Benjamin's essay can be useful if adapted and applied by writers and developers to produce meaningful narrative games; to do this, I continue to draw on research on the educational uses of games and on strategies for providing moral and experiential education. While some of these strategies are designed for the classroom, I suggest they, like Benjamin's fundamentals, are good models for what might be possible in thoughtfully designed narrative games. Both advocates and critics of video games often assume that games offer a richer, more powerful, and more seductive form of storytelling. This can be seen as a danger, as in efforts to regulate violent video games, or as an opportunity, as in the advocacy for the adoption of educational games. This shared assumption is backed up by some research, although the range of games that serve as effective learning tools is much narrower than the range of games that are touted as effective learning tools. This may owe in part to the conditions under which these games are deployed. The success of the early computer game *The Oregon Trail* (Minnesota Educational Computing Consortium, 1974; see Figure 1) as both a widely circulated educational tool and popular obsession provides a tantalizing example of what might be possible. The game ultimately sold some 65 million copies and taught, at the very least, that those westbound along the original Oregon Trail of westward expansion faced significant hardships (Campbell 2013b). However, while games like *The Oregon Trail* offer skills and, to some extent, knowledge, I would argue that they fail to offer counsel. However, this does not mean that games cannot do so, only that these particular games do not. Research on curriculum development for English language arts classes suggests the possibility. Ryan et al. (2002) suggest thoughtful curriculum can provide teachers and students with opportunities to not only cover the required subjects, but to also provide character education and reflection on moral values; Mantle-Bromley and Foster (2005) argue that language arts teachers are uniquely positioned to provide education on matters of democracy and social justice because of the importance of literacy and storytelling in building an understanding of the broader world.

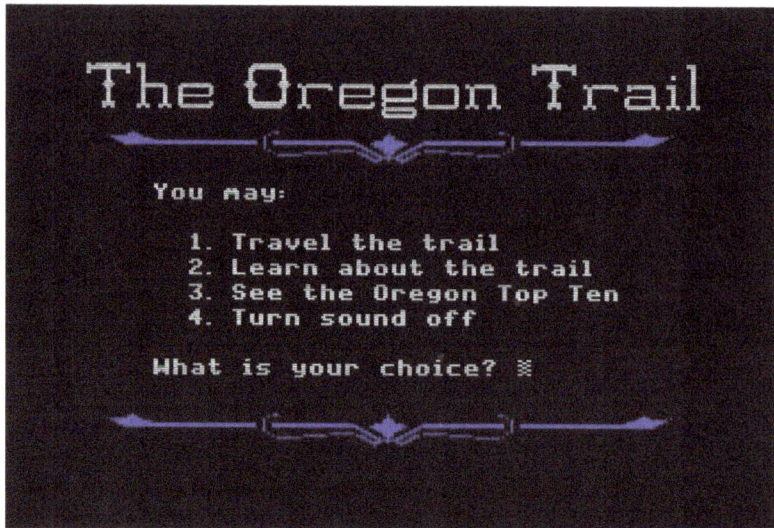

Figure 1. This screen capture from *The Oregon Trail* shows the game's simple interface.

One of the promises of effective game design has been the idea that games can provide experiential knowledge; this echoes Benjamin's assertion that true storytellers draw on the well of experience. The use of simulators for training in fields like flight and medicine has proven effective because they engage students in an experience that closely mirrors real surgical or flight practices while offering additional learning opportunities (Dennis and Harris 1998; Hays et al. 1992; Issenberg et al. 1999; Issenberg et al. 2005). Further, students in these areas are actively invested in learning the material; someone who has enrolled in flight school, for example, clearly wants to learn to fly a plane and so is more likely to retain information from a flight simulation than someone who has not demonstrated such interest. *The Oregon Trail* is a kind of simulator; you, too, can die of dysentery and hunt squirrels in a pixilated wild west. In this, the game teaches the dangers of disease and difficulties of resource management that plagued pioneers. This is a lesson of a kind. Typing games and the numerous games that quiz children on times tables and subtraction problems are also offering lessons, even as many function as glorified flashcards intercut with games.

However, the most effective games are often those built around rich stories, and educational research backs up Benjamin's assertion that storytelling is an effective pedagogical tool. This is no surprise: Studies suggest, for example, that readers of narrative fiction and viewers of television of drama are more empathetic (Black and Barnes 2015). Problem solving is also key to mediated learning experiences. In one study, Bransford et al. (1989) note that the most effective efforts to encourage learners to access relevant knowledge involved "problem-oriented acquisition experiences". These processes presented students with problems to solve rather than lists of facts, what Benjamin might have dismissed as information. The students who solved problems proved better at accessing and applying relevant information. Games, both those that are deliberately educational and those that exist for reasons more of entertainment or art, can be an excellent medium for providing problems to solve. Game mechanics like resource management, trading, role playing, territorial acquisition, and others can all offer compelling problems for players to tackle. What players can gain from solving these types of problems varies widely; most games aspire to at least provide some brief amusement, but others can immerse players in long-running campaigns or rich storyworlds (Long 2016). I would argue that this problem-solving function is a key component both for Benjamin's idealized storyteller—who offers truths without explanation and avoids dispensing information—and for effective games.

Games invested in biographical, historical, or sociological events can present particularly nettlesome problems. The pen-and-paper role-playing game *Dog Eat Dog* (Liwanag Press, 2013) pits the majority of players against a single player as they are cast respectively as the colonized population and colonizing force. In *Papers, Please* (3309 LLC, 2013), the player works as an immigration officer who must decide which immigrants to admit and deny. *Reigns: Her Majesty* explicitly grapples with the extent to which powerful women are often seen as wives more than leaders and, therefore, have to wield power quite differently (Devolver Digital, 2017). Games like these model complex cultural and political problems with a profound human toll. The player faced with addressing these is asked to consider not only their complexity, but their emotional weight. The play of these games can be deeply uncomfortable—in *Dog Eat Dog* one of the players' first tasks is to identify the wealthiest player and cast him as the colonizer—but they also engage players in the workings of a fictionalized representation of a difficult reality while frequently refusing to tell players what to make of those difficulties. In short, they demand that players solve problems, they provide experiential knowledge and, at least potentially, counsel, about complicated social and cultural issues even while engaging and entertaining players.

Benjamin's evocation of storytelling suggests that storytellers can do much the same, and this is why "The Storyteller" can be seen as a useful reference and model for writers and developers interested in the types of counsel, of wisdom, of moral education that games might be able to offer, whether explicitly framed as educational games or not. Benjamin's characteristics of a storyteller can be adapted to describe the characteristics of a storytelling game. In Table 2, I propose a list of key characteristics of effective storytelling games.

Table 2. A possible adaptation of Benjamin's storytelling characteristics for the development of immersive game narratives.

Key Characteristics of Storytelling Games: Proposed Model
Draw on and provide experiential knowledge
Present useful knowledge in the form of morals, practical advice, or proverbs or maxims
Evoke oral traditions
Avoid over explanation of the stories told or their lessons
Provides an experience that is distinct from that available in other games; is artisanal in its presentation
Provides opportunities for human connection and recognition
Carefully and effectively uses multimedia
Engages an audience by providing an immersive, narrative experience that is carefully integrated with the game's rules

These characteristics allow for a broad range of idiosyncratic approaches, but they emphasize opportunities for self-reflection and exploration. These games are often lessons without answers. They make use of the affordances of interactive media while drawing on the best of older traditions and strive to provide experiential knowledge often necessary for cultivating empathy and understanding. There is a subtlety both to Benjamin-style storytelling and to the best of empathy games. They may offer multiple answers or no answers at all, leaving the solutions open to the player. A number of recent games at least aspire to offer counsel through engaging game narratives. I focus on the games mentioned here not because they are the only ones that aspire to offer the kind of rich narrative experience that this Benjamin-derived model asks for, but because they offer a particularly high number of salient examples.

These games can be at times impressionistic in refusing to offer a clear-cut resolution or lesson. In this, they mirror Benjamin's beloved stories, while deviating from industry norms that continue to celebrate good vs. evil superhero values and emphasize simple win/loss dichotomies. The most effective narrative games are often much subtler and less easily recognizable. While some potentially provocative games adhere to the standards of recognized genres—*3rd World Farmer* (Independent, 2005), for example, is a resource-management-driven farming sim—others present intimate, ambiguous tales through the medium of the game. In this, they both are artisanal in the sense of providing distinct experiences and experiential. The ambiguity of games like *I Get This Call Every Day* (Independent, 2013) does not provide players with lessons, but rather invites them to reflect and reach their own conclusions. Both *3rd World Farmer* and *I Get This Call Every Day* present complex narrative worlds even while dealing with daily realities. In *3rd World Farmer*, the player is tasked with maintaining a small family farm in the face of harsh weather, disease, militant uprisings, theft, and political corruption; the impact of these factors on the farm and the family that lives there is relayed through orderly charts that summarize the underlying horrors. Crops fail. The money runs out. Family members die. *I Get This Call Every Day* is focused on the developer's experience working in a call center (see Figure 2). The calls presented were fabricated and scripted, but the fictionalized call center was so believable that the developer was fired from his job, in part because of allegations that he was relaying real calls (Campbell 2013a).

Figure 2. The opening screen for *I Get This Call Every Day* places the player in a first-person perspective at a call desk.

Depression Quest, like many games that explore lived human experiences, is focused on a particular hardship. In it, the player assumes the role of a depressed twentysomething. The game offers players frustration, recognition, and reassurance. If the player makes choices that help the character to improve their life, more pleasant options and scenarios emerge. If the players' choices result in the character's options becoming more limited, those unavailable options will be shown struck through in red (see Figure 3). The game has a soundtrack of faint atmospheric music in a minor key. As the character becomes more depressed, the images embedded in the game become more and more obscured by static; if the character becomes less depressed, the images grow clearer. Through these mechanics and through stylistic and narrative choices, the game seeks to provide a bit of experiential knowledge of depression for players. When the game was released, blog posts and articles often recounted the extent to which players used the game to recognize depression in themselves or work out a path towards treatment (Klepek 2015).

You have to be awake for work in a mere 8 hours, and you know that your work is so much worse on only a few hours sleep.

What do you do?

1: Force yourself to sleep.
2: Go to bed. It shouldn't be that hard.
3: Just close your eyes and let it happen. Why won't your thoughts back off for five seconds?
4: Snap out of it. What is wrong with you? Why can't you stop stressing out for five seconds?
5: You're probably going to go into work tomorrow exhausted and fuck everything up and get fired.
6: Go to your computer. Sleep is clearly not happening no matter how long you lay here.

Depression Quest

an interactive (non)fiction about living with depression

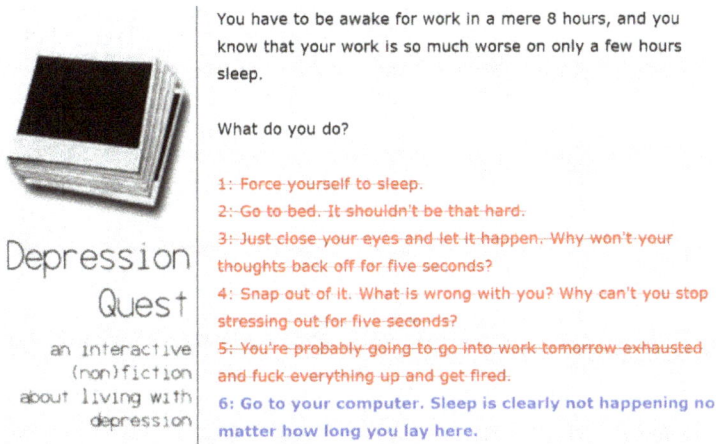

Figure 3. *Depression Quest* steadily eliminates options as the game unfolds.

Some research on games shows they can be effective at fostering empathy (Flanagan et al. 2008; Greitemeyer et al. 2010). In doing so, the most effective of these games may include facts without focusing on them, concentrating instead on immersive game play that invites players to experience feelings. In this way, at their best, they—like Benjamin-type storytelling—require reflection and invite the audience to make their own sense of the experience. They also provide seemingly personalized experiences, sometimes exposing the designer or developer in the process. If players of *Depression Quest* recognize themselves in the game's struggling protagonist, they are also recognizing the life experience of developer Zoe Quinn, who has been open about the high extent to which the game is autobiographical. There are morals and fables to be learned from games, even in those that refuse to provide clear answers. Too often, educational games provide rote information or pedantic definitives. Some of the best narrative games relay experiences by putting the player in another person's situation and inviting the players to make their own conclusions. They provide a framework in which the player can understand their world differently.

Syrian Journey: Choose Your Own Escape Route (2015), distributed by the BBC, challenges players to make the "right" decisions as they flee as refugees from Syria. In Richard Hofmeier's *Cart Life*, the player is shoved into the brutalities of trying to run a small retail business while maintaining a life and receives an at times grueling lesson in the realities of life under late model capitalism. Both of these games present realities through graphic styles that are easily identifiable. They have a distinct aesthetic and feel deeply personal. There is a real intimacy to the experiences these games provide, in part because they invite players to consider what someone else's life is like. They tell stories through immersive, mediated experiences. At both their most reassuring and their grimmest, these games provide opportunities for human connection, for making people feel less alone as they plunge into stories that provide a flash of recognition. In this, perhaps they offer counsel, wisdom, the kind of moral education that so much relies upon.

5. Conclusions

I return now to my original focus on Benjamin, on McMurtry, on that Dairy Queen along a dusty highway in Archer City. The promise of storytelling, as Benjamin and McMurtry view it, is powerful; it is a tool for forming communities and establishing networks, for making brutal places less so, for preserving folklore and tradition, for providing a sense of place and comfort. Discussion of the possibilities of innovative, immersive, experimental games often focuses on their potential instrumentality, and at points games may be effective in this way, in teaching division or geography to grade schoolers or helping adults to prepare for job tasks. But games like these often fail to be playful. They also fall short of the deeper potential of games as an immersive storytelling medium that could help us to explore values, wisdom, and our own inner lives. This is not a call to value one kind of games over another, but rather it is a call to think of games as part of a broader cultural web of storytelling; to look back to oral traditions and practices of community as a source not only of abstract inspiration, but concrete practice. We learn from one another, but we also learn from play, as do most intelligent animals. This is why are impressed when cephalopods and dolphins make toys from the items in their tanks or grackles roll down the windshields of snow-covered cars. It is also why, in thinking about developing serious games or meaningful games or learning games or any games at all, we should think broadly, not just about the information they might impart, but the experiences and wisdom they can provide.

Funding: This research received no external funding.

Conflicts of Interest: The author declares no conflict of interest.

References

Benjamin, Walter. 2006. The Storyteller. In *The Novel: An Anthology of Criticism and Theory 1900–2000*. Edited by Dorothy J. Hale. Malden: Blackwell Publishing, pp. 361–78.

Black, Jessica, and Jennifer L. Barnes. 2015. Fiction and Social Cognition: The Effect of Viewing Award-Winning Television Dramas on Theory of Mind. *Psychology of Aesthetics Creativity and the Arts* 9: 423. [CrossRef]

Bransford, John D., Jeffrey J. Franks, Nancy J. Vye, and Robert D. Sherwood. 1989. New Approaches to Instruction: Because Wisdom Can't Be Told. In *Similarity and Analogical Reasoning*. Edited by Stella Vosniadou and Andrew Ortony. Cambridge: Cambridge University Press, pp. 470–97.

Broadhead, Pat, Justine Howard, and Elizabeth Wood, eds. 2010. *Play and Learning in the Early Years*. London: SAGE Publications.

Brown, Gillian. 1997. Fables and the Forming of Americans. *MFS Modern Fiction Studies* 43: 115–41. [CrossRef]

Callois, Roger. 2006. The Definition of Play and the Classification of Games. In *The Game Design Reader: A Rules of Play Anthology*. Edited by Katie Salen and Eric Zimmerman. Cambridge: MIT Press, pp. 122–55.

Campbell, Collin. 2013a. Fired For Making A Game: The Inside Story of I Get This Call Every Day. *Polygon*. March 7. Available online: http://www.polygon.com/features/2013/3/7/4071136/he-got-fired-for-making-a-game-i-get-this-call (accessed on 19 February 2015).

Campbell, Collin. 2013b. The Oregon Trail Was Made in Just Two Weeks. *Polygon*. July 31. Available online: http://www.polygon.com/2013/7/31/4575810/the-oregon-trail-was-made-in-just-two-weeks (accessed on 18 February 2015).

Cook, Guy. 2000. *Language Play, Language Learning*. London: Oxford University Press.

Dennis, Kerry A., and Don Harris. 1998. Computer-based simulation as an adjunct to ab initio flight training. *The International Journal of Aviation Psychology* 8: 261–76. [CrossRef]

deWinter, Jennifer, Carly A. Kocurek, and Randall Nichols. 2014. Taylorism 2.0: Gamification, Scientific Management and the Capitalist Appropriation of Play. *The Journal of Gaming and Virtual Worlds* 6: 109–27. [CrossRef]

Elkind, David. 2007. *The Power of Play: Learning What Comes Naturally*. New York: Da Capo Press.

Flanagan, Mary, Daniel Howe, and Helen Nissenbaum. 2008. Embodying values in technology: Theory and practice. *Information Technology and Moral Philosophy*, 322–53. [CrossRef]

Gee, James Paul. 2003. What video games have to teach us about learning and literacy. *Computers in Entertainment (CIE)* 1: 20–22. [CrossRef]

Greitemeyer, Tobias, Silvia Osswald, and Markus Brauer. 2010. Playing Prosocial Video Games Increases Empathy and Decreases Schadenfreude. *Emotion* 10: 796–802. [CrossRef] [PubMed]

Grossberg, Lawrence. 1986. On postmodernism and articulation: An interview with Stuart Hall. *Journal of Communication Inquiry* 10: 45–60. [CrossRef]

Hays, Robert T., John W. Jacobs, Carolyn Prince, and Eduardo Salas. 1992. Flight Simulator Training Effectiveness: A Meta-analysis. *Military Psychology* 4: 63–74. [CrossRef]

Huizinga, Johan. 1971. *Homo Ludens: A Study of the Play Element in Culture*. Boston: Beacon Press.

Issenberg, S. Barry, William C. McGaghie, Ian R. Hart, Joan W. Mayer, Joel M. Felner, Emil R. Petrusa, Robert A. Waugh, Donald D. Brown, Robert R. Safford, Ira H. Gessner, and et al. 1999. Simulation Technology for Health Care Professional Skills Training and Assessment. *JAMA* 282: 861–66. [CrossRef] [PubMed]

Issenberg, S. Barry, William C. Mcgaghie, Emil R. Petrusa, David Lee Gordon, and Ross J. Scalese. 2005. Features and Uses of High-fidelity Medical Simulations That Lead to Effective Learning: A BEME Systematic Review. *Medical Teacher* 27: 10–28. [CrossRef] [PubMed]

Juul, Jesper. 2005. *Half-Real: Video Games between Real Rules and Fictional Worlds*. Cambridge: The MIT Press.

Klepek, Patrick. 2015. They Made a Game That Understands Me. *Giant Bomb*. April 10. Available online: http://www.giantbomb.com/articles/they-made-a-game-that-understands-me/1100-4619/ (accessed on 19 February 2015).

Linderoth, Jonas. 2012. The Effort of Being in a Fictional World: Upkeyings and Laminated Frames in MMORPGs. *Symbolic Interaction* 35: 474–92. [CrossRef]

Long, Geoffrey. 2016. Creating Worlds in Which to Play: Using Transmedia Aesthetics to Grow Stories into Storyworlds. In *The Rise of Transtexts: Challenges and Opportunities*. Edited by Benjamin W. L. Derhy Kurtz and Mélanie Bourdaa. New York: Routledge, pp. 139–52.

Magnuson, Cale D., and Lynn A. Barnett. 2013. The Playful Advantage: How Playfulness Enhances Coping with Stress. *Leisure Studies* 35: 129–44. [CrossRef]

Mantle-Bromley, Corinne, and Ann M. Foster. 2005. Educating for Democracy: The Vital Role of the Language Arts Teacher. *The English Journal* 94: 70–74. [CrossRef]

Mayo, Merrilea J. 2007. Games for Science and Engineering Education. *Communications of the ACM* 50: 30–35. [CrossRef]

McGonigal, Jane. 2011. *Reality is Broken: Why Games Make Us Better and How They Can Change the World*. London: Penguin.

McMurtry, Larry. 1999. *Walter Benjamin at the Dairy Queen: Reflections at Sixty and Beyond*. New York: Touchstone.

Mouffe, Chantal, ed. 1979. Hegemony and Ideology in Gramsci. In *Gramsci and Marxist Theory*. London: Routledge, pp. 168–204.

Prensky, Marc. 2006. *Don't Bother Me, Mom, I'm Learning! How Computer and Video Games Are Preparing Your Kids for 21st Century Success and How You Can Help!* New York: Paragon House.

Proyer, René T. 2013. The Well-being of Playful Adults: Adult Playfulness, Subjective Well-being, Physical Well-being, and the Pursuit of Enjoyable Activities. *European Journal of Humour* 1: 84–98. [CrossRef]

Rieber, Lloyd P. 1996. Seriously Considering Play: Designing Interactive Learning Environments Based on the Blending of Microworlds, Simulations, and Games. *Educational Technology Research and Development* 44: 43–58. [CrossRef]

Rodgers, Daniel T. 1980. Socializing Middle-class Children: Institutions, Fables, and Work Values in Nineteenth-century America. *Journal of Social History* 13: 354–67. [CrossRef]

Ryan, Marie-Laure. 2001. *Narrative as Virtual Reality: Immersion and Interactivity in Literature and Electronic Media*. Baltimore: The Johns Hopkins University Press.

Ryan, Francis J., John J. Sweeder, and Maryanne R. Bednar. 2002. Character Education in the English Language Arts Classroom. *Counterpoints* 122: 91–114.

Schrier, Karen S. 2016. *Knowledge Games: How Playing Games Can Solve Problems, Create Insight, and Make Change*. Baltimore: Johns Hopkins University Press.

Shaffer, David Williamson, Richard Halverson, Kurt R. Squire, and James P. Gee. 2005. *Video Games and the Future of Learning*. WCER Working Paper No. 2005-4. Madison: Wisconsin Center for Education Research.

Short, Jeremy C., and David J. Ketchen. 2005. Teaching Timeless Truths through Classic Literature: Aesop's Fables and Strategic Management. *Journal of Management Education* 29: 816–32. [CrossRef]

Singer, Dorothy G., Roberta Michnick Golinkoff, and Kathy Hirsh-Pasek, eds. 2006. *Play = Learning: How Play Motivates and Enhances Children's Cognitive and Social-Emotional Growth*. London: Oxford University Press.

Trujillo, Karen, Barbara Chamberlin, Karin Wiburg, and Amanda Armstrong. 2016. Measurement in Learning Games Evolution: Review of Methodologies Used in Determining Effectiveness of Math Snacks Games and Animations. *Technology, Knowledge and Learning* 21: 1–20. [CrossRef]

Vermeule, Blakey. 2009. *Why Do We Care About Literary Characters?* Baltimore: Johns Hopkins University Press.

Whyte, Douglas A. 1995. Stories, Fables, and Fairy Tales as Teaching Tools. *Human Service Education: A Journal of the National Organization for Human Service Education* 15: 43–46.

Zunshine, Lisa. 2006. *Why We Read Fiction: Theory of Mind and the Novel.* Columbus: The Ohio State University Press.

Article

A Redneck Head on a Nazi Body. Subversive Ludo-Narrative Strategies in *Wolfenstein II: The New Colossus*

Hans-Joachim Backe

Center for Computer Games Research, IT University of Copenhagen, 2300 Copenhagen, Denmark; hanj@itu.dk

Received: 13 July 2018; Accepted: 19 October 2018; Published: 6 November 2018

Abstract: This article argues that *Wolfenstein: The New Colossus*, a AAA First-Person Shooter, is not only politically themed, but presents in itself a critical engagement with the politics of its genre and its player base. Developed at the height of #Gamergate, the game is interpreted as a response to reactionary discourses about gender and ability in both mainstream games and the hardcore gamer community. *The New Colossus* replaces affirmation of masculine empowerment with intersectional ambiguities, foregrounding discourses of feminism and disability. To provoke its players without completely alienating them, the game employs strategies of carnivalesque aesthetics—especially ambivalence and grotesque excess. Analyzing the game in the light of Bakhtinian theory shows how *The New Colossus* reappropriates genre conventions pertaining to able-bodiedness and masculinity and how it "resolves" these issue by grafting the player character's head on a vat-grown Nazi supersoldier-body. The breaches of genre conventions on the narrative level are supported by intentionally awkward and punishing mechanics, resulting in a ludo-narrative aesthetic of defamiliarization commensurate to a grotesque story about subversion and revolt. Echoing the ritualistic cycle of death and rebirth at the heart of carnivalesque aesthetics, *The New Colossus* is nothing short of an ideological re-invention of the genre.

Keywords: game narrative; politics; gender; ability; cyborg; defamiliarization; carnivalesque; Gamergate; Bakhtin; Haraway; AAA; FPS

1. Shooting Virtual Nazis as Entertainment and/or Politics

When Grant Tavinor wrote in 2009 that "Nazis, aliens, monsters, zombies, genetically manipulated mutants [fall] somewhat outside the purview of regular morality" (Tavinor 2009, pp. 165–66), he was very carefully establishing a baseline for "legitimate enemies" (Pötzsch and Šisler 2016, p. 14) in digital games. Since the 1980s, "fighting the good war against unequivocally evil Nazi soldiers" (Pötzsch and Šisler 2016, p. 7) has been a prevalent trope in digital games, where "the 'Good War' narrative is taken to a hyperbolic extreme" (Salvati and Bullinger 2013, p. 163). No game epitomizes this hyperbole better than *Wolfenstein 3D* (id Software 1992), which not only provided the template for the whole genre of First-Person Shooters (Wolf 2008, p. 156; Pinchbeck 2013, p. 9), but also set the bar for portrayals of fighting Nazis by eventually pitting its player character BJ Blazkowicz against a cybernetically enhanced Adolf Hitler.

Given how unquestionably the *Wolfenstein* games have always been "anti-Nazi games" (Wolf 2008, p. 209), it is poignant that the latest entry in the long-running series, *Wolfenstein II: The New Colossus* (MachineGames 2017), provoked the outrage of "Alt-Right" sympathizers. Moving beyond the by-now commonplace heated discussions on user forums and Reddit, *The New Colossus* became the target of coordinated attacks on social media (Maiberg 2017) and was review-bombed (Moseman 2017), i.e., subjected to mass-postings of strategically negative reviews to "punish" the developers. While the young Swedish developer team at MachineGames downplayed the political aspects of their product, publisher Bethesda Softworks was remarkably vocal about not only its continuing support of both the game and its developers, but also about the game's timeliness and topicality, aggressively emphasizing its political dimension (Batchelor 2017). While some commentators characterized this as nothing more than clever marketing, large parts of the games press and some independent developers expressed their support, often contextualizing the game within the increasing acceptance of Alt-Right demagogues by right wing mainstream politicians (Gaynor 2018).

Considered in the light of the political controversy surrounding it, reviews of the game show that—just like any other serious cultural product—its merit as an element of a socio-political debate and as a work of art are inextricably entangled. Doubts about the sincerity of *The New Colossus*'s anti-totalitarian message are frequently connected with aesthetic value judgments, such as that its "serious commentary seems ultimately written in service of its pulpy action" (A. Robertson 2017). This ambivalence and insecurity about *The New Colossus*'s goals and achievements are echoed where it has been considered solely on its qualities as a game. Even when going so far as to call it exemplary of what AAA games—the game industry's equivalent of a Hollywood blockbuster movie—in 2017 should be doing (Francis 2017; McKeand 2017), the praise lavished upon it bespeaks some reservations about "vexing decisions—small issues with writing, the anticlimactic pacing, over-reliance on simplistic stealth, and the unnecessary decision to pull control from the player—[which] hold Wolfenstein back from its potential status as the quintessential modern First-Person Shooter" (Brynard 2018).

The argument presented here is that the ambivalence evoked by the "vexing decisions" of *The New Colossus*'s design team is intentional, as a way of exploring "political themes and topical issues [which] rarely find their way into AAA blockbusters" (Batchelor 2017). I show how the ludic and narrative elements of the game are carefully orchestrated to make them (as MachineGames formulate their design philosophy) "pull in the same direction at the same time" (Graft 2014) to create a First-Person Shooter that critiques its legacy, its conventions, and even its players, without breaking with any of them.

The argument I present here is that *The New Colossus* is not quite "an exercise in deconstructing" (Evans-Thirlwell 2017) its characters and its generic roots, but rather one of defamiliarizing them.[1] *The New Colossus* takes the treatment of World War II and Nazi ideology from the camp of its predecessors (Wolf 2008, p. 156) to an aesthetic of the "grotesque, cathartic, beautiful, horrible and shocking" (Smith 2017), or, more precisely, the carnivalesque in the sense of Mikhail Bakhtin. Following earlier studies into the use of the carnivalesque as an aesthetics of defamiliarization in digital games (Klevjer 2006; Majkowski 2014), I show how MachineGames reappropriate the genre conventions of First-Person Shooters (e.g., a white male protagonist killing hundreds of literally faceless enemies) by deconstructing and reconstructing them: the masculinity, whiteness, and able-bodiedness of the player character are problematized and reframed in the light of contemporary sensibilities about gender, race, and ability. Similar to the pre-modern tradition of the carnival, *The New Colossus* calls its own (generic and societal) foundations into question through provocation, grotesquery, and inversal, not staging a coup or revolution, but fulfilling a necessary function as both an outlet for dissatisfaction and a stimulation of discussions. In analogy to the carnival's imaginary, which centers upon the ritualistic cycle of death and rebirth (Bakhtin 1984, p. 164), *The New Colossus* sets in scene the symbolic death and—importantly—rebirth of First-Person Shooter (in the following: FPS) conventions as something

---

[1]   I opt for the term defamiliarization instead of the closely related terms alienation and e(n)strangement because each of them stands in a distinct, often medium-specific tradition and is alternatively used in a very general or a very specific sense (Pötzsch 2017). For the purpose of the argument presented here, defamiliarization is meant as a "making strange" of signs in the spirit of Shklovsky's *ostranenie* (Shklovsky 2017), but also older traditions going back at least to first generation English Romanticism (Bogdanov 2005), i.e., the notion of using elements of a system in a manner that makes them individually perceptible, moving them from something appearing as natural to something strange and inviting reflection. One additional reason for privileging Shklovsky in this article is that his theories on distancing effects have been shown to be (despite some differences) both historically and argumentatively compatible with Bakhtin's (Emerson 2005).

which (similar to the pre-modern governmental structures the original carnival targeted) only change over time and as a part of slow societal shifts in awareness and sensibilities.

The following argument proceeds in six steps: First, I situate *The New Colossus* both as a game dealing with history and as a cultural artefact of a specific historical period. Second, I point out the paratextual markers that indicate the intentionality of the observed elements. Third, I introduce the basics of Bakhtinian thought and its application to games. Fourth and fifth, I analyze the narrative (foregrounding the character constellation, the plot structure, and the metaphorical dimension) and the game mechanics, showing how they correlate to create calculated ambivalence. Finally, I discuss two key sequences of the game to show how carnivalesque aesthetics tie together the overall design of *The New Colossus*. The goal is to expose the construction principles behind the game's "vexing decisions" through a close reading of its narrative and gameplay, and to show that, while MachineGames might not be familiar with the theories of Bakhtin and Haraway I draw upon, their game unquestionably shows their investedness in discussions about games and gender, race, and ability.

2. Aesthetics for Challenging Gamer Masculinity

Given that *The New Colossus* is a game about Nazis and has been a point of contention in current political debates about far-right issues, the fact that I chose an aesthetic instead of a historical angle to discuss the game might need some explanation.

First, *The New Colossus* takes a different approach than most other historical, war-themed games: Instead of building upon historical accuracy as a starting point from which to allow players the creation of their own counterfactual histories (Rejack 2007; Apperley 2018), *The New Colossus* puts players into a linearly scripted counterfactual history (J. Robertson 2017). *The New Colossus* is set in the 1960s of an alternate timeline where Nazi Germany won World War II and colonized the United States. This major departure from actual history is introduced in the predecessor, *The New Order*, through a narrative strategy that ties the player's perspective to that of the player character, US special forces soldier BJ Blazkowicz. In *The New Order*'s initial stages, BJ is seen to suffer head trauma, and when he wakes up from a coma after ten years, the world around him has changed dramatically, in ways that the player discovers together with BJ. In *The New Colossus*, BJ is firmly established as a Resistance member, hunted by the world-wide Nazi regime as a terrorist, and executing attacks that rival the enemy's in scale—including detonating a nuclear warhead in a populated area. The goal of BJ's violence is exclusively political, as he and his Resistance cell, the "Kreisau Circle," strive toward mobilizing the American public into civil unrest or even outright revolution against the Nazi occupiers.

Reviewers expressed concern that the game's lack of realism might be standing in the way of a critical engagement with politics (E. Smith 2017). In historical game studies, though, the kind of counterfactuality employed in *The New Colossus* has been characterized as a strategy that on the contrary encourages "reflection because it deals specifically with the representation of history" (Apperley 2013, p. 190). By not "only" deviating from history through gameplay, but choosing a counterfactual historical starting point, such games are "encouraging reflection on historical rigor by providing a platform for dialogue around plausibility" (Apperley 2013, p. 190). In other words, despite its departure from historical events, *The New Colossus* obviously deals with history (and especially fascism and colonialism), and there would be many ways to approach the game from within the wide field of historical game studies with its pluralist research interests and methods (Chapman et al. 2016), as well as postcolonial game studies (Mukherjee 2017).[2]

---

2   The complex position in game history that *The New Colossus* occupies would well be worth studying. Considering it as a part of a genealogy, it is the direct descendent of *Wolfenstein 3D*, and hence not only generically, but prototypically a First-Person Shooter. The continuity within the Wolfenstein series is complicated by the fact that it had its origin already in an often ignored 2D action adventure, *Castle Wolfenstein* (Muse Software 1981), and that the full title of the newest game *Wolfenstein II: The New Colossus* indicates that MachineGames' first game, *Wolfenstein: The New Order* (MachineGames 2014), is considered rather a reboot than a sequel within the series (although on the narrative level, it continues the story of BJ Blazkowicz from the earlier games, rudimentary as it may have been). Put in a production context, it is reported that for their first

The choice of an aesthetic over a historical approach is based on two observations. The first observation concerns the tone of the game's engagement with history, which is nothing short of farcical. The scene that encapsulates this best shows an aged Adolf Hitler trying out actors for a film he is producing, an auto-hagiography praising his terminal victory over evil. He has written the script himself, secluded in the new Nazi headquarters on Venus—the only place he is thought to be safe from BJ. Hitler is portrayed as frail and confused, making an entrance in dirty underwear and a bathrobe, only to throw up on the carpet. It is simultaneously frightening and ridiculous to see Hitler give a confused speech while waving a gun around, standing next to a pool of his own vomit in his nightdress, and eventually killing one of the actors in a flight of rage (Figure 1) before being led away like a child. This ambivalence in the portrayal of Hitler (as well as historical events and characters in general) situates the game less in a historiographical than a satirical tradition—one which, as I argue, is drawing heavily on the carnivalesque tradition.[3]

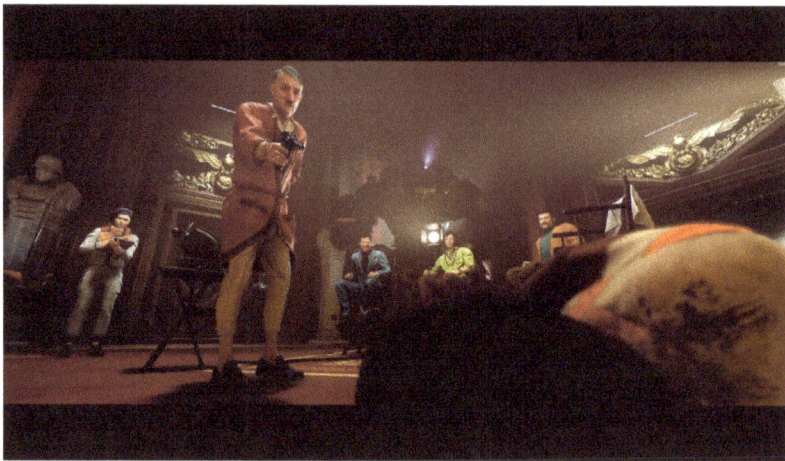

Figure 1. Hitler in his bathrobe killing an actor.

The second observation is, as Pete Hines of Bethesda put it, that it is "pure coincidence that Nazis are marching in the streets of America this year" (Batchelor 2017). Even though the game engages throughout with "the awful Nazi regime's twisted ideology" (McKeand 2017), and although there are some hints at contemporary world politics to be found—one of the many newspaper clips scattered throughout the gameworld alludes to the Trump administration (Evans-Thirlwell 2017)—I argue that those elements are the backdrop of the game's political discourse, not its center. Once we look beyond the facile assumption that the game caused controversy because of its portrayal of Nazism, we can see that most criticism leveled against it can be traced back to departures from the standards of the FPS genre.

---

game, *The New Order*, "developer MachineGames was tasked with making Nazis feel like meaningful enemies instead of warmed-over cannon fodder" (A. Robertson 2017). Given that it was the first production of MachineGames (Graft 2014), expectations were low—in the words of one reviewer, "a dumb shooter with dumb characters—Duke Nukem vs fascists" (McKeand 2017)—which helped the critical and commercial success of the game's careful balancing act between paying homage to *Wolfenstein 3D*'s iconic status and gentle updates to gameplay, production values, and cultural sensibilities. All these factors were conducive to MachineGames' ability to produce a risky project like *The New Colossus*, and receive the support of their publisher.

[3] Another notable departure from the majority of war-themed historical games is that, whereas those gloss over the fact that they are less reflections of actual history than of their mediated representations—what Salvati and Bullinger call metonymically "BrandWWII" (Salvati and Bullinger 2013)—*The New Colossus* thematizes the importance of media for our cultural imaginary of history, from the film-shoot to omnipresent advertisements, newspapers, and TV shows.

The New Colossus deviates from generic norms even more than its already slightly unconventional predecessor: Often hopelessly outnumbered, even BJ Blazkowicz, the epitome of the gung-ho shooter character, needs to resort to stealth in *The New Colossus*, all the more so because he no longer recovers fully from the wounds he has suffered, has his health-value permanently lowered, and even starts the game in a wheelchair. Not only mere fans of the game, but professional reviewers criticized these design decisions, remarking that "the stealth mechanics are stale and superficial" and that players "have already completed about half the game by the time it decides to let you feel truly powerful" (Brynard 2018). Even to professionals, it is apparently unthinkable that making the FPS player feel disempowered might be one of *The New Colossus*'s design goals. The game's narrative points in this direction, as it not only portrays BJ as disillusioned and suicidal, but relegates him to the role of a brute enforcer, a part player within a multi-ethnic cast led by strong, idiosyncratic female characters (J. Robertson 2017)—a treatment of game characters less in line with conventions of AAA than what Dyer-Witheford and de Peuter call "games of multitude" (Dyer-Witheford and Peuter 2009, p. 188).

These two observations about the game's take on history and genre—that *The New Colossus* is actively pursuing ambivalence in its portrayal of history and breaks with conventions of its genre in ways that leave even professional reviewers alienated—become even more telling when the time of production is contextualized not only within world politics, but within game(r) culture.

The New Colossus entered production right after the release of its predecessor, i.e., in the summer of 2014, the origin of the #Gamergate movement. By now well-documented and chronicled (Mortensen 2015), #Gamergate marks a paradigm shift in the public discourse about games. The driving force behind it were fears of loss of identity and privilege of "hardcore gamers"—predominantly white, cis-gender males from the global north, often lifelong players of "real games" (Shaw 2013), such as the "violently gory and technologically complex genre of FPS titles" (Dymek 2012, p. 39). Their fear of disenfranchisement was not new; what changed in the summer of 2014 was both the extent to which whole networks of gamers acted upon their convictions by harassing prominent Others, and that previously latent Fascist sentiments became verbalized, with far-right mass-media such as Breitbart.com providing prominence and public support (Mortensen 2015, p. 2).

Hardcore gamer identity and masculinity discourses have historically been strongly entangled. As Newman's study of early home console culture shows, already in the 1970s, "[v]ideo games would invite players to act out fantasies of masculine empowerment" (Newman 2017, p. 67). Despite the by-now established statistical diversity of players of digital games, the development and especially marketing of games has carried forward a culture in which a "male player is generally addressed [. . .], even when female main characters are represented (typically sexualized)" (Newman and Vanderhoef 2014, p. 381). The marginalization of the "obscure subcultural" (Voorhees 2012, p. 92) hardcore gamer created a problematic identity for them:

> Hardcore video game culture privileges an idealized hegemonic masculinity even while that culture contends with a stereotype of the gamer—the name for someone seriously invested in hardcore PC, Xbox 360, or PlayStation 3 games in particular—as immature, lazy, and boyish. Helen Thornham (2009) argues that in response to the infantilizing of digital games, gamers rationalize and normalize their play to establish an aura of legitimacy.
>
> (Newman and Vanderhoef 2014, p. 383)

As such, even though they are doubtlessly the "dominant fundamental group" recognized and given "'spontaneous' consent" within the hegemony (Lears 1985) of gamer discourse, the identity of hardcore gamers is plagued by (self-)doubt and needs constant affirmation of its values. It is therefore unsurprising that hardcore FPS games have been identified as a primary arena for affirming masculinity and patriarchal ideals. By positioning "the masculinized gamer as a defender of patriarchal subjectivity" (Spittle 2011, p. 323), especially horror and military themed games have fostered the development of aggressive (and gendered) player communities (Dyer-Witheford and Peuter 2009, pp. 82–85).

With #Gamergate, some self-declared hardcore gamer spokespeople reinterpreted these latent, historically grown traditions of unreflected identity politics in AAA games as an unavoidable fact and vehemently requested that they be affirmed and propagated—a position that must have provoked the politically sensitive developers at MachineGames. Already committed to developing a historically and military themed FPS, they bent the rules of the genre as far as possible in ways that foreground the stereotypes hardcore gamers were taking for granted, yet without completely deviating from the established formulas. Science-Fiction-themed FPS in the tradition of *System Shock* (Looking Glass Studios 1994) have frequently bent the genre rules to a greater degree. To have its desired effect, the game needed to work as a FPS and still appeal to its core target audience to be played by them, because "the nuances and aesthetics of the contemporary video game medium are imperceptible to most parts of society" (Dymek 2012, p. 51), i.e., only they are able to understand the significance of *The New Colossus*'s iconoclasm. I show that carnivalesque aesthetics allows the game to offer up ridicule and confrontationalism with a gesture of jest, a "yes, but" resolution of conflicting positions. Before exploring this aesthetic strategy, though, it seems necessary to point out how *The New Colossus* invites players to read it as a serious and critical text.

3. Invitation to Play: Paratextual Markers of Difference

As mentioned already in the Introduction, even overwhelmingly positive reviews of *The New Colossus* voice a certain degree of puzzlement over the grotesque narrative, perceived inconsistencies, and some unpleasant game mechanics. I propose to read the inconsistencies and perceived flaws (especially, as I argue in Section 6, the much-criticized stealth system) of *The New Colossus* as intentional elements meant to provoke the players. I argue that such a reading of the game is justified because its immediate, primary paratexts—its title and the end-credits song—situate the game as a political, subversive cultural product, and act as very visible signposts inviting a deep (and benevolent) reading of the game.

"The New Colossus" is the title of Emma Lazarus' sonnet engraved into the foundations of the Statue of Liberty. The source of the oft-quoted "Give me your tired, your poor//Your huddled masses," the sonnet is emblematic for American values of a bygone past, above all the promise of shelter and fairness to refugees. Read before the background of the game's narrative, Lazarus' title forms an ironic counterpart to the Nazi-ruled USA of *The New Colossus*'s imperialism and forced integration into a Germanic cultural domain. Within the greater cultural context of the game's time of release, though, the irony extends to the xenophobic, nationalistic tendencies on the rise worldwide, from tensions in the EU as a reaction to the Syrian refugee crisis to Brexit and, maybe most of all, the Trump Administration's Mexican border-wall and no-tolerance position on immigration.

While the title opens the political dimension of the game, its end credits hint at its intended mode of interpretation. The end credit's soundtrack is a cover version of Twisted Sister's "We're not gonna take it," in a performance credited to the apocryphal band Veilröth, featuring influential extreme Metal guitarist Fredrik Thordendal of the Swedish band Meshuggah. The song's origin, history, and interpretation create a network of contradictions that all but enforces critical engagement: Lyrically a protest song for teenagers against the suppression by adults, "We're not gonna take it" gained additional prominence and momentum at the time of its release in 1984 through Twisted Sister's band image and its provoking play with gender stereotypes. Coming from the band's singer, cross-dressing icon Dee Snyder, the rejection of outdated values of propriety and decency gained an additional gender-component. How easily the actual subject matter and gender subtext can be ignored is nowhere more apparent than in the song's use by the Trump presidential campaign: ostensibly intending it to be nothing but a general declaration of dissent, Trump played the song at the end of his rallies—a practice ultimately prohibited by Snyder (Diaz 2015). The cover version at the end of *The New Colossus* takes the glam/punk song and re-interprets it with down-tuned staccato guitars and a completely new middle section as a challenging, progressive-rock soundscape. The on-the-nose choice of music is counteracted by the unexpected interpretation in a way that eludes facile explanations to the same degree as the song's history of interpretation and use. In other words, the choice of music mirrors the controversial, highly context-dependent configuration *The New Colossus* has been situated in by its developers, and the re-interpretation of it parallels the game's reformulation of its genre traditions. If one follows the reading of the game proposed here, "We're not gonna take it" thus becomes a message from game developers to #Gamergate's conflation of gamer identity and reactionary ideology.

4. Carnivalesque Aesthetics and Games

The carnivalesque has long been established as a means for confronting hegemonic structures. Mikhail Bakhtin's reflections upon the carnival practices of the late Middle Ages and Renaissance come out of his studies of François Rabelais's satires. Bakhtin shows how the pre-modern humoristic sensibilities of Rabelais' texts (with their explicit treatment of bodily functions and physical excesses) are, on the one hand, rooted in old folk traditions of the carnival and have had, on the other hand, aesthetic influence on modern realism. Bakhtin argues that Rabelais' texts are prime examples of the carnivalesque, "an aesthetic of mockery, inversion and excess, grown out of the body-based and grotesque elements of popular culture in the middle ages and the renaissance" (Klevjer 2006).

The carnivalesque tradition is, to Bakhtin, part of an older, more general practice of societal resistance, the "culture of laughter," where the calcified relationships of power between groups and classes are ridiculed and, as a result, called into question. In laughing about authority, its claim to formulating universal truths is undermined: "The opposition between the unofficial culture of laughter and the official culture of order thus appears to be one between a culture of ambivalence and a culture of monovalence" (Lachmann 1988, p. 130). The ambivalence created by this kind of laughter produces a crisis with the possibility of "a shift of world orders. Laughter embraces both poles of change, it deals with the very process of change, with crisis itself. Combined in the act of carnival laughter are death and rebirth, negation (a smirk) and affirmation (rejoicing laughter)" (Bakhtin 1984, p. 127). In other words, ridiculing an authority and its power-structures is seen as productive and empowering by Bakhtin, the fertile ground of a ritualistically reoccurring cycle of change.

In the context of late Medieval community founded on religious principles, the festivities of the carnival allow for a radicalization of the principles of the (counter-)culture of laughter. In the carnival, "dogma, hegemony, and authority are dispersed through ridicule and laughter" (Lachmann 1988, p. 130). In this "spectacular feast of inversion and parody of high culture," the power of laughter is amplified to allow for a "complete withdrawal from the present order" (Lachmann 1988, p. 118). However, Bakhtin observes, the carnival itself is merely an emblematic prototype of the carnivalesque, which therefore is less a practice situated in a specific historical setting "as it is a certain kind of spirit, an aesthetic of vulgar, popular gaiety which is identifiable in the writings of Rabelais. Central to this spirit is the appreciation of what Bakhtin labels *grotesque realism*, an attitude that turns the vulgarity of excrement, orifice and bodily dismemberment into a joyful affirmation of the materiality of the body" (Klevjer 2006).

As an artistic style, this grotesque realism opposes what Bakhtin terms classical realism: instead of the celebration of timeless virtues and constant truths that dominates classical texts, grotesque realism "concentrates on the fleeting nature of both the body and the social order in which the body is currently positioned" (Majkowski 2015, p. 31). Grotesque realism operates with a repertoire of motives revolving around physicality and reversals of positions or polarities: "All the images of carnival are dualistic; they unite within themselves both poles of change and crisis: birth and death [...], blessing and curse [...], praise and abuse, youth and old age, top and bottom, face and backside, stupidity and wisdom" (Bakhtin 1984, p. 126). By "combining what should not be combined, presenting moments of humiliation, describing carnal erotic and gastric excess as well as mutilation and various deformations," grotesque realism presents the human body "as constantly connected to the world and other bodies, always unready, becoming, giving birth, dying, and being recreated" (Majkowski 2015, p. 31).

Bakhtin's concepts have been applied to digital games by some scholars, with different results. Probably the most opposed takes on the carnivalesque potential of games are those of Rune Klevjer and

Tomasz Majkowski. Discussing exclusively First-Person Shooters and connecting Bakhtin with Victor Turner, Rune Klevjer describes the carnivalesque in games as a liminal contribution to a ritualistic negotiation between parts of a culture. The First-Person Shooter genre combines, according to Klevjer, a "spectacular and modern-ritualistic celebration of modern violence and power" with "cultural contradictions, parody and play, and does not seem to be entirely defined by traditionally militaristic and imperialist ideologies," which makes him propose that "the FPS-aesthetic delineates a liminal space of techno-romantic power-play, a space where dominant ideologies are celebrated and negated" (Klevjer 2006).

Klevjer is, however, skeptical about the actual manifestation of this potentially carnivalesque ambivalence, which he underscores by injecting Turner's idea of liminality into Bakhtin's theory. Turner distinguishes famously between traditional rituals, which create liminal spaces, and modern practices that resemble them, yet are something different, i.e., merely liminoid, because they are "most often commodities which the consumer can *choose* to buy into or not" (Klevjer 2006). To complicate matters, morally imperative cultural forms (such as the satire) can transcend from this stage to one of pseudo-liminality, which is infused with value-arguments. To Klevjer, the "FPS-Adventure absolutely qualifies as such a "pseudo-liminal" form of play. It is a strictly commodified and industrially manufactured piece of entertainment software, providing an artificial realm of ritualistic performance that is both nostalgic and hyper-modern" (Klevjer 2006). In an involved rhetorical move, Klevjer refocuses the carnivalesque element of digital games from the game artefact to the player. He maintains that the

> grotesque element renders the mastery of the player visible, immediate and spectacular. Carnival is the perfect ingredient in techno-fetishist forms of play, augmenting the simulated power fantasies. The abstractness and invisibility of modern technological power is transformed into a simulated realm of mythic heroism and violence, where it suddenly becomes something concrete, magical and terrifying. There is no doubt, then, that the run-and-gun First Person Shooter is inherently conformist and affirmative as a cultural form [. . .]. (Klevjer 2006)

Thus, even while Klevjer sees in FPS games a potential to "open up to the modern individual a playful space of potentially transgressive practice" (Klevjer 2006), he categorically denies them the ability to be carnivalistic in the same way that Bakhtin sees in Rabelais and Dostoevski.

Tomasz Majkowski has taken the exact opposite position in a number of recent papers, where he describes digital games as a privileged locus of the carnivalesque. His starting point is a view of digital games as inherently parodistic, in the sense of a "self-awareness of storytelling." Both game designers and players have to be highly aware of generic conventions of both games and narratives, because "to successfully navigate the game, the player needs to identify the situation they are in and, moreover, predict the possible narrative or mechanic solutions. This ostentatious clarity additionally increases the tension between game and its references, thematising its own object, that is the ways of constructing and carrying out the storylines" (Majkowski 2014, p. 2). To Majkowski, this is not only manifest in the worldbuilding and narrative, but extends to the selection practices inherent in setting up the rule systems of ludic simulations. He sees in them parodistic (or, to go with a term not explicitly used by him, but suggested in his description, caricaturistic) strategies already in the act of translating the disorganized multiplicity of reality into the rule-bound interactions of gameworlds: "The very mechanism of the successful construction of a video game stems from parody: it relies on isolating from the chaos of reality some clear and easily distinguished rules and forging them into a coherent system governed by stated, larger-than-life rules" (Majkowski 2014, p. 1).

Majkowski concedes that the treatment of bodies in games is generally different from in the carnivalesque tradition. Both for reasons of gameplay and social acceptance as an entertainment commodity, "the lower stratum of the body" and its functions (especially fornication and defecation) are almost absent. The foregrounding of the human body in its imperfections and changeability that dominates grotesque realism can, however, still be found in digital games, in avatar-based games even at their very core: "At the centre of the gameplay there is therefore a body: of the hero, sometimes present on the screen in its entirety, perceived from the outside, and sometimes cut into pieces and fragmentary (and so degraded), in a perspective suggesting a bodily sameness of the player and the hero" (Majkowski 2014, p. 3). Additionally, the "lower stratum" of the body emphasized in traditional grotesque realism is alluded to in the hypersexualized and hypertrophic design of female and male bodies in games (Majkowski 2014, p. 4). Taken together, the "various grotesque deformations of bodies in mainstream, high-budget video games, such as over-muscled male protagonists, hypersexual women and hideous or inhuman enemies, as well as the strange obsession with producing photorealistic settings, fall firmly into this aesthetic" (Majkowski 2015, p. 27).

Majkowski identifies three common tropes that resonate with the carnivalesque: First, the perfectibility of the protagonist through improved equipment and leveling up is an expression of the carnivalesque emphasis of the constant becoming of the human body. Second, the segmentation of (mostly enemy) bodies draws attention to body parts and their no longer actualized functions, similar to the explicit treatment of (especially the lower) body in carnival practices. Third, the hierarchy of enemies that gets climbed and toppled (by overcoming regular foes, mini-bosses, and bosses) is carnivalesque in itself, because "the hero fulfils their carnivalesque mission in deconstructing the hierarchical order, exposing its most important defect: the seeming difference in quality between two ends of the social ladder is in actuality a difference in quantity" (Majkowski 2015, p. 34).

Where Klevjer re-interprets the gameplay of digital games as rituals and therefore concludes that only in transgressive play, games can be the locus of carnival, Majkowski stresses the difference between the tradition of the carnival and the carnivalesque aesthetics of grotesque realist fiction: "Games seem to be closer to narrative forms which, as Bakhtin writes, are more carnivalesque than a carnival per se. Therefore, some phenomena, clearly observed in street festivities, are problematized or presented as metaphors. [...] On the level of narrative, the collective body finds its equivalent in the polyphony and heteroglossia of the novel, that is in the equality of various points of view and socially rooted languages which are not given into the regime of ideological speech and official hierarchy" (Majkowski 2015, p. 36). The parodistic foregrounding of the game narrative's artifice allows for the carnivalesque potential of games to unfold: "In this way, for the duration of the game, the player is freed from conventional rules governing the everyday and placed in a space in which they can act in a manner usually forbidden: above all they can murder and destroy and devote themselves to limitless, positively-valued devouring" (Majkowski 2014, p. 3).

In this, Majkowski addresses the performative dimension of the play act, yet arrives at a different conclusion than Klevjer. To Majkowski, violent gameplay in action games is not so much subjugated to a cultural hegemony of techno-fetishism as it "erodes moral and social authorities and in the atmosphere of a merry but cruel carnivalesque laughter [...] it opens up a space of free destructive action, whose aim seems to be a temporary, but significant empowerment of the player, who in the world of seriousness answers to social rules. The obscene laughter has healing qualities, and an openly parodist, non-compromising game seems to be a substitute for holy days, loosening the corset of rules and allowing for their self-restitution in the atmosphere of merry play" (Majkowski 2014, pp. 8–9).

Majkowski's argument relativizes Klevjer's to a certain degree, especially when one considers that the latter's insistence on established carnivalesque practices runs counter to Bakhtin's observation that these are always subject to constant developments and reinterpretations.[4] Bakhtin already distinguishes between the carnival proper and carnivalesque strategies, which can be deployed very flexibly, which is not only expressed in Bakhtin's writings, but forms their basis. While his work masks as a description of a folk culture tradition, it is a critique of Stalin-era cultural hegemony, allowing

---

[4] As Renate Lachmann emphasizes, the carnival is to Bakhtin one specific step in the tradition of the culture of laughter, not its "pure" or final form: "Bakhtin attempts to document how the experience of ambivalence in folk culture always derived from a conflict with agelastic [laughter-averse] culture. This conflict took place in such a way that the concrete expressions invented by folk culture always corresponded to the official forms prevailing at the time" (Lachmann 1988, p. 132).

Bakhtin to circumvent censorship and to formulate a tongue-in-cheek deconstruction of homogenizing Stalinist discourse (Lachmann 1988, pp. 116–20).

Klevjer's second point of contention, the friction between the counter-cultural potential of the excesses of digital games and their situatedness in an extension of the military-industrial complex, is where *The New Colossus* deviates from the patterns Klevjer identifies in the FPS tradition. In the next section, I show how the game reflects upon the technology-driven action of the FPS genre by problematizing discourses of masculinity and ability through the destabilizing ridicule Bakhtin describes.

5. Breaking with the Conventions of the American Aryan Hero

In Section 3, I argue that the ambiguous paratexts challenge players to assume an underlying subtext in all of *The New Colossus* and thus engage with it critically. This section reads the game's narrative level in this fashion, outlining the very clear positions it takes on issues that other games (and its own predecessors) have long ignored.

The themes of fascism, oppression, racism, and, in general terms, othering, become tangible already in the diversity of its cast of characters. That despite this diversity the player character is still white, hyper-masculine, and cis-gender might at first seem like a concession to player demographics and genre conventions. Given how radically this character is exposed to criticism and deconstructed, not the least through situating him among very diverse characters, the opposite seems to be the case. Instead of flirting with ideas of white, male supremacy, the game continuously exposes Nazi rhetoric[5] and central values of fascist and supremacist ideology such as masculine virility (Spackman 1997). One particularly obvious instance is when an SS-officer in a conversation with player character BJ Blazkowicz compliments him on his "very Aryan face," putting the finger on one of the ironies of the game series', the fact that the great American hero incorporates every ideal of the Nazi master-race (see Figure 2). As Edwin Evans-Thirlwell remarks in one of the most insightful early analyses of the game, *The New Colossus* is caught in a Foucauldian differential of power that resembles that of its protagonist: "To take up arms against a regime is therefore to risk perpetuating that logic, as MachineGames' portrayal of BJ as a latent fascist acknowledges" (Evans-Thirlwell 2017).

In the previous game, *The New Order*, BJ indeed starts out as a perfect image of Aryan body ideals. At the beginning of the *The New Colossus*, though, he is on the brink of death, and throughout half of the campaign, his derelict body is basically kept alive by machines. In the initial gameplay sections, the player controls BJ in a wheelchair, where he is weakened and his range of motion limited (see Figure 3). This creates a striking contrast to the traditions of body representations in FPS games, which rely on stark othering in their ableist, heteronormative image of the player character: In the depiction of opponents, FPS games overwhelmingly employ aesthetics of the abject and the uncanny, dehumanizing or demonizing the other (Brock 2011; Spittle 2011; Carr 2014). The avatar body, on the other hand, is mostly unseen, yet implied to be near ideal or perfectible, allowing for affirmation of values and a feeling of security: "By donning another corporeality, that of the avatar, players can experience just what a superhard and agile body can do—perform a hyperviolent masculinity in a space that allows them to contest the waning dominance of white heteronormativity, free from the disapproving eye of the 'other,' or the unwelcome gaze of the gay male" (Burrill 2008, p. 79).[6]

---

[5] Not the least because of how widespread and diversified Nazi strategies of denigrating and dehumanizing people rhetorically are (Casmir 1968), its treatment in *The New Colossus* could be the subject of a paper of its own. For an exemplary discussion of one strategy, the "kill the rats" rhetoric, see (Francis 2017).

[6] This emphasis of heteronormativity and hypermasculinity is incidentally reminiscent of Fascist gender performativity, which was driven by (besides factors such as reproduction politics) a fear to be perceived itself as queer (Herzog 2011, p. 73).

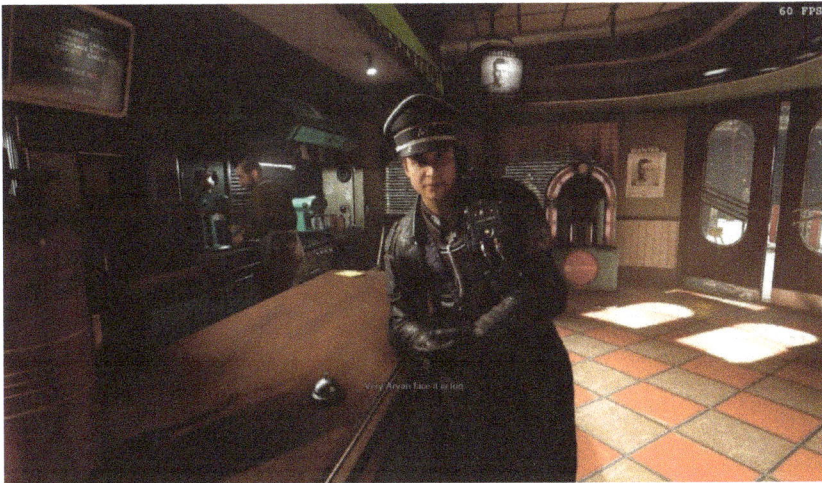

Figure 2. A Nazi officer complimenting the player character upon his Aryan facial features.

Figure 3. Hero in wheelchair, bathrobe, and catheter.

The decision to start the game by depriving BJ Blazkowicz of his able-bodiedness is more than a gameplay twist on FPS conventions (which I discuss in the next section), it caricatures the promise of improvement and perfectibility implicit in the standardized alternative corporeality of hardcore games. Instead of offering the player an avatar who is better than them in basically every way and can act as a foil for projections of masculine power fantasies, *The New Colossus* re-contextualizes BJs body in the alternative corporeality of disability. Disability studies emphasizes "the active transformation of life that the alternative corporealities of disability creatively entail" (Mitchell and Snyder 2015, p. 2), i.e., the ingenuity and tenacity it takes to navigate a society built upon implicit standards of able-bodiedness (Siebers 2008). It would be naive to assume that putting BJ in a wheelchair was a realistic simulation of disability, but it does not have to be; it radically runs counter to the player expectations of an FPS avatar body as hyper-able and lets players experience being in a physical environment that does not accommodate one's corporeality.

That BJ remains a viable FPS avatar despite the limitations to his mobility is due to technology. His dependence on technology is very apparent in the big picture, where he is able to move first in the wheelchair and then a power armor, before eventually having his head attached to a vat-grown Nazi supersoldier-body, in a procedure that combines advanced surgery and cabbalistic science-magic. Emphasizing the technological basis of movement of the FPS avatar through the wheelchair stresses not only an overall dependence on tools—because once he is equipped with weapons and traps, BJ is very well capable of dealing with his situation. It also suggests that *The New Colossus*'s avatar is always a cyborg, first in a mundane way of technological augmentation, then a militaristic power-fantasy, and eventually a more fundamental vision of near-immortality through putting a consciousness into a new body. The realization that BJ is always already a cyborg draws attention to the fact that the "archetype of the cyborg warrior has acquired a fundamental position within the FPS genre" (Klevjer 2006). Cybernetic technologies are indeed central to countless games of the genre, and in many variations, from the iconic power-armors of *Half-Life* (Valve 1998) and *Doom* (id Software 2016), to more ostensibly realistic near-future and far-future militaristic visions of armored infantry in games such as *Call of Duty: Advanced Warfare* (Sledgehammer Games 2014) and *Titanfall* (Respawn Entertainment 2014), and even voluntary and involuntary extensive body-modifications in *Deus Ex* (Ion Storm 2000) or *Quake 4* (Raven Software 2005). Klevjer highlights that the trope of the cyborg externalizes and stylizes a dependency on technology that is inherent in digital games and the act of playing them: "The fantasies performed are fantasies about abilities, made possible by the representational and procedural powers of the computer. In this sense, therefore, all computer game avatars—and all computer game players—are cyborgs" (Klevjer 2006).

Klevjer's consequential (albeit radical) suggestion of extending the cyborgism of the avatar to the player resonates strongly with the close association between the FPS avatar's able-bodiedness and the masculinity discourses of hardcore gaming discussed in Section 2. As "discourses of disability and ability connect with other aspects of subjectivity including ethnicity and gender" (Carr 2014, EN 8), BJ's disability puts a spotlight on his masculinity, which both through the vicarious cyborgism identified by Klevjer and the discursive masculinization of hardcore gamers suggests connections to the gender identity of the players.[7] Put differently, the way in which BJ Blazkowicz is a cyborg in *The New Colossus* stands less in the tradition of the techno-fetishist, hyper-ableist masculine power-fantasies Klevjer identifies as typical of FPS games than in that of Donna Haraway's feminist and post-humanist "Cyborg Manifesto" (Haraway 1991).

Haraway's essay takes its point of departure in the historical moment of a "radical change in American white heterosexuality" which coincides with a blurring of "the boundary between physical and non-physical" (Haraway 1991, p. 153). Just as sexual identity is discussed in the early 1990s as all-encompassing and infinitely more complex than previously considered, technological visions of the future turn out to have been realized in unexpected ways that have not yet been noticed by society. Instead of a utopian step of technologically driven evolution producing unambiguously new human–machine hybrids, the reality of cyborgs is one of "ubiquity and invisibility," in which they are "as hard to see politically as materially. They are about consciousness—or its simulation. They are floating signifiers" (Haraway 1991, 153). Radicalizing the idea of the cyborg to a much farther degree than even Klevjer, Haraway states that her "cyborg myth is about transgressed boundaries, potent

---

7   Jordan Wood's analysis of *The Binding of Isaac*—something of a polar opposite of a AAA FPS—shows an even more clear
     alternative to the heteronormative and hypermasculine stylization of the avatar. Wood argues compellingly for how
     the ordeals of a naked pre-teen boy in "randomly generated levels of psychosexual, scatological horror" (Wood 2017, p.
     222) are challenging stereotypes of masculinity to the point where they "represent queer becoming" (Wood 2017, p. 218).
     Full of "radical rejection of heteronormative safety" (Wood 2017, p. 225), the game negates with its rogue-like structure
     heteronormative narratives of linear progression and improvement (Wood 2017, p. 224) and couples gains in Isaac's powers
     to "highly visible, grotesque alterations to his corporeality" (Wood 2017, p. 224). Although *The Binding of Isaac* is more
     radical in its departure from norms, it is remarkable how similar the strategies employed in *The New Colossus* are in their
     connection of masculinity and ability discourses with scatological and grotesque imagery.

fusions, and dangerous possibilities which progressive people might explore as one part of needed political work" (Haraway 1991, p. 154).

As I show in detail further down in this section, *The New Colossus*'s protagonists are exactly this, a group of progressive people who risk everything to effect political change. Transgressing boundaries of race, class, and ability, and disregarding conventions of gendered behavior, they personify the danger of "impurity" feared by Nazi ideologues. They are a prototypical example of the macroscopic dimension of Haraway's cyborg, a communal body not unlike the Hobbesian Leviathan. What distinguishes this type of communal union from other models is that it is formed by neither necessity nor blood "but by choice, the appeal of one chemical nuclear group for another" (Haraway 1991, p. 155). In Haraway's ideal, groups are united by "affinity, not identity" (Haraway 1991, p. 155)—an ideal that is made topical throughout *The New Colossus*'s portrayal and discussion of the founding principles of respectively Resistance and Nazi communities.

It might seem far-fetched to invoke complex post-structuralist concepts of the cyborg in the discussion of *The New Colossus*, as if I were suggesting that MachineGames actively engaged with Bakhtin, Haraway, or Klevjer. More likely than not, this was not the case. However, the sensibilities with which complex topics such as intersectionality and community building are anchored in the game can be outlined more clearly before the background of these theoretical and ideological frameworks—especially in their conjunction, which is mirrored in the closely intertwined themes and motifs of the narrative.

Only in the light of theories of cyborgism and the association of player identity and generic treatments of masculinity, the permutations of BJ's body become coherently meaningful. Giving the avatar a disability allows the game to show that, similar to any alternative corporeality, digital play needs technological support to function according to expectations. Exchanging the wheelchair for the power suit comes down to replacing a mundane, obvious, and clumsy prosthetic for a (in game conventions) more common, easier to ignore, elegant prosthetic which quickly become transparently normalized as a part of the player character's body. However, *The New Colossus* finds ways of having the power armor draw attention to itself when BJ fruitlessly tries to hide it away under clothes. When it rips through the heavy leather jacket, it obviously resists the illusion of normalcy, giving visibility to its otherness compared to a common human body. When BJ re-attains the semblance of normalcy through a synthetically crafted body created in Nazi laboratories, his post-human status becomes less visible, yet still far from hidden, as the connection between his head and the vat-grown body is clearly visible above his collar. To complete the post-human, post-gender argument, BJ's previously central virility is no longer performed on-screen in the love-making that was prominent in *The New Order*, but transcended into the pregnancy of his girlfriend Anya. Especially after the body-graft, his sexuality goes unmentioned, at least hinting at the possibility that the artificial body might be effectively sexless. While the cyborg-dimension of BJ's body certainly is a metaphor for the player–avatar relationship as Klevjer posits, it is not one of friction-less identity or empowerment. At no point is BJ the invulnerable *Übermensch* of Aryan propaganda and FPS stereotype, but rather its reversal and ironization.[8]

As mentioned in the beginning of this section, BJ's weakness and humanity become even more noticeable because of the diverse cast of characters he is embedded in. While rather one-dimensional on their own, as a rather large ensemble, they form a kaleidoscope of personalities.

No-one in this game is fully rounded as a character—in isolation, each is too shallow to match our own complexities—although each exhibits their own defining characteristic. Irene Engel has the apathy, Anya the empathy, Set the curiosity, Super Spesh the paranoia, Sigrun

---

8   This affects not only BJ: In one of the two possible versions of the gameworld, the Fergus timeline, Fergus Reid receives a prosthetic arm which will not cooperate, and is identified by him as female. Combined with his constant clashing with Resistance leader Grace Walker, this lets Fergus emerge as an alternative to BJ's acceptance of post-human or at least gender-positive thinking. Fergus is the caricature of the war hero caught in a pointless performance of masculine stereotypes in the face of damage to his physical integrity and a subversion of his androcentric world view.

Engel the naivety, BJ's father owns the hatred and fear, BJ himself is consumed by loss and sadness. Together, they form what most would consider to be some of the key facets of humanity—for better or worse. (J. Robertson 2017)

Beyond their personalities, the many ethnicities, beliefs, and body-types represented by them makes *The New Colossus* an example for what Dyer-Witheford and de Peuter call "games of multitude" (Dyer-Witheford and Peuter 2009, p. 188), i.e., digital games that go out of their way to not privilege a certain, usually American or European, white ethnic identity. Even though it focuses on cis-gender characters, the game puts questions of gender front and center. Together with his physical integrity, BJ's masculinity in terms of social roles and behavioral patterns is a central locus of defamiliarization of genre tropes.

This discourse already begins in *The New Order*, where BJ becomes a member of the Kreisau circle, a Resistance cell led by a woman, Caroline Becker. Caroline's paraplegic body puts her initially in a wheelchair and later in the power armor BJ "inherits" from her after her death. BJ follows therefore quite literally in Caroline's footsteps, but just as he is happy to serve under her para-military leadership, he makes her his spiritual leader after her death, talking to her in his thoughts in what amounts to prayers for guidance. Both physically (as wearer of the power suit) and spiritually (as temporary leader of the Resistance cell), BJ tries to fill the void left by her. The power suit proves to only be a makeshift solution for his problems, and his leadership cannot live up to Caroline's example, so he gladly steps down as soon as another leader is available: Grace Walker, an African-American Resistance fighter whose politics combine patriotism, feminism and Marxism.

The female leaders are only one way in which *The New Colossus* reverses the stereotyped gender-roles commonly found in mainstream entertainment. The most important characters in relation to BJ are women, his enemy, his leader, and his lover, yet all of them in ways that do not conform to clichéd roles. BJ's Nemesis is SS-General Irene Engel, a cruel, sadistic Nazi-stereotype whose obsession with the American soldier has unmistakably sexual undertones. Instead of portraying her as hysteric, pining, or with other behavioral patterns traditionally coded as expressive of female sexuality, she is an aggressive sexual predator. Several times throughout the course of *The New Colossus*, BJ is exposed naked and vulnerable in front of Engel, who even commits acts of sexual violence against him, "kissing" him with Caroline's head after decapitating her, and simulating oral rape with a gun (see Figure 4). In a series of very different breaches of convention, Grace Walker, the eventual leader of BJ's Resistance cell, is introduced by giving an exposition of the horrors of war for the population of a city subjected to a nuclear attack, and doing so while breastfeeding her infant child and smoking. Her anti-patriarchal stance is poignantly comprised in the end of her initial conversation, when BJ unthinkingly compliments her courage by calling her actions "ballsy." This provokes a diatribe from Grace in which she eloquently juxtaposes the vulnerability, frailty, and ugliness of testicles to their metaphorical grandeur. BJ's girlfriend Anya is initially introduced as his nurse in *The New Order*, and while she already in the first game develops into a fierce combatant in her own right, the sequel shows her as a third-trimester pregnant Valkyrie equaling BJ in every aspect. Throughout the campaign, she is hinted at performing acts of heroism equivalent to BJ's, but off-screen, an unsung heroine, coming only to the fore when really needed. She does so in the very end, as discussed in the final section of this article.

The game goes so far as to make BJ symbolically disavow patriarchal order. BJ's childhood is shown in flashbacks to have been dominated by the violence of his father, an immigrant to the US who denied his Eastern-European roots to the point where he allied himself with the Nazi oppressors and sold out his wife to them for personal gain. When BJ kills his father, he does so in great part to avenge his mother, who had not only remained faithful to her Polish heritage, but also to her Jewish faith. BJ choses his mother's ethnic and religious heritage for himself, to the point of marrying her self-sufficient, new-woman mirror image Anya in the end.

Figure 4. Irene Engel's sexually charged assault on BJ Blazkowicz.

6. Mechanics of Withdrawal

The New Colossus would already be noteworthy if it only offered a critique of the politics of its genre on the level of its narrative, but the game goes further than this. The gameplay mirrors the aesthetic devices of the narrative in exactly the points that critics sometimes perceived as flawed or problematic. Three design decisions particularly stand out in this respect: health management, stealth mechanics, and equipment limitations.

For the majority of the game, the avatar is confined to a wheelchair or artificially empowered by an actuator-driven suit of armor. The wheelchair restricts the player's agility, forcing her to act more strategically and carefully than in a traditional FPS (like the predecessor *The New Order*), and while movement in the power armor is comparatively unrestrained, it is still clunky and somewhat imprecise. Throughout these sections, the weakness of BJ is signified ludically by halving his maximum health value. Gameplay-wise, this is offset by both the ability to wear armor (and quite a lot of it when wearing the power suit) and temporarily boosting the health-value beyond its maximum value. However, seeing the health counter trickling down to 50 has not only the gameplay function of making the avatar less resilient, but psychologically reinforcing an awareness of the frailty of the human body—a memento mori quite unheard of in the gung-ho world of First-Person Shooters. The physical restrictions imposed on the avatar by, e.g., the wheelchair might be argued to be not carrying any game-extrinsic meaning. Bo Kampmann Walther has argued for what he calls "dynamics of recursivity" (Walther 2007), meaning that game elements always refer first and foremost recursively to the rules governing them. The extra restrictions imposed on the avatarial body through the wheelchair would in this logic be transparent and normalized, because within the ludic structures of *The New Colossus*, they are no different from all the other artificially imposed constraints typical of goal-oriented play that players submit to in what Bernard Suits calls the "lusory attitude" (Suits 2005, pp. 54–55). *The New Colossus*, however, does not allow for the naturalization of some game elements (like the wheelchair) because it changes them before repetition could make them conventionalized, and uses the narrative to remind the player of their additional significance.

The stealth mechanics of *The New Order* drew significant criticism for being clumsy and awkward, if not downright broken. While not a dedicated First-Person stealth game in the tradition of *Thief: The Dark Project* (Looking Glass Studios 1999), *The New Colossus* encourages stealthy gameplay in several ways, such as introducing it in tutorial sections and awarding achievements for stealth kills, yet also on a more universal level, given that the high difficulty of fights especially against mini-bosses and bosses makes avoiding open fire-fights often more of a necessity than a stylistic choice. At the same time, taking cover and sneaking are implemented without much feedback on the level of the interface, so that detection happens easily and will not be communicated to the player in the efficient and forgiving manner that has become customary in recent stealth games. This results in a stealth feature that is, ironically, as unpredictable, dangerous, and challenging as the fights, often leading to failure in situations that should be simple enough. Some enemies, especially the Zitadelle- and Zerstörer-class robots, can be easily avoided through stealth, making it effectively possible to choose which bosses to fight. The stealth mechanics thus offer at the same time a choice to avoid fighting in a combat-oriented game, characterizing this approach as a valid alternative solution, yet also signaling that this is not the strong suit of the player character or the game. Similar to BJ, the player is forced outside her element by the events of the game, and not offering a perfectly balanced and polished way of dealing with these challenges becomes less of a shortcoming than a ludic analogy to the narrative about limits, challenges, and (dis-)abilities.

The third strategy of *The New Colossus* that might appear as a shortcoming is the omission of some weapons from the previous game. Missing a sniper rifle, heavy machine gun, and rocket launcher, the second game features a slightly reduced inventory in terms of sheer numbers, which, however, is offset by allowing the fewer weapons to be freely combined with each other in dual-wielding configurations. As with the health and stealth mechanics, this not only has (in this case positive) gameplay ramifications, but results in a procedural rhetoric that exchanges fascist ideals of purity and strength in numbers for strength through diversity. *The New Colossus* delivers a similar message when introducing its BFG class weapon, the Übergewehr, in only one level late in the game, when the weapon can be found in a research lab on Venus. Only available once, rather cumbersome, effectively overpowered and not very useful in the narrow corridors of the space station, and impossible to keep when leaving the level, the super-weapon becomes an almost useless symbol of the self-defeating nature of "superior force."

The design strategy of withholding or subtracting gameplay is furthermore tied into the history of the series. This is again most easy to demonstrate in direct comparison between the two most recent games in the series. Both feature a playable version of Wolfenstein 3D. In *The New Order*, it is only one level, which is implemented as a well-hidden Easter-egg quite late in the campaign, and is contextualized as a nightmare in which BJ relives his own past. In *The New Colossus*, the whole game is implemented as an in-game arcade machine, and completely re-contextualized as a cultural product of the alternate history of the game: entitled "Wolfstone 3D," the game allows the player to control "Elite Hans," a German soldier hunting for public enemy number one BJ Blazkowicz, or, as the Nazi propaganda apparatus calls him, Terror Billy.

As with its general relationship to history, the refashioning of the predecessor as "Wolfstone 3D" allows *The New Colossus* to attain an ironic distance to the political as well as medial past, which are highlighted and amplified, e.g., by comments of BJ's about the stupendous fidelity of the game's graphics. In the context of *The New Colossus*' own game mechanics, a subtler difference between the two different re-envisioned *Wolfenstein 3D*s appears especially noteworthy: In *The New Order*, the controls and weapons available to the player in the dream sequence match those of the rest of the game, giving BJ, e.g., the ability to lean around corners, updating the gameplay and making it effectively somewhat easier. In *The New Colossus*, the rendition of the original game is faithful, even where the gameplay is outdated and the controls less than perfect. The irony of "Wolfstone 3D" is thus heightened by the fact that this version of the game, despite its Nazi reskin, is the more faithful rendition of the original, compared to which the dream sequence in *The New Order* appears as a power fantasy. Similarly, the previously mentioned chagrin directed at the game's stealth mechanics ignores that the implementation of stealth in *The New Order* is rather faithful to the *actual* original game, the 2D action-adventure *Castle Wolfenstein*, which pioneered this mechanic: "Castle Wolfenstein's legacy can't be overestimated, particularly in regard to its integration of basic stealth elements into its gameplay" (Loguidice and Barton 2012, p. 24).

A final procedural statement connected to the "Wolfstone 3D" arcade machine is that it is located in the headquarters of the Kreisau Circle, right next to an allied entertainment machine, a pinball with the name "Yes we can!" This machine is, however, out of order, creating another, this time extremely game-specific, commentary on contemporary politics: The machine named after the political leitmotif of the Obama-era is no longer accessible, cannot be engaged with anymore, and all that remains is a historically revisionist arcade-shooter that draws us in with its technological achievement and graphical fidelity to make the player feel immersed, while ignoring the dubious political message (see Figure 5).[9] MachineGames' use of an arcade as a metaphor for the shift in the American political landscape between the Obama and Trump administrations, hidden in plain sight in the middle of a mainstream digital game, is a perfectly elegant display of game design mastery.

Figure 5. The in-game arcade with the "Wolfstone 3D" and "Yes We Can!" machines.

7. The Carnivalesque Climax of *The New Colossus*

Similar to all carnivalesque, *The New Colossus* is an expression of counter-cultural thinking (Lachmann 1988), which the game foregrounds by dealing with counter-cultures in its narrative—the Resistance against the Nazi-regime, Marxist and Feminist intellectuals, and beat and rock sentiments—which should not be in any way controversial in our age, yet are set in scene in a way that insinuates contemporary reactionary tendencies.

The New Colossus resists a homogeneous, facile reading of its topics by injecting its narrative with moments of crass humor and grotesquery typical of traditions of the carnivalesque. Some of the characters are so over-the-top—especially conspiracy theorist Super Spesh and communist preacher Horton Boone—as to be caricatures. The specifically carnivalesque dimension of the characters in the game is easiest to demonstrate in Scientist Set Roth's pet, Shoshana. While the hybrid animal with a cat's head on a monkey body is on the one hand a plot device foreshadowing BJ's body-graft, her body is, conceptually speaking, combining generally incompatible realms to produce something "unnatural" which allows reflection on accepted norms and standards. To draw attention to her, the game not only features her prominently in many cut-scenes, her name also appears on the score-board of competitions of the Kreisau-circle (e.g., a shooting gallery). The advertisements for German products and service in the armed forces as well as the "Aryanized" reimaginations of pop music classics (turning

---

9   For a more in-depth analysis of the context the game puts its "arcade" in, see (Evans-Thirlwell 2017).

e.g., the Beatles into Die Käfer) are often non-sequitur, throwaway comic relief rather than political commentary, in a similar way as the whole sequence in which BJ auditions for the role of himself in a movie produced by Hitler personally. However, they use key techniques of the carnivalesque like the reversal of hierarchies as well as humor centered around lower bodily functions and excrement.

One character is particularly noteworthy as carnivalesque: Sigrun, General Engel's daughter, stands in a humoristic tradition of painting the female body as grotesque by focusing on her sexuality, her physicality, and her bodily fluids (Rowe 2011). Already at the time of her introduction, her obesity and her sexual appetite are stressed, together with her bookishness and her resistance to control through figures of power, in her case her mother. She is a prototype of the trope of the "unruly woman," which "can be seen as prototype of woman as subject—transgressive above all when she lays claim to her own desire" (Rowe 2011, p. 31). In many instances, Sigrun's obesity, chattiness, and lack of self-control are shown or referenced for comical effect, in sometimes clearly boundary-crossing ways as when she and her lover are interrupted in their lovemaking. However, in a carnivalesque act of reversal, Sigrun becomes the subject of a political discourse in unexpected ways. Grace distrusts Sigrun for being the daughter of a German officer and calls her a Nazi at every given opportunity, until Sigrun eventually physically attacks Grace in an act of helpless defiance. The arguments Sigrun raises in her anger all point toward polemics against minorities: She resists being labeled something she is not, being treated as a lesser being or even less than human—clear references to a fascist rhetoric of subjugation, which she, the daughter of a powerful German Nazi official, should both be immune against and ignorant to. That it is not Sigrun but Grace who relapses into this mindset of (to put it in a reversal of Haraway's categories) identity instead of affinity, is the completion of carnivalesque logic, the reversal of the reversal. Sigrun and Grace have exchanged their social positions for their polar opposites, yet those new positions are not stable and need challenging and possibly revising through ridicule, degradation, and potentially violence.

Finally, there are two sequences in which the carnivalesque is presented in its pure form. The first is BJ's birthday party, which quickly develops into a sequence of drinking-contests, pig-riding, casual sex, fighting, plus puke-and-poop jokes. In addition to the overall grotesquery, there are again several instances of reversals of hierarchy, from the explicit reversal of priorities from fighting for liberation to celebrating BJ's birthday to the pacifist, mentally handicapped Max Hass beating BJ in a fistfight.

The second sequence is the final battle, in which carnivalesque aesthetic is most pronounced. In the pivotal cut-scene, Blazkowicz is saved by his pregnant girlfriend Anya several times in a row, first by single-handedly defeating half a dozen of high-level enemies, before protecting him from an explosion with her body. Stripped of her burnt clothes, splattered in blood, her face a hollow-cheeked mask reminiscent of a skull, Anya straddles BJ below her pregnant body in an imagery typical of carnivalesque ritual birth (Bakhtin 1984, p. 126), with her dual-wielded guns and the oft-mentioned twins in her belly adding the trope of duality to that of reversal of roles and ritual rebirth (see Figure 6). As Bakhtin describes it: "In living carnival images, death itself is pregnant and gives birth, and the mother's womb giving birth becomes a grave. Precisely such images are produced by creative ambivalent carnival laughter, in which mockery and triumph, praise and abuse are inseparably fused" (Bakhtin 1984, p. 164). Anya's selfless protection of BJ is an almost comically out-of-proportion act of heroism which simultaneously characterizes her as the true hero of the story and ridicules not only BJ's, but, by extension, the player's efforts and the genre tropes of the First-Person Shooter, by deflating the final climax both narratively and ludically in a deus-ex-machina-moment. The fight has been won, evil has been defeated, yet the victory falls dramatically flat because it is not earned by player or character in any way. Turning the conventions of dramatic and ludic closure on its head, *The New Colossus* in its final scene once more challenges its players' preconceptions about their roles in the newest take on the genre maybe most intimately associated with male hard-core-gamer identity.

Figure 6. Anya as the carnivalesque female, birthing death.

8. Conclusions

The aim of my argument was to show that *The New Colossus* is definitely not "just" an AAA shooter, and neither a parody nor deconstruction of the genre or its series, but a reaction to contemporary cultural developments presented as a piece of carnivalesque culture in the strict sense: a liminally positioned contribution to a ritualistically conducted negotiation between parts of a culture.

I have argued that reading *The New Colossus*'s departure from traditions of affirmative masculinity in FPS games as a response to a co-option of AAA game development by reactionary hardcore gamers is justified by the time of its development, which coincided with the radicalization of gamer culture in the #Gamergate events. *The New Colossus* reverses many of its genre conventions and challenges its core player base, drawing upon the clout of major publisher backing, being situated in a long-running, influential franchise, and following a commercially and critically acclaimed predecessor. The game eschews downright deconstruction of its generic roots in favor of defamiliarization achieved by embracing the Bakhtinian carnivalesque. Not only does the ambiguity of the carnivalesque leave room for conservative players to experience the game without feeling personally attacked in their values and preferences, thus ensuring that the game would not be impalpable to the players it addresses both aesthetically and ideologically. It also allows the norms and implicit value system of FPS games in general to be as idiosyncratic and contradictory as they are. Grotesque elements challenge players and shatter expected coherence into a multitude of ambivalences, and genre tropes get replaced by their reversals, yet all of that happens playfully, temporarily. At the end, everything is as it should be—the Nazis have been temporarily defeated, BJ (and with him, implicitly, the player) is celebrated as a hero—because, after the carnival, everything returns to the way it was.

However, this restitution is only an outward appearance, because the assumed normalcy has been shaken up, has been shown to be a hegemonic construct. *The New Order* highlights that, as Klevjer has observed, every avatar is a cyborg, and in doing so moves the treatment of cyborgs in the FPS genre from its techno-fetishistic, affirmatively hypermasculine standard to Haraway's vision of the cyborg as an inherently hybridized, multiplicitous subject which rejects and disproves notions of normalcy. Nothing makes this clearer than how misplaced those elements of FPS conventions feel that MachineGames uncritically retain. As one review shrewdly points out, the game's conventions of culturally coding levels of difficulty are conservative and run counter to the game's politics: "Sticking a bonnet on BJ [as a visualization of the lowest difficulty setting] and infantilizing the player by analogy isn't exactly an invitation to explore playing Wolfenstein 2 differently. Even just calling one difficulty setting 'normal' implies the others are deviant. When you're fighting to liberate the country from people who believe in eugenics in a game that celebrates difference and diversity, moralizing the difficulty around the struggle (easy equals lazy/bad, hard equals virtuous/good) feels archaic" (Gach 2017). It says a lot about the sophistication the overall engagement with stereotypes and norms in a game when the cultural conventions exposed in the difficulty selection become visible as a misstep against identity sensitivities.

This analysis has demonstrated that *The New Colossus* manages to connect a high-concept narrative with matching gameplay, and in doing so imbues everything the player does with anti-supremacist subtext: the cripple vanquishes the superhuman, female affinity beats male militarism, diversity trumps strength in numbers, etc. *The New Colossus* uses the carnivalesque in a fashion that permeates the game as a whole, allowing the player to indulge in inherently ridiculous acts that invite being laughed at as well as laughed about, paving the way for a reflective, responsible engagement with cultural and media history that simultaneously foregrounds the shortcomings and strengths of its own medium. MachineGames thus achieve a rare success: they deconstruct their heritage without destroying or negating it, and give form to an ideal of "affinity, not identity" (Haraway 1991, p. 155) instead of preaching it. Only time will tell if their attempt to lead by example has been fruitful.

Funding: This research received no external funding.

Conflicts of Interest: The author declares no conflict of interest.

References

Apperley, Tom. 2013. Modding the Historians' Code: Historical Verisimilitude and the Counterfactual Imagination. In *Playing with the Past. Digital Games and the Simulation of History*. Edited by Mathew Wilhelm Kapell and Andrew B. R. Elliott. New York and London: Bloomsbury, pp. 185–98.

Apperley, Tom. 2018. Counterfactual communities: Strategy games, paratexts and the player's experience of history. *Open Library of Humanities* 41: 1–22. [CrossRef]

Bakhtin, Michail Michajlovič. 1984. *Rabelais and His World*. Bloomington: Indiana University Press.

Batchelor, James. 2017. 'It's Disturbing that Wolfenstein can Be Considered a Controversial Political Statement.' Bethesda Marketing Boss Pete Hines Discusses Publisher's Marketing for Upcoming anti-Nazi Shooter. *Gamesindustry.biz*. Available online: https://www.gamesindustry.biz/articles/2017-10-06-bethesda-were-not-afraid-of-being-openly-anti-nazi (accessed on 6 October 2017).

Bogdanov, Alexei. 2005. Ostranenie, Kenosis, and Dialogue: The Metaphysics of Formalism According to Shklovsky. *The Slavic and East European Journal* 49: 48–62. [CrossRef]

Brock, André. 2011. 'When Keeping it Real Goes Wrong': Resident Evil 5, Racial Representation, and Gamers. *Games and Culture* 6: 429–52. [CrossRef]

Brynard, Alec. 2018. How Wolfenstein II: The New Colossus JUST Misses the Mark. *Critical Hit*. Available online: https://www.criticalhit.net/features/wolfenstein-ii-new-colossus-just-misses-mark/ (accessed on 22 January 2018).

Burrill, Derek A. 2008. *Die Tryin': Videogames, Masculinity, Culture*. New York: Peter Lang.

Carr, Diane. 2014. Ability, Disability and Dead Space. *Game Studies*. 14/2. Available online: http://gamestudies.org/1402/articles/carr (accessed on 28 October 2018).

Casmir, Fred L. 1968. Nazi Rhetoric. A Rhetoric of Fear. *Today's Speech* 16: 15–18. [CrossRef]

Chapman, Adam, Anna Foka, and Jonathan Westin. 2016. Introduction: What is historical game studies? *Rethinking History* 21: 358–71. [CrossRef]

Diaz, Daniella. 2015. Dee Snider to Trump: I May Not Take It Anymore. *CNN*. Available online: https://edition.cnn.com/2015/12/10/politics/dee-snider-donald-trump-twisted-sister/index.html (accessed on 10 December 2015).

Dyer-Witheford, Nick, and Greig de Peuter. 2009. *Games of Empire. Global Capitalism and Video Games*. Minneapolis: University of Minnesota Press.

Dymek, Mikolaj. 2012. The Video Game Industry. Formation, Present State, and Future. In *The Video Game Industry*. Edited by Peter Zackariasson and Timothy L. Wilson. New York and London: Routledge, pp. 34–56.

Emerson, Caryl. 2005. Shklovsky's ostranenie, Bakhtin's vnenakhodimost' (How Distance Serves an Aesthetics of Arousal Differently from an Aesthetics Based on Pain). *Poetics Today* 26: 637–64. [CrossRef]

Evans-Thirlwell, Edwin. 2017. How Wolfenstein: The New Colossus Takes the White Dudebro Hero Apart. Available online: https://www.rockpapershotgun.com/2017/12/28/wolfenstein-2-the-new-colossus-politics/ (accessed on 28 December 2017).

Francis, Bryant. 2017. Wolfenstein II: A Good Argument for Games to Get Political. Available online: https://www.gamasutra.com/blogs/BryantFrancis/20171030/308635/Wolfenstein_II_A_good_argument_for_games_to_get_political.php (accessed on 30 October 2017).

Gach, Ethan. 2017. It Might Be Time to Rethink Difficulty Menus. Available online: https://kotaku.com/it-might-be-time-to-rethink-difficulty-menus-1820961183 (accessed on 3 December 2017).

Gaynor, Steve. 2018. Wolfenstein Raises the Question: When Did Punching Nazis Become Controversial? Available online: https://www.polygon.com/2018/1/11/16874580/wolfenstein-2-best-video-games-2017-year-in-review (accessed on 11 January 2018).

Graft, Kris. 2014. Being BJ Blazkowicz: Storytelling in Wolfenstein: The New Order. Available online: https://www.gamasutra.com/view/news/218899/Being_BJ_Blazkowicz_Storytelling_in_Wolfenstein_The_New_Order.php (accessed on 5 June 2014).

Haraway, Donna. 1991. The Cyborg Manifesto. In *Simians, Cyborgs, and Women: The Reinvention of Nature*. New York: Routledge, pp. 149–82.

Herzog, Dagmar. 2011. *Sexuality in Europe. A Twentieth Century History*. Cambridge: Cambridge University Press.

id Software. 1992. *Wolfenstein 3D*. Garland: Apogee Software.

id Software. 2016. *Doom*. Rockville: Bethesda Softworks.

Ion Storm. 2000. *Deus Ex*. London: Eidos Interactive.

Klevjer, Rune. 2006. Dancing with the Modern Grotesque. War, Work, Play and Ritual in the Run-and-Gun First Person Shooter. Available online: http://folk.uib.no/smkrk/docs/dancing.htm (accessed on 13 July 2018).

Lachmann, Renate. 1988. Bakhtin and carnival: Culture as counter-culture. *Cultural Critique* 11: 115–52. [CrossRef]

Lears, T. J. Jackson. 1985. The Concept of Cultural Hegemony: Problems and Possibilities. *The American Historical Review* 90: 567–93. [CrossRef]

Loguidice, Bill, and Matt Barton. 2012. *Vintage Games: An Insider Look at the History of Grand Theft Auto, Super Mario, and the Most Influential Games of All Time*. Burlington: Focal Press.

Looking Glass Studios. 1994. *System Shock*. Austin: Origin Systems.

Looking Glass Studios. 1999. *Thief: The Dark Project*. London: Eidos Interactive.

MachineGames. 2014. *Wolfenstein: The New Order*. Rockville: Bethesda.

MachineGames. 2017. *Wolfenstein II: The New Colossus*. Rockville: Bethesda.

Maiberg, Emanuel. 2017. The Alt-Right Thinks 'Wolfenstein: The New Colossus' Is Racist to White People. Available online: https://motherboard.vice.com/en_us/article/mbj9xv/the-alt-right-thinks-wolfenstein-the-new-colossus-is-racist-to-white-people (accessed on 12 June 2017).

Majkowski, Tomasz Z. 2014. Freedom of Destruction and Carnivalesque in Video Games. In Proceedings of the 8th International Conference on the Philosophy of Computer Games, Istanbul, November 3–15; Available online: http://gamephilosophy2014.org/wp-content/uploads/2014/11/Tomasz-Z-Majkowski-2014.-Freedom-of-Destruction-and-Carnivalesque-in-Video-Games.-PCG2014.pdf (accessed on 13 July 2018).

Majkowski, Tomasz Z. 2015. *Grotesque Realism and Carnality: Bakhtinian Inspirations in Video Game Studies*. Edited by Tomáš Bártek, Jan Miškov and Jaroslav Švelch. Brno: Masaryk University, pp. 27–43.

McKeand, Kirk. 2017. What 'Unfiltered Creative Expression' Means for Wolfenstein 2's Depiction of Nazism. Available online: https://www.pcgamesn.com/wolfenstein-2-the-new-colossus/wolfenstein-2-political-themes (accessed on 5 September 2017).

Mitchell, David T., and Sharon L. Snyder. 2015. *The Biopolitics of Disability. Neoliberalism, Ablenationalism, and Peripheral Embodiment*. Ann Arbor: University of Michigan Press.

Mortensen, Torill Elvira. 2015. Anger, Fear, and Games. The Long Event of #GamerGate. *Games and Culture*. [CrossRef]

Moseman, Andrew. 2017. People Are Bombarding Nazi-Killing Game 'Wolfenstein II' with Bad Reviews Because It's about Killing Nazis. Available online: https://www.popularmechanics.com/culture/gaming/news/a28808/people-are-bombarding/ (accessed on 27 October 2017).

Mukherjee, Souvik. 2017. *Videogames and Postcolonialism. Empire Plays Back*. Basingstoke: Palgrave Macmillan.

Muse Software. 1981. *Castle Wolfenstein*. Baltimore: Muse Software.

Newman, Michael Z. 2017. *Atari Age. The Emergence of Video Games in America*. Cambridge: MIT Press.

Newman, Michael Z., and John Vanderhoef. 2014. "Masculinity." *The Routledge Companion to Video Game Studies*. Edited by Mark J. P. Wolf and Bernard Perron. New York and London: Routledge, pp. 380–87.

Pinchbeck, Dan. 2013. *DOOM. SCARYDARKFAST*. Ann Arbor: University of Michigan Press.

Pötzsch, Holger. 2017. Playing Games with Shklovsky, Brecht, and Boal: Ostranenie, V-Effect, and Spect-Actors as Analytical Tools for Game Studies. *Game Studies*. 17/2. Available online: http://gamestudies.org/1702/articles/potzsch (accessed on 28 October 2018).

Pötzsch, Holger, and Vít Šisler. 2016. Playing Cultural Memory: Framing History in Call of Duty: Black Ops and Czechoslovakia 38–89: Assassination. *Games and Culture*, 1–23. [CrossRef]

Raven Software. 2005. *Quake 4*. Santa Monica: Activision.

Rejack, Brian. 2007. Toward a virtual reenactment of history: Video games and the recreation of the past. *Rethinking History* 11: 411–25. [CrossRef]

Respawn Entertainment. 2014. *Titanfall*. Redwood City: Electronic Arts.

Robertson, Adi. 2017. Wolfenstein II Wants to Laugh at the Present without Commenting on It. Available online: https://www.theverge.com/2017/7/27/15958176/wolfenstein-ii-the-new-colossus-gameplay-preview-nazi-punching (accessed on 27 July 2017).

Robertson, John. 2017. Wolfenstein 2's Linearity Is What Makes It a Game Worth Talking about. Available online: https://www.pcgamesn.com/wolfenstein-2-the-new-colossus/wolfenstein-ii-linearity (accessed on 24 January 2018).

Rowe, Kathleen. 2011. *The Unruly Woman: Gender and the Genres of Laughter*. Austin: University of Texas Press.

Salvati, Andrew J., and Jonathan M. Bullinger. 2013. Selective Authenticity and the Playable Past. In *Playing with the Past. Digital Games and the Simulation of History*. Edited by Mathew Wilhelm Kapell and Andrew B. R. Elliott. New York and London: Bloomsbury, pp. 153–67.

Shaw, Adrienne. 2013. On Not Becoming Gamers: Moving beyond the constructed Audience. *Ada: A Journal of Gender, New Media, and Technology* 2. [CrossRef]

Shklovsky, Viktor. 2017. *A Reader*. Edited by Alexandra Berlina. London: Bloomsbury.

Siebers, Tobin. 2008. *Disability Theory*. Ann Arbor: University of Michigan Press.

Sledgehammer Games. 2014. *Call of Duty: Advanced Warfare*. Santa Monica: Activision.

Smith, Adam. 2017. Wot I Think: Wolfenstein 2: The New Colossus. Available online: https://www.rockpapershotgun.com/2017/10/26/wolfenstein-2-the-new-colossus-review-pc/ (accessed on 26 October 2017).

Smith, Edward. 2017. Why 'Wolfenstein II' Should Embrace Reality, Not Escapism. Available online: https://www.rollingstone.com/glixel/news/why-wolfenstein-ii-should-embrace-reality-not-escapism-w496096 (accessed on 10 August 2017).

Spackman, Barbara. 1997. *Fascist Virilities. Rhetoric, Ideology, and Social Fantasy in Italy*. Minnesota: University of Minnesota Press.

Spittle, Steve. 2011. 'Did This Game Scare You? Because it Sure as Hell Scared Me!' F.E.A.R., the Abject and the Uncanny. *Games and Culture* 6: 312–26. [CrossRef]

Suits, Bernard. 2005. *The Grasshopper: Games, Life and Utopia*. Peterborough: Broadview Press.

Tavinor, Grant. 2009. *The Art of Videogames*. Malden: Wiley-Blackwell.

Valve. 1998. *Half-Life*. Bellevue: Sierra Entertainment.

Voorhees, G. 2012. Monsters, Nazis and Tangos: The normalization of the first-person shooter. In *Guns, Grenades and Grunts: First Person Shooter Games*. Edited by Gerald Voorhees, Josh Call and Katie Whitlock. New York: Continuum International, pp. 89–111.

Walther, Bo Kampmann. 2007. Self-Reference in Computer Games: A Formalistic Approach. In *Self-Reference in the Media*. Edited by Nina Bishara and Winfried Nöth. Berlin and New York: Mouton de Gruyter, pp. 219–36.

Wolf, Mark J. P. 2008. *The Video Game Explosion. A History from Pong to Playstation and Beyond*. Westport: Greenwood Press.

Wood, Jordan. 2017. Romancing an Empire, Becoming Isaac. The Queer Possibilities of Jade Empire and The Binding of Isaac. In *Gaming Representation: Race, Gender, and Sexuality in Video Games*. Edited by Jennifer Malkowski and TreaAndrea M. Russworm. Bloomington: Indiana University Press.

MDPI

St. Alban-Anlage 66

4052 Basel

Switzerland

Tel. +41 61 683 77 34

Fax +41 61 302 89 18

www.mdpi.com

Arts Editorial Office

E-mail: arts@mdpi.com

www.mdpi.com/journal/arts

www.ingramcontent.com/pod-product-compliance
Lightning Source LLC
Chambersburg PA
CBHW051315020426
42333CB00028B/3353